REDEMPTION IN IRISH HISTORY

John Mark Alder

Freedom is so splendid a thing that one cannot worthily state it in the terms of a definition; one has to write it in some flaming symbol or to sing it in music riotous with the uproar of heaven.

Patrick Pearse

Redemption in Irish History

John Marsden

DOMINICAN PUBLICATIONS

First published (2005) by
Dominican Publications
42 Parnell Square
Dublin 1

ISBN 1-871552-89-3

British Library Cataloguing in Publications Data.
A catalogue record for this book is available
from the British Library.

Cover design by Bill Bolger

Printed in Ireland by
The Leinster Leader Ltd
Naas, Co. Kildare.

The front cover is from a design by Harry Clarke for a stained glass panel
illustrating the lines 'I have heard a sound of wailing in unnumbered / Hovels,
and I must go down, down I know not where', from W. B. Yeats' play, *The
Countess Cathleen*, in the *Geneva Window*. The design, in pencil and watercolour,
was produced *c.* 1928.

Contents

Preface

This book began life as a course in Irish Contextual Theology at the Church of Ireland Theological College in Dublin, which trains Anglican clergy for the whole of Ireland. Whilst theology is in fact always 'contextual', there is merit in labouring the point in circumstances where historical, political and cultural factors have not always been given due attention. It was evident in teaching this course that before a theological dialogue could ensue we needed first of all to wrestle with divergent readings of Irish history. This was accommodated by devoting the first term to history and the second term to theological reflection. I am indebted to the students for their lively contributions in what were at times heated debates.

Ray Refausée, Heather Smith and Susan Hood at the Representative Church Body Library of the Church of Ireland gave invaluable help in locating relevant sources. At various stages a number of people were kind enough to respond to questions I raised with them about different aspects of my work. I would like to record my thanks to Denis Carroll, Terry Eagleton, Michael Hurley, Ken Kearon, Kieran Kennedy, Dáire Keogh, Declan Kiberd, Terence McCaughey, Gerry O'Hanlon, the late Ronald Preston, and Bernard Treacy.

Finally, earlier versions of parts of some chapters appeared in articles in *Doctrine & Life*, *The Heythrop Journal*, *Search* and *Studies*, and I would like to express my thanks to the editors.

John Marsden
All Saints' Day, 2004

r

Introduction

Although for many people the word 'redemption' is seen in terms of personal salvation and the hope for eternal life, this is scarcely an adequate summation of the Christian hope, which also affirms that the divine love and purpose seek the redemptive transformation of *this* world. It should always be remembered that in its repudiation of dualism from Irenaeus onwards,[1] Christianity rejected the Gnostic notion that the creation is somehow intractable, intrinsically evil and therefore irredeemable. There is therefore no warrant for a privatised spirituality that excludes the corporate political domain and the legitimate earthly hopes for a greater justice and human flourishing.

In the last few decades this wider perspective has received renewed attention largely through the influence of the Liberation Theology that has emerged from the poorer countries of the southern hemisphere. Through the work of the religious orders, whose members have often worked in countries where liberation theology has been strongly represented, the insights of this new style of theology and pastoral practice have already enriched the Irish Church. In 1987 Denis Carroll's timely study, *What Is Liberation Theology?*, went some way to introducing some of the main themes of liberation theology to an Irish audience. Carroll readily concedes that liberation theology is not for 'easy export'.[2] It is therefore encouraging that in recent years, most notably through the work of Enda McDonagh and Terence McCaughey,[3] there have been some significant contributions to developing a more prophetic and socially aware theology in Ireland.

To date, though, it remains the case that comparatively little has been written which specifically aims to apply the methodology and themes of

1. See Chapter 7, p. 123.
2. (Dublin: Mercier Press, 1987), p. 5. Dermot Lane and Donal Dorr have also published significant work in this regard. See D. Lane, *Foundations for a Social Theology: Praxis, Process and Salvation* (Dublin: Gill and Macmillan, 1984); D. Dorr, *Option for the Poor: A Hundred Years of Vatican Social Teaching*, rev. ed. (Dublin: Gill and Macmillan, 1992).
3. See Terence McCaughey, *Memory and Redemption: Church, Politics and Prophetic Theology in Ireland* (Dublin: Gill and Macmillan, 1993) and Enda McDonagh, *The Gracing of Society* (Dublin: Gill and Macmillan, 1989).

liberation theology to the Irish context: indeed some commentators would question the wisdom of doing so.[4] To begin with, there is the question of whether a Marxist-inspired methodology used in Latin America is appropriate in a European setting. In addition to this there is the concern that the divergences in religious and political identity in Northern Ireland make a liberation theology model inappropriate because, as Gabriel Daly puts it, 'communities are divided'.[5] The treatment of liberation theology in Chapter Ten below acknowledges these complexities, but maintains that the methodology of liberation theology can be satisfactorily developed, adapted and applied. Moreover, the attempt to draw out some of the implications of doing so shows that an indigenous usage of the insights of liberation theology, adapted to the exigencies of Ireland's economic, political and cultural situation, is not only urgently needed but central to the renewal of the Irish Church.

Since its emergence in Latin America in the late 1960s, in response to the wish to develop a more socially concerned Christian witness in the context of poverty and injustice, liberation theology has insisted that theology should adopt a *praxis* orientation, i.e., one that is rooted in an active involvement and solidarity with the oppressed, which leads on to social analysis, and in turn informs theological reflection and pastoral action.[6] When this theological method is more fully considered in Chapter Ten, the point is made that the specific social analysis that is deployed may take a variety of forms and that the collapse of communism has not somehow suddenly removed the need for significant programmes of political, social and economic reform.

Liberation theology is a highly variegated phenomenon and a critical use of its insights does not imply an endorsement of the grander claims of some of its exponents to 'epistemological privilege', or subscribing to

4. A useful start was made by the Irish Theological Association which held conferences on liberation theology in 1977 and 1984. See D. Lane, ed., *Liberation Theology: An Irish Dialogue* (Dublin: Gill and Macmillan, 1977) and E. McDonagh, ed., *Irish Challenges to Theology*, (Dublin: Dominican Publications, 1986).
5 . See his paper at the 1984 I.T.A. conference 'Towards an Irish Theology – Some Questions of Method' in E. McDonagh, ed., *Irish Challenges to Theology*, pp. 88-101 (99).
6. The notion of 'praxis' here is of Marxist provenance and associated with Marx's rejection of abstract and contemplative forms of materialism that fail to see the importance of practical sensuous human activity. Marx's *Theses on Feuerbach* presents his viewpoint and closes with the famous eleventh thesis that reads: 'Hitherto the philosophers have only interpreted the world, in various ways; the point is to change it.'

a naïve utopianism. What can be embraced is an appreciation of the moral and political significance of the voice of the socially excluded and the bearing this should have on our thinking, orientation and priorities. Liberation theologians rightly insist that theology should not be done in abstraction. Theological reflection should always be contextual, i.e., rooted in both a critical engagement with and an analysis of a given socio-political context. A vital task for a Christian theology in Ireland is therefore to identify a level of political thinking commensurate with the contemporary situation. Christian discipleship would be fundamentally flawed if it exempted itself from this crucial exercise. Yet all too often the call to salvation is presented in terms of an individualistic gospel that ignores questions of social responsibility. This criticism applies to much of Protestantism in Ireland and also to a regressive conservatism within Roman Catholicism that too often seems more preoccupied with sexual morality than social justice. This kind of pietistic retreat is a poor substitute for embarking upon the serious wrestling with economic, political and cultural questions that should be central to Christian mission.

In Ireland the task of articulating a social and political analysis is admittedly complicated by the fact there exist two state jurisdictions, which correspond to two competing political identities. In order to understand better these differing conceptions of national identity, an examination of Irish history will be needed to elucidate how exactly it is that these divergences have evolved.

The methodological interests already adverted to will have their bearing on the conduct of historical enquiry and justify the primacy given to a 'committed' reading of Irish history 'from below' in any attempt to develop a theological interpretation of Irish history. In a sectarian state ruled by a narrow Ascendancy élite, dissent was as widespread as it was inevitable. As we shall see, it was the dynamism and vitality in the struggle of the oppressed (which in Ireland included the large body of politically excluded citizenry) that provided the catalyst and energies for the campaigns that produced political change.

The particular exigencies of Irish history must of course be seen in their wider setting and this study begins with a discussion of the way in which Irish society was convulsed by the democratic revolutionary tide associated with the Enlightenment and French Revolution. What Wolfe

Tone described as 'an oppressed, insulted and plundered nation' proved particularly receptive to the new political radicalism.[7] During this period the United Irish Society set itself the aim of uniting people of all religious persuasions in a polity that was pluralist, democratic and cosmopolitan in outlook. Thus at its inception Irish nationalism was a culturally inclusive democratic movement. This ideal stands in sharp contrast with the bifurcation of Irish political culture that became institutionalised in the creation of a Protestant unionist state in the North and an independent Irish state with a predominantly Roman Catholic ethos.

The revolutionary ferment of the 1790s was undoubtedly the highwater mark of democratic thinking in Ireland. The period since then can be understood as a long and often tortuous unfolding of democratic politics through bitter political struggle and protracted social conflict that were sustained by popular discontent. During this process the old Ascendancy structure was progressively weakened through Catholic Emancipation, the abolition of tithes, the disestablishment of the Church of Ireland, the partial resolution of the land question and, finally, the struggle for the extension of democracy that eventually led to the foundation of an independent Irish state in the South. With the failure of Partition and the unravelling of a Protestant hegemony in the North, after the violent interlude of the Troubles, the return to constitutional politics has at last created the conditions for a peaceful movement in the direction of a sustainable democratic politics.

A theology that wishes to be contextual, as we have seen, cannot avoid at least some examination of the historical events that have done so much to shape the contemporary cultural and political situation. Moreover, since an effective social and political analysis will need to be historically rooted, this has its claims on the organisation of material, with theological concerns rightly introduced only at a later stage. The need for such an historical approach is underlined by the fact that because of demographic and other factors, people in Ireland have too often only been exposed to sectarian versions of their history, with home, school and community sometimes all reinforcing prejudice. If only in broad outline, some treatment of the salient events that have shaped modern Ire-

    7. *Life of Theobald Wolfe Tone:Compiled and arranged by William Theobald Wolfe Tone*, edited by T. Bartlett (Dublin: Lilliput Press, 1998), pp. 39f.

land is therefore needed.

Following the treatment of the 1790s in the opening chapter, the second chapter of this study considers some of the key developments that have shaped the evolution of Irish politics in the nineteenth and early-twentieth centuries: the Tithe War, O'Connell's Emancipation and Repeal agitations, the Young Ireland Movement, Fenianism, changes in the three main ecclesial traditions, Parnell's land and constitutional campaigns, the Gaelic revival and the nationalist resurgence before the Easter Rising. The origin of modern unionism in response to the Home Rule crises of the late-nineteenth and early-twentieth centuries is also considered in this chapter. Prior to this period, political divisions in Ulster had found expression through the mainstream British political parties. It was the fear of a Catholic-dominated Dublin Parliament that resulted in unionism emerging as a potent political force, which in alliance with a popular loyalism, mobilised a cross-class opposition to Home Rule. Alongside the revival of old religious cleavages, powerful economic interests were brought into play, with the North-East perceiving ties to Empire as central to the region's commercial and industrial well-being

In Chapters Three and Four on Patrick Pearse and James Connolly – the founders of the Irish Republic – the opportunity is taken to reflect at greater depth on some of the questions surrounding the relationship of religion to both national and social aspirations. The provisional nature of all claims to national self-determination and the danger of an idolatrous assertion of national identity are addressed through an assessment of Pearse, while in an evaluation of Connolly's socialist vision the supposed conflict between Christianity and socialist aspirations is discussed. On the wider question of their vision of nationalism, Pearse's efforts to rouse a rather too quiescent people in danger of internalising their oppression through accepting their subordinate status, and Connolly's creative attempt to link the day-to-day economic struggles of the marginalised with aspirations for national and democratic freedoms, shows the significance they both attached to securing the widest possible popular mandate. Pearse's talk in his later plays and drama of 'a risen people' might have been given more practical expression by Connolly the trade unionist and socialist, but they were both committed to a reading of history from below.

Chapter Five looks at the degree to which in the twentieth-century Irish nationalism might be considered Gaelic and Catholic, and charts the move to a greater pluralism in Irish society, with the 'yes' vote in the 1995 Irish divorce referendum being seen as something of a watershed. In addition to an interest in the differing conceptions of political identity that have shaped Irish history, throughout the text an effort has been made to address economic and social issues, which in a society as riven with conflict and inequality as Ireland, have never been far away. The more advanced elements in the United Irish Society considered significant measures of social improvement to be the natural accompaniment of the extension of democracy. This social radicalism was informed by a religious conviction of the dignity of the human person, which implied rights of a social as well as a political nature. From within the Young Ireland movement of the 1840s, the egalitarian thrust within the nationalist tradition was developed by James Fintan Lalor, who championed the case for land redistribution amid the trauma of an Ireland torn apart by famine. In the era of Parnell the land and constitutional agitation were brought into a powerful coalition that was responsible for a series of Land Acts that did much to transform agrarian conditions.

To assist in relating broader social themes to the contemporary situation, Chapter Six includes an extended discussion of social and political inequality in modern Ireland. This provides an opportunity to try to understand why it is that the Irish Free State and the Republic have had such a poor record on poverty and inequality. Unionism's record in power and the history of the Northern State is also considered (a critical examination of the various strands within contemporary unionism is left for Chapter Ten). Why was social inequality allowed to persist for so long in Northern Ireland, when the despair and hopelessness of unemployment and disadvantage have been such potent factors in fuelling conflict? The opportunity now provided both North and South by more advantageous economic circumstances to address the historical legacy of deprivation, brings to centre-stage the question of how the fruits of economic growth are to be shared. Here the need for a renewal of social democracy, which in Ireland for historical reasons has been relatively lacking, is identified as an important corrective to too great a reliance on the free market.

These wide-ranging reflections help set the agenda for the remaining chapters, which introduce theological themes and attempt to relate the fortunes of social justice and democratic politics in Ireland to what we mean by redemption. Some of the larger theological issues that are identified include: the significance of eschatological hope in relation to political and social ideals; an examination of the relationship between political liberty and millenarian hope in Ireland; the tension between understanding the human creature as sinner and as *imago Dei*, and the implications this might have for Christian hope and democratic politics; a treatment of the themes of remembrance and redemption in relation to the tragedy of the Great Famine; applying the Just War tradition to a consideration of paramilitary violence in Northern Ireland; the development and adaptation of perspectives from liberation theology in an Irish context and their relevance for the search for peace; the relationship between socio-economic liberation and the Christian understanding of salvation; articulating a social and political analysis that might adequately inform theological reflection; delineating forms of political identity that are genuinely liberative and consistent with a democratic polity and those that are not; and finally a consideration of ecumenical witness in the context of an understanding of the Church as a sacrament of the unity of the whole human family and the implications of this for the Irish Church.

The contention that much more work needs to be done in developing a specifically Irish contextual theology that utilizes the aims and methods of liberation theology is illustrated by the fact that several of the subjects tackled in this text have involved traversing relatively uncharted waters.

There remain, of course, many issues that have not been addressed. For example, gender and sexual inequality persists in manifold forms: despite increased participation in the workforce, the marginalisation experienced by women remains significant and more needs to be done to promote equality of opportunity and equal pay;[8] for men, the deep-seated prejudice regarding their role within the family means that the parental rights and nurturing roles of fathers are too often dismissed out

8. See M. MacCurtain and D. Ó' Corráin, eds., *Women in Irish Society: The Historical Dimension* (Dublin: The Women's Press, 1978).

of hand, either in the name of a homespun sexual stereotyping or a perverted feminism; the unacceptable delay in the decriminalization of homosexuality and the lack of tolerance of non-hetrosexual relationships have left scars still in need of healing. As for children, their abuse whether sexual, physical, emotional, or by way of neglect, is only just beginning to be acknowledged, and in all four regards it has been the State itself through acquiescing with a culture of abuse that has been the prime offender.

Another area where liberative energies are to be welcomed stems from the fact that as well as being political and economic, alienation is very often cultural, and if a more free and inclusive polity is to be created within Irish society then the work of cultural reconstruction this will entail is something with which theology should be involved. The richness of modern Irish literature suggests that the material is certainly there for constructing more inclusive and less alienating forms of cultural identity. Recent contributions in the study of Irish literature, like Declan Kiberd's, which draw attention to Protestant influences in Irish writing, would suggest that there already exist important signposts for those wishing to point towards a richer cultural diversity.[9] Valuable insights can also be drawn from the attempts of writers such as Roddy Doyle to articulate aspects of Irish working class experience in ways which not only show the harsh realities of life that many people face, but also the compassion and human understanding that can contribute to a sense of communal solidarity.[10]

Although such major areas of concern should ideally have been incorporated into this work, it seemed better to finish a more restricted project than run the risk of taking on a task which might have proved beyond my abilities and stamina.

As regards the inter-disciplinary nature of this study, this is something for which no apology should be made, since intellectual disciplines should not be allowed to sit sleepily alongside one another. History, political theory and theology will only be enriched by the right sort of dialogue,

9. See *Inventing Ireland: the Literature of the Modern Nation* (London: Vintage, 1996). For a useful discussion of issues of culture and identity in an Irish context see Declan Kiberd and Edna Longley, *Multi-Culturalism: The View from the Two Irelands* (Cork: Cork University Press, 2001).

10. For example *The Barrytown Trilogy: The Commitments, The Snapper, The Van* (London: Minerva, 1992).

which gets scholarship away from the trends of specialization whereby more and more is known about less and less.

Not possessing the skills of a professional historian, whilst making use of the writings of leading figures of the 1790s and the 1916 generation, more generally it seemed wiser largely to rely on some of the better secondary source material available. Thankfully, in recent years there have been important breakthroughs in the study of Irish history. Scholarship is less patrician and, influenced by historians like E. P. Thompson, work which gives greater attention to the popular classes has proved significant.[11] The remarkably advanced political culture of the late eighteenth century and the manner in which it embraced a wide social constituency is now more fully appreciated. One consequence of this is that revisionist polemic which fails to acknowledge the diversity and depth of the Irish nationalist tradition has begun to look distinctly dated. The cosmopolitan outlook of early Irish republicanism is something that has the potential to embrace both nationalist and unionist in the common search for a viable democratic polity. It was after all parliamentary reform under the Crown which constituted its founding ideal.

In this increasingly secular age, to venture a theological interpretation of Irish history will no doubt strike many as rather odd. As in any discipline, history has its divergent schools, and all attempts at interpretation are, as a matter of course, hotly contested. In approaching history with the conviction that what is at one level a description of human activity, is at another level the outworking of divine redemptive purpose, the requirements of scholarly neutrality have admittedly been transgressed. This text cannot realistically venture into many of the larger issues that a theology of history would undoubtedly pose, though if only in a preliminary manner the plausibility of such an approach should at the outset at least be outlined.

There is a growing body of opinion that a case can be made for a reading of the Old Testament prophetic tradition that yields a strong theology of history. Following the identity-defining Exodus narrative, which gives Israel its sense of destiny, we find a distinct broadening in the prophetic literature whereby divine saving action begins to embrace

---

11. See Nancy Curtin's introductory essay in her *The United Irishmen: Popular Politics in Ulster and Dublin 1791-1799* (Oxford: Clarendon Press, 2001) pp. 1-12.

other nations. We see this in Amos, where the scope of Yahweh's liberative design is extended to Israel's neighbours. In similar fashion in Isaiah, as both Walter Eichrodt and Gerhard von Rad have observed, we find a universalising of Israel's faith in providence with the divine salvific purpose extending onto the stage of world history.[12]

One of the most recent advocates of the need for a theology of history is Wolfhart Pannenberg.[13] Pannenberg decries the retreat of theology into the narrower and less world-affirming confines of a salvation history (*heilsgeschichte*) that has been reduced to a distinct strand within universal history. His endeavour adapts Hegel through introducing a Christology whereby the Christ event is understood as an anticipation of 'the end of history'. Whatever the difficulties of such attempts to understand the totality of history in redemptive terms, the wider reference entailed in relation to what is perceived as salvific purpose is to be welcomed.

Reinhold Niebuhr would be a good example of a theologian who deemed it essential that Christianity should address the larger questions of human social destiny, no matter how fraught this task may be. For Niebuhr, it was the great primary themes of creation, fall, atonement and eschatology, which provided the framework within which a realistic assessment might be made of the Christian hope and of the scope and limits of human destiny.[14] When confronted with the horrors of human history and the potential of human beings for both good and evil, Niebuhr's realism (provided it does not relapse into pessimism) is an essential ingredient of any theology of history. Such a note of qualification does not, however, rule out understanding history in redemptive terms, even if such an understanding must be able to incorporate what Paul Tillich would describe as the 'tragic' elements of human existence and recognise that the fulfillment of the Kingdom of God remains only partial within human history.[15]

Since any claim concerning redemptive history must be a qualified

---

12. See Raymond Plant's discussion of recent Old Testament scholarship in *Politics, Theology and History* (Cambridge: Cambridge University Press, 2001) pp. 25ff.
13. Plant includes a treatment of Pannenberg's theology of history (see ibid, p. 79ff.).
14. See K. Durkin, *Reinhold Niebuhr* (London: Geoffrey Chapman, 1989), pp. 95ff.
15. For a fuller treatment of Tillich's eschatology which draws particularly on his earlier work see J. Marsden, *Marxian and Christian Utopianism: Toward a Socialist Political Theology* (New York: Monthly Review Press, 1991), pp. 105ff.

one, rather than make too overt an attempt to relate Irish history to a perception of redemptive purpose, I have been content to allow such a perspective to inform the ordering of chapters and arrangement of material, and leave the reader to judge how illuminating or otherwise the exercise has been. Those at least who are open to the wider claims and social reference of Christian theology, will, I hope, applaud such an effort, even if my overall theological balance and the judgements implicit in my treatment of material have less to commend them.

It might be thought that the contemporary scholarly community would reject outright such an approach to history. Here, two points can be made. First, Christians are not the only ones concerned with socially emancipatory readings of history, and this creates fruitful scope for constructive dialogue. Second, fortunately, most historians would now more readily concede that the writing of history is never a neutral exercise. Both these observations remind us that it is important to recognise that we have a living and dynamic relationship with the historical past. Reassessments of historical judgements are rarely without political import for matters of current debate. The past is full of menace and has its claims upon the present since dangerous memories can pose awkward questions about our contemporary identity. We do not have to pause for thought for very long before we realise this is certainly true of Irish history. Has the Republic of Ireland subordinated or even abandoned its founding social vision to the claims of the market economy? Have nationalists and unionists in Northern Ireland properly acknowledged the need to abandon the sectarian mentality of former times that wanted a victory for one side over the other? There is a battle still going on concerning Irish identity, and James Joyce's comment about going 'to forge in the smithy of my soul the uncreated conscience of my race' reminds us that this has always been the case.[16]

Whilst the perspective from which this study has been approached has been readily acknowledged, some reference to the confessional context in which it has been written is also appropriate. Writing as a member of the Church of Ireland carries its own obligations, not least of which is a readiness to express regrets concerning the past. Although the Estab-

16. *Portrait of the Artist as a Young Man*, introduction by S. Deane (Harmondsworth: Penguin, 1992), pp. 275f.

lished Church produced some towering figures, like Wolfe Tone and
Thomas Russell, it was also the religion of an oppressive ruling élite that
grossly betrayed Gospel values. If Anglicanism is to have a creditable future in Irish society, it will need to come to terms with its inglorious and
vainglorious past.

When what remained of the former Ascendancy structure finally col-
lapsed in the South with the creation of the Free State, by and large the
Church of Ireland kept its head down, and showed little sign of positively identifying with the new dispensation. With the passage of time
things have improved, especially as the Republic has become more ready
to shed the trappings of a confessional state and embrace a pluralist
outlook. This is to be welcomed, but there must be a real question mark
as to whether Irish Anglicans have thought through its full implications.
Should members of Church of Ireland in the Republic now be more
forthright in their endorsement of the republican ethos of the Irish State?
What view should now be taken of the 1916 Rising and figures like Pearse
and Connolly who were the founders of the Irish Republic? How can
Irish Anglicans best come to terms with their Church's former role as
part of a privileged Ascendancy structure, which continued (albeit in
modified form) in Northern Ireland through an inbuilt majority at
Stormont? Those who do not find the insights offered in this study persuasive can hardly deny the pertinence of these kinds of questions.

Anglicans in Northern Ireland also need to re-examine their identity
and role in the light of changing circumstances. Here the Church of
Ireland will need to become more than a body with a pastoral word for
'our people', if it is to make its contribution to the creation of a genuinely democratic polity. There may be two main religious traditions but
there is only one political community. Too often in the past statements
by Church leaders have been confined[17] to speaking on behalf of their
own religious constituency, whether it be Cardinal Cahal Daly raising

---

17. Pertinent in this regard is the submission to the Opsahl Commission of the Corrymeela
     Community, which recommended 'the development of social programmes across
     community boundaries between Church congregations and parishes, and attempts
     by the Church leaderships to act together when making comment on political, secu-
     rity and legal matters. Otherwise, the sociological and psychological forces of division
     will automatically proclaim another message – namely solidarity with our own cul-
     tural/religious group.' See *A Citizens' Inquiry: The Opsahl Report on Northern Ireland*,
     ed. A. Pollak (Dublin: Lilliput, 1993), p. 347.

important issues concerning the treatment of IRA prisoners or Archbishop Robert Eames drawing attention to Protestant fears and insecurities that too often are not fully appreciated. The difficulty here is that
the Churches are in danger of being perceived as little more than chap-
lains to the warring tribes.

The commitment of Church leaders to making pronouncements often in an ecumenical setting goes some way to striking a more positive
note, though even this contribution is undermined if the Churches themselves, as institutions, do not show a willingness to embrace change and
identify with the interest of the wider community. Education, alone, is
indication enough that the Churches have too often in fact exercised a
profoundly divisive role with little recognition of the value of inter-de-
nominational initiatives. As Duncan Forrester has noted, when children
are separately educated 'misunderstandings and suspicions inevitably arise
and the community building function of education is compromised.'[18]
The way in which denominational divisions have done so much to reinforce political divisions is borne out by sociological research conducted
by Duncan Morrow.[19] If Christians were more ready to speak up for the
interests of those who are not members of their denomination, it might
do much to subvert the existing relationship between religious affiliation and political allegiance which has done so much to polarise society
in Northern Ireland.

Christian witness in Ireland has been hampered in another major respect through the way in which there has been far too much easy talk
about reconciliation that has not addressed the underlying injustices in
Irish society. Often it has been the politicians who have reminded the
Church that forgiveness is a *political* act that finds its context in the acknowledgement and also the correction of unjust situations. This is in
fact evident from the order of penitential liturgies, where repentance
and a commitment to amendment of life *precede* forgiveness and is only
meaningful if there is a proper recognition of the wrongs of the past
combined with a readiness to embrace real change. As Gerry O'Hanlon
has argued, for genuine reconciliation to be achieved the question of

18. 'Politics and Reconciliation' in M. Hurley, ed., *Reconciliation in Religion and Society*
(Belfast: Institute of Irish Studies, 1994), pp. 111-122 (115).
19. *The Churches and Inter-Community Relationships* (Coleraine: University of Ulster, 1994).

injustice must first be addressed: restoration of a sundered relationship can take place only after the situation of oppression has been overcome.[20] Such considerations point to the theological warrant for the lengthy treatment of economic issues in Chapter Six.

The final chapter concludes its treatment of liberation theology with an extended discussion of those respects in which the ecumenical movement in Ireland has failed. Ways in which the overall mission of the Church is seriously compromised are identified and specific recommendations made. Most notably, it is argued that a willingness by the Protestant Churches to formally distance themselves from the Orange Order and by the Roman Catholic Church to be more generous in sharing Communion, would do much to give substance to the condemnation of the corrosive sectarianism that has so bedevilled Irish society.

The situation in Northern Ireland should not of course be presented as solely a conflict over religious or even political identity. It needs to be more widely acknowledged that Northern Ireland is the only remaining part of Western Europe that has yet to enjoy a fully democratic polity. The Government of Ireland Act which made provision for a Northern Parliament bequeathed a model of parliamentary representation that was too close to that of Westminster and it was subsequently adapted in ways that made it wholly inappropriate given the political demography of Northern Ireland. Thankfully, power-sharing, the new executive and institutions, police reform and wider social and economic reforms, now hold out the prospect of a successful democratisation of the Northern State.

The Churches have not tended to see things in this focussed way and have too often been content to try to mediate tensions between the nationalist and unionist traditions by simply calling for greater mutual understanding. This reveals an assessment of the situation that shows all too little understanding, insofar as it does not properly acknowledge the historic injustices and inadequate political structures that have existed. Nor does it attempt to discriminate between the different strands of both traditions in order to make a vigorous case for more generous conceptions of political community within both traditions. Regrettably, the fail-

---

20. 'Justice and Reconciliation' in M. Hurley, ed., *Reconciliation in Religion and Society*, pp. 48-67.

ure of Protestant Church leaders to prevent the use of churches by the Orange Order in association with parades, is too often paralleled by their reluctance to criticise prominent unionist politicians who foolishly associate the unionist cause with the sectarian bandwagon. Yet it is clarity on these issues that is desperately needed if any substance is to be brought to the stance of the Churches in the turmoil of politics in Northern Ireland. In the case of the Church of Ireland, it is particularly disappointing that despite the counterweight of the Southern Province, it has too often remained captive to the political allegiances of its own constituency and failed to articulate an adequate critique of the political and economic injustices of the Northern State or recognise the need to apologise for its part in them.

By way of conclusion of this introduction, it should be noted that a theology that is truly contextual is never far from what are more universal and perennial themes. This work may relate to a specific cultural context, but many of the concerns that are addressed clearly have a much wider relevance. For example, should not all nationalist movements be judged by the way in which they advance democratic interests, permit multi-ethnicity, defend social rights and aspirations, and respect religious pluralism? Why did Europeans – fifty years after the historic defeat of fascism – not oppose with greater vigour ethnic cleansing and political philosophies founded on racist principles? Why have the absence of democratic rights and a recognition of the place for multi-culturalism within the institutions of the State been allowed to distort politics in the Middle East? In the light of the Irish experience, ought we to tolerate famine in our world today, when collectively we have the means to prevent it? Finally, in an increasingly interdependent world, where sovereignty is widely diffused, what is being done to control multi-national and other global forces that shape so much of all of our lives? Healthy forms of nationalism have the self-confidence to be alive to these sorts of questions and have long since put tribalism behind them.

CHAPTER ONE

The Union of Religious Creeds

Theobald Wolfe Tone and the Origins of the Irish Republican Tradition

Mourn, lost Hibernia, ever mourn
thy freedom lost, thy laurels torn,
thy warriors sunk on Aughrim's Plains,
and Britain loading thee with chains.

'The Tears of Hibernia for the Battle of Aughrim'
Thomas Russell

THE SEVENTEENTH AND EIGHTEENTH-CENTURY BACKGROUND

The Boyne, Aughrim and the conclusion of the Williamite Wars in the Treaty of Limerick in 1691, heralded the triumph of a Protestant Ascendancy in Ireland which excluded both Dissenter and Catholic. Although in the wider British context the accession of William of Orange to the throne represented an advance for democratic interests, in Ireland it proved to be a victory for reaction and colonial subordination, with the subsequent introduction of penal laws denying the political and property rights of the mass of the population.

In the latter half of the eighteenth century the American Revolution had alerted the ruling élite in Ireland to the attractions of having a greater say in their own affairs and this assertiveness was bound to attract wide support. The Volunteer movement, founded to guard Ireland against any designs of the King of France while British troops were deployed abroad, soon proved to be something of a doubled-edged sword. Subservience to London rankled with many of the armed gentry, and the advocates of greater autonomy for the Dublin Parliament obtained important freedoms for the Irish legislature. These achievements were effectively neutralised, however, since patronage was successfully used to ensure the loyalty of the Ascendancy élite, thus isolating the lower ranks of the Volunteer movement which included the more restive and reform-minded elements within Presbyterianism.

With regard to political theory, it was the ideas of John Locke, most notably his contract theory of government, which encouraged the growing desire for greater independence among Protestants. As early as 1698, William Molyneux in his *The Case of Ireland's being bound by Acts of Parliament in England, stated*, had argued that the Irish people's contract was directly with the Crown, and therefore Ireland, which was a separate kingdom, should not be subject to the English Parliament. Thus began the campaign which was later to result in the short-lived gains that arose from the granting of legislative independence for the Irish Parliament in 1782/3.[1]

Presbyterianism had good reason to sympathise with those who advocated reform. Its acute sense of grievance against the ruling Ascendancy and its own democratic procedures for Church government made it receptive to more progressive political thinking. Moreover, given the close associations between Ulster and Scotland, it is not surprising that in the eighteenth century Ulster Presbyterianism was influenced by Enlightenment thought. Many of the clergy were educated at the Universities of Glasgow and Edinburgh and thus had direct experience of the Scottish Enlightenment. As early as the 1720s, the controversy surrounding adherence to the Westminster Confession had resulted in the formation of 'New Light' non-subscribing Presbyterianism. This more libertarian strand, which welcomed much of the new thinking of the Enlightenment, quickly became a significant force within Presbyterianism, and later in the century was to contribute to the rising Protestant assertiveness and radicalism which produced the Volunteer and the United Irish movements. Even the more theologically conservative ministers sometimes held advanced views when it came to political matters.[2]

Locke's contract theory had a wide appeal within Presbyterianism. As did the republican thought of Francis Hutcheson, who taught at a Dissenting academy in Dublin and later as Professor of Moral Philosophy at

1. M. Elliott, *Watchmen in Sion: The Protestant Idea of Liberty* (Derry: A Field Day Pamphlet, No. 8, 1985), p. 18.
2. Elliott, *Watchmen in Sion*, pp. 5ff.; J. Smyth, *The Men of No Property: Irish Radicals and Popular Politics in the Late Eighteenth Century* (London: Macmillan, 1992), pp. 80ff; and D. Dickson, D. Keogh and K. Whelan, eds, *The United Irishmen: Republicanism, Radicalism and Rebellion* (Dublin, Lilliput Press: 1993), Chapters 3 and 4.

Glasgow. In his development of social contract theory Hutcheson taught a doctrine of resistance, which was deemed to be justified in circumstances where government had betrayed the trust of the people.[3] It was also increasingly recognised that a contract theory of government implied the involvement of the majority, and towards the end of the eighteenth century while most Protestants still saw Catholics as a threat to their interests, the case for the inclusion of the Catholic population in reform aspirations was gaining ground.[4] These issues were fervently debated within the Volunteer movement which included within its ranks members strongly sympathetic to radical republican ideas.[5] Thus in Ireland the democratic revolutionary current transforming European society in the aftermath of the French Revolution fused with a native republican tradition.

THE 1798 REBELLION:

THEOBALD WOLFE TONE AND THE UNITED IRISH SOCIETY

The life and thought of Theobald Wolfe Tone might seem an odd place to begin a consideration of the republican rebellion of 1798. For the three years from 1795-98, Tone was in America and France, and, following his capture at sea in 1798, he was ignominiously transported to Dublin where he was swiftly tried and sentenced to death. When he heard details of the carnage that had raged in Ireland, he indicated his shock and regret, saying that he had only sought an open and honourable conflict, with aid of France, to remove the English connection.[6] It was only after the publication of his Journal in 1826 and the intense interest shown

3. Elliott, *Watchmen in Sion*, pp. 12ff. In his *Short Introduction to Moral Philosophy*, Hutcheson wrote: 'When the common rights of the community are trampled upon ... then as the governor is plainly perfidious to his trust, he has forfeited all the power committed. In every sort of government the people have the right of defending themselves against the abuse of power.' Quoted by Pieter Tesch in 'Presbyterian Radicalism' in Dickson, Keogh and Whelan, *The United Irishmen*, pp. 33-48 (38).
4. Elliott, *Watchmen in Sion*, pp. 17f.
5. On the Volunteer movement and its importance for later developments see A. Stewart, *A Deeper Silence: The Hidden Roots of the United Irish Movement* (London: Faber and Faber, 1993). Although Stewart's argument concerning the influence of Presbyterianism, the Volunteer movement and Masonry is perhaps overstated, he highlights significant continuities with the later radicalism of the 1790s.
6. For a major biography of Tone see Marianne Elliott, *Wolfe Tone: Prophet of Irish Independence* (New Haven and London: Yale University Press, 1989). For Tone's words of regret during his trial see p. 393.

by the Young Irelanders in the 1840s, that the process which was to estab-
lish Tone as the founder of Irish republican tradition really began.[7]

Tone's subsequent reputation was, however, a well deserved one. The
passage of his thought from reform sympathies to forthright republicanism, the break with the Protestant Ascendancy in the furtherance of a
political movement that would unite Catholic, Protestant and Dissenter,
and the willingness to countenance an alliance with revolutionary France
in the interests of an independent Ireland – all these describe more than
biographical details. They document the birth of modern Irish republicanism, which at its inception was remarkably cosmopolitan in perspective.

The process whereby the revolution in political consciousness associated with the European Enlightenment and French Revolution established its roots in Irish soil, introducing into Irish culture the same aspiration for national freedom and democratic rights that was sweeping
through European society, is of course more than Tone's story. The United
Irish Society – of which Tone was scarcely the most prominent member –
produced a whole series of leaders of stature. It was Tone's talents as a
popular writer and political thinker who skillfully pressed home the case
for the inclusion of Catholics within the reform movement, along with
the circumstances that led to him representing the international dimension to the political conflict of his generation, which marked him out
and thereby justify the kindness of posterity.

Theobald Wolfe Tone was born in 1763 in Dublin. His father was a
coach builder with small landed interests, and a member of the established Church of Ireland. His family was thus part of the lower ranks of
the Ascendancy order. Tone entered Trinity College in 1781. After two
years at the Middle Temple in London, he returned to Dublin, where he
took his law exams and was called to the Bar in 1789. At this stage in his
career, law was not particularly exciting or lucrative, and Tone lacked
the patience to cultivate prospects for advancement.

Tone's energies needed a wider outlet, which he was soon to find
through the invitation to write a pamphlet for the Irish Whig opposition, reviewing the conduct of the Government. The pamphlet was published in April 1790. In this, his first foray upon the political stage, Tone

7. Ibid., pp. 411ff.

commended the Whig opposition for defending the wider interests of the people, and lambasted the corruption of the current administration, which he compared unfavourably with the Parliament of 1782 that had at least achieved a degree of autonomy for Irish interests. Given that the Irish Whigs shared the Government's commitment to the Protestant Ascendancy and the English connection, this pamphlet only shows Tone to be of reformist sympathies, though in places, such as his appeal to 'the great body of the people', his language points in more radical directions.[8]

The growing impact of the French revolution, the widespread interest in Thomas Paine's *Rights of Man*, and the mounting pressure for Catholic emancipation, all made 1791 a year of rapid political development. In his Journal, Tone refers to the marked effect of both the French Revolution and Paine's work in Ireland, and on himself personally.

> In England, Burke had the triumph completely to decide the public .... But matters were very different in Ireland, an oppressed, insulted and plundered nation.... In a little time the French Revolution became the test of every man's political creed, and the nation was fairly divided into two great parties, the Aristocrats and Democrats (epithets borrowed from France) ... It is needless, I believe, to say that I was a Democrat from the very commencement.[9]

It was during this period that Tone forged a number of political friendships and associations – most notably with Thomas Russell and William Drennan – who were later to be instrumental with Tone in the formation of the United Irish Society in October 1791. The circle of Tone's associates in this period was indeed an ever-widening one, and demarcating the lines of influence is no easy task. Tone's gift was his pen, and his ability to synthesise ideas concisely meant that he was entrusted with the task of framing the declaration and resolutions of the new society. The document had three central resolutions:

> *First, Resolved,* That the weight of English influence in the Government of this country is so great, as to require a cordial union among

---

8. T. Bartlett, editor, *Life of Theobald Wolfe Tone: Compiled and arranged by William Theobald Wolfe Tone* (Dublin: Lilliput Press, 1998), pp. 247 ff (264).
9. Ibid., pp. 39f.

all the people of Ireland to maintain that balance which is essential to the preservation of our liberties, and the extension of our commerce.

Second, That the sole constitutional mode by which this influence can be opposed, is by a complete and radical reform of the representation of the people in Parliament.

Third, That no reform is practicable, efficacious, or just, which shall not include Irishmen of every *religious* persuasion.[10]

Tone regarded the overcoming of the religious cleavages in Irish society as fundamental. In this he was influenced by the closest of his political confidants, Thomas Russell. Although the word 'Catholic' had not been expressly mentioned in the Resolutions, implicitly bringing the Catholic question to the forefront was not without controversy among the constituency to which the United Irish Society appealed.[11]

Throughout the summer of 1791 Tone had in fact been focussing his attention on the Catholic question and this provided the occasion for writing his *Argument on Behalf of the Catholics of Ireland,* published in August 1791. Tone primarily sought to address Ulster-Dissenter opinion, which, despite its radical political outlook, was divided on the emancipation issue. He argued that while the proximate source of Ireland's troubles was the corrupting influence of English rule, that rule was based on the disunity of Irish society, 'our own intestine division'. The Government had been able to reverse the gains made by the Irish Parliament in 1782 because Parliament was unrepresentative, easily manipulated and unable to marshal the interests of the whole country. Similarly, the Volunteer Movement had failed because it was 'built on too narrow a foundation'. 'No reform can ever be obtained', Tone argued, 'which shall not comprehensively embrace Irishmen of all denominations.'

As a Protestant himself, Tone understood the anxiety that the prospect of Catholic emancipation provoked in the mind of the Dissenter. Indeed, the persuasiveness of his appeal derives from the way he succeeds in associating himself with his audience, as, for example, when he speaks of confronting the 'ghastly spectre of our distempered imagina-

---

10. Ibid., pp. 248 ff. Elliott, *Wolfe Tone,* pp. 124ff. and 139ff.
11. In his Journal Tone gives a report of some of the not always convivial conversation that took place on this matter. Bartlett (ed.), *Life of Theobald Wolfe Tone.* p. 126. See R. Jacob, *The Rise of the United Irishmen 1791-4* (London: George Harrap, 1937), pp. 68ff.

tion'. To the objection that the Catholics' loyalty to the pope allies them to a foreign power, he cites the burning of the pope's effigy in France and the way in which Catholics and Protestants were working together in the French Assembly. To the fear that land titles would be contested, he points to the self-interest of those Catholics who had themselves invested in land. To the argument that on account of their ignorance Catholics were not ready for liberty, he emphasises the disingenuousness of this viewpoint, given that it is the Protestants who have denied Catholics the opportunity for education, and rejoins with a Painite stress upon on the rights of man. To the case that emancipation would mean that the Catholics would swamp the legislature, he reminds his hearers of the property qualification.[12]

Although Tone was by no means the first to observe that the disunion of religious creeds was the basis of English influence and Ascendancy power, he presented the argument with a clarity and precision that had hitherto been lacking. The appeal to natural rights was Tone's strongest argument, since this was the very ground on which the Dissenters sought redress for their own grievances. The pamphlet also gives us some insight into the degree of pragmatism in Tone's radicalism: he always wished to carry his hearers with him and his discussion of the property qualification for the franchise shows him ready to assuage more moderate opinion. It should also be noted that the October Resolutions of the United Irish Society envisaged only parliamentary reform as the means of redressing Ireland's grievances. In this respect, however, there is evidence that Tone's own thinking was in advance of many within the United Irish Society. In a letter to Thomas Russell, enclosed with the first draft of the Resolutions, Tone comments that the 'bane of Irish prosperity is the influence of England' and indicates his personal 'wish for separation', while conceding that such an opinion was 'for the present too hardy'.[13] Tone's separatism flowed directly from his adhesion to democratic principles – independence was necessary to secure the extension of political liberty.

Tone's *Argument* was a bestseller, with distribution reaching sixteen thousand.[14] Not surprisingly, given his skill as a publicist and his sympathy for their cause, Tone was soon approached by leading Catholics, and

12. Bartlett, *Life of Theobald Wolfe Tone*, pp. 278ff. (279, 285f).
13. See Jacob, *The Rise of the United Irishmen*, pp. 61f.
14. Elliott, *Wolfe Tone*, p. 129.

in 1792 he was appointed Secretary of the Catholic Committee. The authorities at Dublin Castle had every reason to take a close interest in Tone's work for Catholic emancipation and his participation in the United Irish Society. Implicated in a treasonable correspondence and facing possible trial, he was in June 1795 forced to leave Irish soil. As he bade farewell to Belfast colleagues, he joined with them in a solemn oath 'never to desist in our efforts until we had subverted the authority of England over our country and asserted her independence.'[15] In his Memoir of August 1796, we find Tone's famous summary of the political principles he had held since 1791:

> To subvert the tyranny of our execrable government, to break the connection with England, the never-failing source of all our political evils, and to assert the independence of my country – these were my objects. To unite the whole people of Ireland, to abolish the memory of all past dissensions and to substitute the common name of Irishman in place of the denominations of Protestant, Catholic and Dissenter – these were my means.[16]

In 1795 Tone had left for America where he pursued a diplomatic mission on behalf of the United Irish Society to enlist French military assistance. After obtaining the support of the French Ambassador, he obtained the necessary papers of introduction to the French Government. There followed his extraordinary negotiations with Carnot, his securing the confidence of the French Directory, his introduction to the prestigious General Hoche, his entry into the French Army where he was to reach the rank of Adjutant General, his participation in the ill-fated Bantry Bay expedition, and, finally, his arrest at sea in a later French attempt at intervention in 1798.[17]

Tone's objective of a union of religious creeds had more to contend with than prejudice. Political forces running in precisely the opposite direction were increasingly evident throughout the 1790s. The skilful manipulation of Irish affairs by a government that fully understood that its success lay in playing off one group against another should certainly not be underestimated. There was also in the Orange Order, founded in

15.   Bartlett, *Life of Theobald Wolfe Tone*, pp. 107f.
16.   Ibid., p. 46.
17.   M. Elliott, *Wolfe Tone*, pp. 260ff.

1795, an anti-Catholic organisation ready violently to assert what it perceived as Protestant economic and political interests. Although there had been a history of local disturbance associated with secret societies and land disputes, the Orange Order which was more organised, quickly spread throughout Ulster, and was used by the Government both to foment discord and sometimes as a military force. Many sections of the yeomanry in fact consisted of Orange Clubs.[18]

THE SOCIAL IDEALS OF THE UNITED IRISH MOVEMENT

As early as 1793/4, the Dublin branch of the United Irish Society had issued a manifesto similar to that of the later Chartist movement, advocating voting rights for all adult males, annual parliaments and abolition of the property qualification for parliamentary members.[19] Pitt's policy of repression in the mid-1790s accelerated the process whereby the limited objective of parliamentary reform was gradually replaced by a commitment to the political ideal of republican government that now advocated separation. The Belfast branch of the United Irish Society was to prove more radical than the more aristocratic Dublin membership, some of whom left as republican aspirations deepened.[20]

There existed a considerable diversity of opinion as to the specific measures a republican government should adopt. Some historians characterise the United Irish movement as primarily bourgeois, and argue that political radicalism was not accompanied by a willingness to countenance major social measures. At the other extreme, scholars like Desmond Greaves have suggested that socialist ideas can be found in Wolfe Tone and that the 1798 rebellion involved a proletarian element. The text most frequently quoted in support of this contention records Tone's sentiments in 1796:

> Our independence must be had at all hazards. If the men of property will not support us, they must fall; we can support ourselves by the aid

---

18. See E. Strauss, *Irish Nationalism and British Democracy* (London: Methuen, 1951), pp. 24-6, 53-5.
19. *Northern Star*, 17-20 February 1794.
20. See D. Carroll, *The Man From God Knows Where: Thomas Russell 1767-1803* (Dublin: Gartan, 1995), pp. 60, 70ff.

of that numerous and respectable class of the community, *the men of no property*.[21]

This has been dismissed as no more than an expression of exaspera-tion and not signalling a shift in Tone's thinking. The truth no doubt lies somewhere in between. It would certainly not be the first occasion in which Tone showed himself to be in advance of some of his contempo-raries, and it would have been surprising if his time in France had not led to a greater appreciation of the role of popular mobilisation. There is, in fact, evidence of a similar shift during the second half of the 1790s in the strategy of the United Irish movement, which was increasingly engaged in forging links with agrarian organisations like the Defenders and other protest groups among the poorer classes.[22] There is no reason why the divisions that had existed in the revolution movement in France between the dominant bourgeois interest, radical Jacobinism and the levelling aspirations of the *sans-culottes*, did not have its parallel within an Irish context. It might be that Tone was realising that the American and French revolutions had promised more than they had delivered and had come to identify the real driving force likely to sustain a republican move-ment as an unprecedented popular mobilisation. Tone's statement, af-ter his arrival in France in 1796, is of relevance: 'I should be glad if the Jacobins were to come again into play, for I think a little more energy just now would do the French Government no harm.'[23]

Tone's friendship with Thomas Russell – with whom he always felt the very closest of affinities – certainly suggests that Tone came to share at least some of the social radicalism for which Russell was well known.[24]

21. Bartlett, *Life of Theobald Wolfe Tone*, p. 494. See also C. Desmond Greaves, *Theobald Wolfe Tone and the Irish Nation*, (Dublin: Connolly Publications, 1989), p. 48.
22. See Nancy Curtin, 'The transformation of the Society of United Irishmen into a Mass-based Revolutionary Organisation, 1794-6', *Irish Historical Studies*, Vol. 24, No. 96 (1985), pp. 463-92; M. Elliott, *Wolfe Tone*, pp. 255 ff; and K. Whelan, 'The United Irishmen, the Enlightenment and Popular Culture' in Dickson, Keogh and Whelan, *The United Irishmen*, pp. 269-296 (especially p. 285).
23. Bartlett, *Life of Theobald Wolfe Tone*, p. 495.
24. Elliott records Tone's assessment of his prized friendship with Russell. 'Russell and I were inseparable, and, as our discussions were mostly political, and our sentiments agreed exactly, we extended our views and fortified each other in the opinions, to the propagation and establishment of which we have ever since been devoted.' (Elliott, *Wolfe Tone*, p. 99). See also her comments on Russell's influence on Tone on p. 232. Despite this, however, Elliott takes the view that 'Tone's radicalism did not go beyond the middling sort and he never lost his dislike of popular tumult.' (p. 232). By 1991 it

Russell's egalitarian ideas were informed by a fervent religious conviction of the dignity of the human person which implied rights of a social
as well as a political nature. In his *A letter to the people of Ireland* he insisted
that since all people are endowed by God with 'the same passions and
the same reason as the great', they are qualified 'for the same liberty,
happiness and virtue'.[25] The attack upon the fitness of the poor for self-
governance was rejected by Russell as an infamy of tyrannical government against the divine purpose. He contrasted the corrupt rule of a
privileged minority with government that excluded no one from the body
politic and was therefore rooted in the interests of all. Although Tone
was more patrician and did not have the empathy for the poor for which
Russell was so renowned, it is likely that if he had he been in Ireland
during the preparations for 1798 he would have been impressed by alliances and bonds of affection Russell had helped forge with the lower
classes.

Russell was part of a wider network within the United Irish Society
that was responsible for shifting policy in more radical directions and
initiating mergers with the Defenders. This circle included James Hope
and Henry Joy McCracken who were both keen advocates of social justice and the need to address the plight of the labouring classes. In the
North there was a Jacobin society of artisans and working men, and a
group known as the Mudler's Club that had Jacobin sympathies, with
whom Russell seems to have had contacts.[26] Economic pressures, which
told particularly harshly on the poorer classes, were certainly evident in
the 1790s[27] and with politicisation did not always lead to sectarianism.

An examination of the writings of the United Irish Society and popular manifestos associated with the movement shows that socially radical

---

would seem that Elliott had adjusted her position on this matter, since here she says
that Russell convinced Tone that 'the future of Irish independence lay with the lower
orders'. See Elliott's foreword in C. J. Woods, ed., *Journals and Memoirs of Thomas
Russell: 1791-5* (Dublin and Belfast: Irish Academic Press, 1991), p. 9.

25. *A letter to the people of Ireland on the present situation of the country* (Belfast, 1796), p. 18.
26. Carroll, *The Man From God Knows Where*, pp. 106ff. and 93.
27. David Dickson cites the sharp growth in population in the second half of the eighteenth century and consequent inflationary pressures. In 1797 one critic of the United
Irish Society described the duty on salt as 'a great means of perverting the minds of
the lower order'. See David Dickson, 'The State of Ireland Before 1798', in Cathal
Póirtéir, ed., *The Great Irish Rebellion of 1798* (Dublin: Mercier Press, 1998), pp. 15-25
(25).

sympathies were in fact entertained in many quarters. This went beyond an attack upon the indulgence of a bloated aristocracy, the corruption of government by patronage and the awarding of massive pensions from public funds. Thomas Addis Emmet anticipated significant measures of social improvement as the natural accompaniment of the extension of democracy and advocated the abolition of tithes and the provision of adequate education. *The Union Doctrine; or Poor Man's Catechism* envisaged similar measures:

> I believe applying the lands of the Church to relieve old age, to give education and protection to infancy, will be more acceptable to an United people, than maintaining lazy hypocrites and ravenous tythe proctors.

The question of land distribution was linked with belief in popular sovereignty. 'The Almighty intended all mankind to lord the soil' and it would be 'unfair for fifty or a hundred men to possess what is for the subsistence of near five millions'.[28]

The wide coalition of interests which the United Irish movement embraced meant that its social radicalism could easily prove divisive. Its members among the commercial classes might have accepted the need for agrarian reform, but this would have fallen a long way short of an attack upon property. Even the likes of Russell, who fervently believed that popular government would lead to more just government with reform measures, was often rather vague when it came to matters of policy. The commitment to removing tithes and countenancing some land redistribution clearly held by many should not be taken to mean that what we are dealing with here is a nascent socialist movement. There is, nonetheless, evidence of ideas as advanced as those found among the Jacobin left in France from which a generation later a recognisably socialist movement did emerge. There is thus every justification for the contention that both Irish democracy and Irish socialism have their roots in the fertile soil of the eighteenth-century republicanism of the United Irish Society.

28. See Smyth, *The Men of No Property*, pp. 167f. See also pp. 94ff.

CHAPTER TWO

Politics and Religion in Ireland

From the Act of Union to the Free State

THE EMMET RISING, AGRARIAN UNREST AND THE TITHE WAR

The events surrounding 1798 provided the pretext for the closure of the
Dublin parliament, though the consolidation of British imperial interests with the Act of Union at the beginning of the new century can scarcely
be said to have ushered in a period of political tranquillity. The United
Irish Society still had many leaders of stature, and discontent was never
far below the surface.

The Emmet insurrection of 1803 is often discounted as a piece of
foolhardy adventurism on the part of an idealistic young man completely
out of touch with the general mood of his country. This reading of events
oversimplifies the situation and does not sit well with the fact that the
preparations for the attempt in 1803 to seize power in Dublin and touch
off a national insurrection would seem to have been quite elaborate.
The Manifesto of the Provisional Government was an impressive constitutional document not without political and moral discrimination in its
articulation of the Rising's aims; a large stand of arms had been amassed
in a depot in Thomas Street and Emmet could have counted on enthusiastic support from the workers in the Liberties district of Dublin; the
redoubtable Michael O'Dwyer in Wicklow and other veterans of 1798
could be relied upon to rally support in the country areas outside Dublin; the legendary Thomas Russell had managed to return to Ireland
from exile and was attempting with James Hope – albeit unsuccessfully –
to enlist support in the North.

In the event, the plan to seize the Castle in Dublin was bungled when
the men who were to supply coaches were challenged by a soldier, whom
they shot; they then fled in panic. The intended seizure of the Castle,
which it was envisaged would provide the psychological blow to spur people into action, had been the centrepiece of the strategy, and the insurrection had to be quickly aborted. There was nonetheless serious fighting in the Liberties.

Embarrassed by their being taken by surprise, the authorities sought to distract public attention by making an example of Emmet.[1]

Although there were no further coordinated attempts at insurrection in the opening decades of the century, there were sporadic disturbances in individual counties that provoked military action to restore order, and agrarian discontent associated with secret societies was widespread. The first of these societies, the Whiteboys, can be traced back to the 1760s. Economic tensions frequently gave rise to forms of protest such as cattle maiming and sometimes summary retribution was meted out to land-lords or agents whose actions were particularly deeply resented.

This violence was usually kept within prescribed limits by these secret organisations. Their role was to regulate relations between landlord and tenant, and informed by a communal vision of justice, they sought to impose what some scholars have described as the 'moral economy' of the masses.[2] Much of the energy and vitality of these movements ex-pressing popular discontent fed into the great political campaigns that followed as the nineteenth century unfolded. Some of these agrarian groups linked their social protests with fervent millenarian-style beliefs. The Rockites, for instance, in the early 1820s circulated pamphlets pre-dicting the impending collapse of Protestantism in the year 1825.[3]

The infamous collection of tithes was to prove a frequent cause for agrarian disquiet. Through this tax the peasantry were expected to sup-port the clergy of the Established Church. As well as being a regressive tax that bore most heavily on those least able to pay it, Catholics and Presbyterians naturally resented having to pay for the upkeep of an es-tablished Church that denounced them as heretics and denied their po-litical rights. What became known as the 'Tithe War' broke out in Graiguenamanagh on the Carlow/Kilkenny border in 1830. The cam-paign for non-payment quickly spread, and when crops and livestock

1. For accounts of the 1803 insurrection see P. Geoghegan, *Robert Emmet: A Life* (Dublin: Gill and Macmillan, 2002); M. Elliott, *Partners in Revolution: the United Irishmen and France* (New Haven and London: Yale University, 1982), pp. 297ff.; H. Landreth, *The Pursuit of Robert Emmet* (Dublin: Browne and Nolan, 1949); and D. Carroll, *The Man From God Knows Where: Thomas Russell 1767-1803* (Dublin: Gartan, 1995), pp. 164ff.

2. See O. MacDonagh, *States of Mind: A Study of the Anglo-Irish Conflict 1780-1980* (London: Allen and Unwin, 1983), pp. 39ff.

3. See K. T. Hoppen, in his *Ireland Since 1800: Conflict and Conformity* (London and New York: Longman, 1989), pp. 44ff.

were seized the violence became more intense. In the North the campaign had interdenominational support, though the Orange Order vigorously opposed it as a threat to Protestant supremacy. It was a member of the Church of Ireland, Sharman Crawford, who pressed the case against tithes in the House of Commons. Such was the popular dissent that by 1838 the Whig administration of Lord Grey had passed a bill reducing tithes and transferring payments to landlords. This only partially resolved the problem, but it did pave the way for further reform and bring an end to the unrest.[4]

CATHOLIC EMANCIPATION AND REPEAL: DANIEL O'CONNELL

Despite the imposition of the Penal Laws over several decades following the Williamite settlement, there existed in Ireland a growing body of Catholics who had managed to prosper. The O'Connells of Iveragh, Co Kerry, were landowners of old Gaelic stock who had acquired strong trading interests. Whilst he certainly had a privileged background, Daniel O'Connell (born 1775) was still very much a product of his Gaelic environment. In infancy he had been fostered out to a peasant family, after which he lived at his uncle's house on the Kerry coast. In later life, although he embraced the wider more cosmopolitan world that politics thrust upon him, he always found refreshment in returning to his native Kerry.[5]

For part of his teenage years O'Connell was educated in France, where he was exposed to a more liberal Catholicism.[6] In 1794 he enrolled at Lincoln's Inn, London, to begin training for the profession in which he was soon to secure such a distinguished reputation. He also attended King's Inn, Dublin, to qualify for the Irish Bar. O'Connell's student years in London and Dublin were to prove crucial for the development of his political ideas. He read widely, and quickly acquainted himself with the democratic ideals so pervasive in the 1790s. William Godwin's *Inquiry concerning Political Justice* was a work he particularly admired, and it is

---

4. See Oliver MacDonagh, 'The Economy and Society, 1830-45' in W. Vaughan, ed., *A New History of Ireland*, Vol. V, *Ireland Under the Union, I 1801-70* (Oxford: Clarendon, 1989), pp. 218-241 (222-5) and F. Campbell, *The Dissenting Voice: Protestant Democracy in Ulster from Plantation to Partition* (Belfast: The Blackstaff Press, 1991), pp. 145ff.
5. F. O'Ferrall, *Daniel O'Connell* (Dublin: Gill and Macmillan, 1981), pp. 4ff.
6. R. Foster, *Modern Ireland 1600-1972* (London: Penguin, 1988), p. 300.

likely that it was Godwin who fortified the emphasis O'Connell came to place on achieving political reforms through moral force. Later in life, O'Connell was keen to distance himself from the aims of the United Irish Society in the 1790s. Although he favoured parliamentary reform, he certainly had no enthusiasm for what he saw as the threat to property that a social revolution along French lines would pose.[7] The situation may not however always have been as clear-cut as this might suggest. Indeed there is evidence that O'Connell was disingenuous about some of his own past associations with the United Irish Society, which would have caused him considerable embarrassment and did not sit well with the political outlook that informed his own campaigning.[8]

O'Connell's first significant intervention on the public stage was a speech in 1800 at a meeting which had been organised to oppose the Act of Union.[9] Not all Roman Catholics had been enticed by the promise of Emancipation, which in the event was not delivered, and O'Connell had no hesitation in joining with those Protestants who wished to make the case for maintaining the independence and liberty of the Irish Parliament. Closing his speech O'Connell declared:

> I know that the Catholics of Ireland still remember that they have a country, and that they will never accept of any advantages as a *sect*, which would debase and destroy them as a *people*.[10]

It was O'Connell's brilliant legal career on the Munster Circuit that established his popular reputation.[11] He was soon regarded as the leading advocate in the land – no mean achievement given the impediments to advancement in the legal profession for a Catholic. O'Connell's commitment to non-violent methods would have been fortified by his legal work, where his willingness, and frequent success, in defending those accused of involvement in agrarian disturbances gave him a direct insight into the often destructive consequences of political discontent. Such

---

7. O'Ferrall, *Daniel O'Connell*, pp. 9-13. For a discussion of O'Connell's emphasis on moral force and his opposition to violence see Maurice O'Connell, *Daniel O'Connell: The man and his politics* (Dublin: The Irish Academic Press, 1990), pp. 61ff.
8. See K. Whelan, *The Tree of Liberty: Radicalism, Catholism and the Construction of Irish Identity 1760-1830* (Cork: Cork University Press, 1996), pp. 150ff.
9. O'Ferrall, *Daniel O'Connell*, pp. 14ff.
10. See M. O'Connell, *Daniel O'Connell: The Man and his Politics*, p. 46.
11. O'Ferrall, *Daniel O'Connell*, pp. 16ff.

trials brought O'Connell national attention, with famous acquittals that made him a folk-hero and earned him the popular title of 'the Counsellor'. It was in the courtroom that O'Connell learned the oratorical skills he was to use to such purpose in his political campaigning.

To place in context O'Connell's contribution to the struggle for Catholic Emancipation it is necessary to recall Pitt's earlier handling of this matter. Following the passing of the Act of Union, the promises that had been made about Catholic Emancipation were not honoured because the cabinet was divided and George III had indicated his opposition. Pitt resigned and his administration fell. The issue was scarcely going to go away and by 1804 influential Catholics were campaigning for new measures. Most adopted a pragmatic line, which would ensure safeguards for ruling Ascendancy interests.

When O'Connell entered the fray he staked his case resolutely on the question of religious liberty. Emancipation was not about the granting of a series of piecemeal concessions but the assertion of fundamental rights. O'Connell knew how to present a case and he eventually succeeded in carrying Catholic opinion. He argued that if Emancipation was limited through governmental powers of veto on clerical appointments and other encroachments that would follow from state financial support, the freedom of the Catholic Church would be compromised. This was unacceptable, since in the absence of Irish independence, the religious liberty of Catholics was the last vestige of liberty left.[12] O'Connell's campaigning mobilised the Catholic population and this in turn helped him win over leading Catholics.

The famine of 1821-2 had undoubtedly increased the militancy of the peasantry and O'Connell was keen to channel these energies. The agitation entered a new phase in 1823 with the formation of the Catholic Association, which achieved a more advanced level of organisation and began to raise large sums of money through subscriptions in what was to become known as the 'Catholic Rent'. With this unprecedented mobilisation, the Emancipation movement now assumed the form of a mass agitation led by the Catholic middle class and enjoying the approval of the Catholic hierarchy. A powerful campaigning infrastructure had been

12. Ibid., p. 30.

forged which could direct the energies of popular discontent towards Parliament and elections.[13]

Although on occasion O'Connell made it clear that he thought that the refusal to grant Catholics their liberties might lead to civil war and was not above brinkmanship, he relied on force of argument and an appeal to the justice of the Catholic cause. Summarising his hopes, he argued that 'there was a moral electricity in the continuous expression of public opinion concentrated upon a single point, perfectly irresistible in its efficacy.'[14]

After a period supporting Protestant pro-Emancipation electoral candidates, in 1828 O'Connell decided to contest the Clare by-election. The existing parliamentary oaths made O'Connell's victory a constitutional embarrassment, since he would be unable to take his seat. Wellington and Peel – albeit with bad grace – were at last convinced that Emancipation must be granted and a bill was passed in 1829.

This victory had a sting in the tail. It was won at the expense of the political rights of the tenantry to whom O'Connell had appealed, since the property qualification for the franchise was raised from forty shillings to ten pounds. Landlords no longer had the same electoral interest in swelling the ranks of their tenants and evictions followed as land was cleared for more profitable grazing.

Emancipation did not bring to an end Protestant dominance in Irish affairs. Although new offices under the Crown were now open to Catholics, government patronage ensured that in practice hopes were frustrated. O'Connell himself saw Catholic Emancipation as a stepping-stone to wider political aims and he quickly set his sights on the more ambitious objective of repeal of the Act of Union.

As an M.P., O'Connell did not confine his attention to Irish matters. On entering parliament he gave his support to electoral reform, Jewish emancipation and the abolition of slavery. He identified closely with the philosophical radicalism of Jeremy Bentham and James Mill. This tells us quite a lot about his political outlook. His commitment to democracy was allied with an individualistic conception of society that stressed the

13. The significance of the famine of 1821-2 is stressed in the treatment of Catholic Emancipation by E. Strauss, *Irish Nationalism and British Democracy* (London: Methuen, 1951), pp. 88-96 (92).
14. O'Ferrall, *Daniel O'Connell*, p. 52.

rights of property and a belief in the unrestrained operations of the market. O'Connell's rather poor record on socially progressive legislation would seem to confirm that his radicalism was very much of the middle class variety.[15] His stance on what he saw as the frequent excesses of trade unionism was one of vehement opposition. 'There was no tyranny', he complained, 'equal to that which was exercised by the trade unionists in Dublin over their fellow labourers.'[16]

The Repeal agitation won widespread popular support that was soon translated into parliamentary seats. O'Connell was able to use the Repeal party at Westminster to obtain concessions, and in 1835 formally supported a Whig administration which introduced a number of favourable measures for Ireland.[17] The changes to the political landscape produced by parliamentary reform and the difficulties rival administrations had in sustaining majorities had made the political system even more susceptible to pressures from below.[18]

When the Tories returned to power in the 1840s, the Repeal Association sponsored a series of mass rallies, known as 'monster meetings', and for a time the momentum seemed to be moving in O'Connell's favour. The Government, alarmed by developments, took decisive action in 1843 by proscribing a meeting at Clontarf and deploying troops. The authorities had braced themselves for the worst and were ready to face down civil disorder or rebellion. O'Connell cancelled the meeting and the subsequent disarray was compounded by his arrest on charges of conspiracy. He conducted his own defence, with some success, but the vitality of youth was no longer there, and on his release he was unable to rejuvenate the Repeal movement, which was in any case overtaken by the tragedy of the Great Famine. O'Connell's health weakened and he died in 1847.

O'Connell's achievement was to sustain a mass movement which mobilised democratic pressures on a hitherto unprecedented scale. By the time of the passing of the Emancipation Act, Ireland had reached a more advanced stage of organised political development than Britain. The for-

---

15. See E. Norman, *A History of Modern Ireland* (London: Penguin, 1971), pp. 57-63.
16. See J. Connolly, *Labour in Ireland* (Dublin: Maunsel, 1917), pp. 145ff. (154).
17. Norman, *A History of Modern Ireland*, pp. 90ff.
18. O. MacDonagh 'The age of O'Connell, 1830-45' in Vaughan, *A New History of Ireland, pp.* 158-68.

mation of Liberal Clubs in Irish constituencies in the run up to Emancipation, made elections more than a series of local contests. Elections were now fought by nationally organised parties – an example which was to be followed in England after the Reform Act of 1832. It was the successes of the O'Connell era in harnessing grass-root energies that paved the way for the later land and constitutional politics of Parnell's Home Rule party.

Despite this undoubtedly impressive record, in some respects at least the O'Connell era left an ambiguous legacy. Most notably, the link between the struggle for democratic rights and the achievement of significant social reform that had been part of the inheritance of the United Irish movement was not adequately sustained by O'Connell, who sometimes resisted measures directed at the improvement of social conditions. This stance had potentially damaging repercussions for the development of the Irish nationalist tradition since it assisted the process whereby the interests of the middle classes came to shape the agenda, though, as we shall see, bringing together imaginatively national and social discontent always remained an effective tactic and the energies thus harnessed sometimes ran in a more radical direction.

The other serious failing was that under O'Connell Irish nationalism had become too closely associated with Roman Catholicism. It is difficult to envisage what other effect championing the rights of Catholics in the context of the Protestant Ascendancy in Ireland could have had. That this was no part of O'Connell's direct intention is evident from a number of factors. First, his entrée into public life had been to oppose the Act of Union, and thus *de facto* to uphold the right of a Dublin Protestant-dominated Parliament. Second, his support for Emancipation was based on liberal ideals and not sectarian interests. Third, he was not without sympathies for measures such as the creation of non-denominational National Schools. Fourth, he was prepared to accept the authority of Rome in spiritual but not in political matters.[19]

Finally, Protestant backing for the Emancipation cause was always

19. In response to the ban on priests attending repeal meetings by Pope Gregory XVI, O'Connell claimed that this was an unjustified interference in Irish affairs and said he would 'take his religion from Rome, but not his politics.' Quoted by James Connolly in P. Berresford Ellis, ed., *James Connolly: Selected Writings* (Harmondsworth: Penguin, 1973), p. 64.

sought and the effort was made to enlist the widest support for Repeal (a substantial number of Repeal Members of Parliament were in fact Protestant).[20]

Echoing the sentiments of the United Irishmen, O'Connell maintained that the Act of Union had been made possible through 'the religious dissensions which the enemies of Ireland have created'.[21] O'Connell in turn was himself to be severely damaged by these dissensions and he scarcely helped matters by relying too readily on the support of his own religious group.[22] His campaigning met with little success in Ulster, and the process whereby he was identified in the public mind with the Catholic interest proved ineluctable. A popular ballad expressed the dominant sentiment:

> The bondage of the Israelites our Saviour he did see,
> He then commanded Moses for to go and set them free,
> And in the same we did remain suffering for our own
> Till God he sent O'Connell, for to free the Church of Rome.[23]

THE YOUNG IRELAND MOVEMENT

The cultural nationalism associated with Herder and German Romanticism had parallels throughout Europe, and the Young Ireland movement should be seen in the wider context of the rapid growth of nationalism throughout the nineteenth century. Through the newspaper, the *Nation*, Young Ireland espoused a form of nationalism, which was at once spiritual, cultural and literary. It exercised a wide appeal among both Protestant and Catholic disaffected intellectuals, and countered the tendency to identify the nationalist cause with Roman Catholicism. Thomas Davis (1814-45), who was the leading thinker of the movement, considered sectarian differences to be corrosive to national unity. The issue came to a head over the question of university education, where Davis argued that the reasons for separate education are

> reasons for separate life, for mutual animosity ... Let those who insist on unqualified separate education follow out their own principles –

20. Norman, *A History of Modern Ireland*, p. 65.
21. O'Ferrall, *Daniel O'Connell*, p. 31.
22. Campbell, *The Dissenting Voice*, pp. 216f.
23. Quoted in Hoppen, *Ireland Since 1800: Conflict and Conformity*, p. 19.

let them prohibit Catholic and Protestant boys from playing, or talk-
ing, or walking together.[24]

The *Nation* informed its readers of its intention to foster a sense of
nationality 'racy of the soil' and 'unshackled by sect or party'.[25] Davis
wished to see a fusion of the ancient Irish and Anglo-Irish, and directed
his literary production accordingly. Admittedly, his enthusiasm for Celtic
culture and desire to combat 'perfidious' Albion, sometimes worked
against this approach, but at heart his was an inclusive nationalism more
in the tradition of the United Irish Society than O'Connellism.[26] Thus
despite its origins within the Repeal agitation, Young Ireland was more
republican and separatist in outlook, and Repeal would have been seen
as a stepping-stone rather than an end in itself. One inquirer who asked
about the tone of the Young Ireland meetings, was given the answer 'Wolfe
Tone'!

It is of course important not to oversimplify and there are in fact
discontinuities as well as continuities. In its preoccupation with cultural
identity, the romantic nationalism of Young Ireland did not always sit
well with the concentration upon democratic and social freedoms which
had characterised the more radical elements within earlier republicanism. Davis did much to bridge this divide. His concept of nationhood as
a spiritual reality did not lead to the glorification of nationality for its
own sake, but to a deepened sense of ethical obligation. Thus in one
poem he writes:

> May Ireland's voice be ever heard
> Amid the world's applause!
> And never be her flag-staff stirred,
> But in an honest cause!
> May freedom be her very breath,
> Be justice ever dear,

---

24. Here I have truncated a quotation made by J. C. Beckett in his *The Making of Modern Ireland, 1603-1923* (London: Faber, 1966), p. 332.
25. See R. Davis, *The Young Ireland Movement* (Dublin: Gill and Macmillan, 1987), p. 25.
26. On occasion Davis did lapse into derogatory racial remarks. For example: 'The Saxon plots a vice where the Celt mediates a complement'. Quoted in Norman, *A History of Modern Ireland*, p. 11. On Young Ireland see also Foster, *Modern Ireland 1600-1972*, pp. 312ff.

> And never an ennobled death
> May son of Ireland fear!
> So the Lord will ever smile.
> With guardian grace upon our isle.[27]

Davis' anti-sectarianism and interest in social justice, although often expressed within a romantic idiom, certainly placed him in sympathy with the political and social ideals of the republican tradition. His nationalism was rooted in a deep humanism and this involved him in passionate protest and fervent appeals on behalf of the poor:

> Aristocracy of Ireland, will ye do nothing? – Will ye do nothing for fear – for pity – for love? Will ye forever abdicate the duty and the joy of making the poor comfortable.[28]

There may be more *noblesse oblige* than socialism in this; nonetheless, Davis' recognition of the unity of the national and social question was to prove influential.

The Young Ireland movement evolved in a number of directions after Davis' death from scarlatina in 1845. James Fintan Lalor (1807-49) is particularly important for the way he developed the egalitarian thrust within Young Ireland by championing land reform and thereby opening up the possibility of forging links with a wider social constituency. Exposed to continental influences through his stay in France, Lalor was an enthusiast for Rousseau. More than anything else, however, it was the tragedy of the Famine that convinced Lalor that former social arrangements must give way to a new basis of social organisation:

> When society fails to perform its duty and fulfil its office of providing for its people; it must take another and more effective form ... then it is time to see it is God's will that society should stand dissolved, and assume another shape and action.[29]

Lalor argued that national freedom would be a sham without the resolution of the land question, and justified his radical policy by an appeal to

---

27. E. Sullivan, *Thomas Davis* (London: Associated University Presses, 1978), pp. 82f.
28. Ibid., p. 55.
29. *James Fintan Lalor: Patriot and Political Essayist. Collected Writings*, introduction by L. Fogarty (Dublin, Talbot Press, 1918), p. 10.

popular sovereignty.

> The principle I state, and mean to stand upon, is this, that the entire ownership of Ireland, moral and material, up to the sun and down to the centre, is vested of right in the people of Ireland; that they, and none but they, are the land-owners and lawmakers of this Island; that all laws are null and void not made by them; and all titles to land invalid not conferred and confirmed by them.[30]

Contrary to the impression this quotation may give, it would be rash to consider Lalor a socialist. His measures were restricted to the redistribution of land on a more equitable basis and he had a rather negative attitude to the new industrialism.

The earlier cooperation of the Young Irelanders with the Repeal agitation had run into difficulties over a whole series of issues. Not least of which was the physical force *versus* constitutionalism debate, which assumed a growing importance. Despite O'Connell's occasional brinkmanship, this controversy had always made a break possible. O'Connell had had direct experience of the bloodshed in 1798, whereas Young Ireland represented a different generation who were more ready to countenance physical force in certain circumstances.[31] In the event, the Young Irelanders' rather bungling insurrectionary activity failed adequately to mobilise popular discontent. The attempt to replicate in Ireland the democratic advances occurring throughout Europe during 1848 was no match for an efficient British intelligence service and massive coercive power.

After the failure of 1848, Young Ireland was a spent force. Nonetheless, if only posthumously, its more prominent members, such as Thomas Davis, found a place among the heroes of the Irish nationalist tradition which their own literary efforts had done so much to invigorate. The ideal of an Irish cultural nationalism was to prove a potent source of future inspiration. In 1916 Arthur Griffith was to write: 'when the Irish read and reflect with Davis, their day of redemption will be at hand.' [32]

---

30. Ibid., pp. 60f. For a discussion of Lalor's social philosophy see D. Buckley, *James Fintan Lalor: Radical* (Cork: Cork University Press, 1990).
31. See T. Moody, *Thomas Davis: 1814-45* (Dublin: Hodges, Figgis and Co., 1945), p. 38.
32. Quoted in Norman in his *A History of Modern Ireland*, p. 137.

FENIANISM

The readiness to create an Irish Republic by armed force links the nationalism of the Young Irelanders with the revolutionary politics of the later Fenian movement. The similarity ends there, since while Fenianism produced a wealth of propaganda, it did not concern itself with cultural and literary activity.

The organisation was founded by James Stephens in 1859 and was sometimes called the Irish Republican Brotherhood. Members took an oath of allegiance and were given military instruction. With the emphasis placed exclusively on the urgency of the need to overthrow British rule in Ireland, constitutionalism was seen as irrelevant, and in language almost millenarian in tone, reference was made to 'the Irish Republic now virtually established'.[33] Secrecy undoubtedly gave the movement an aura of mystique and a notoriety out of all proportion to its actual activity. Although James Stephens and Jeremiah O'Donovan Rossa (another leading Fenian) were both members of the International Workingmen's Association, Fenianism was rather restricted in its social thinking and failed to integrate adequately the national question within a wider political agenda. 'Though it throve on social discontent', J. C. Beckett observed, 'Fenianism had no programme of reform'.[34] Although this is perhaps a little unfair since Fenianism did favour agrarian measures, apart from its later alliance with the Land League, it did not always articulate as effectively as it might have done the rural discontent it had undoubtedly aroused.[35] This was primarily because many Fenians were unprepared to expend energies on reform measures on the basis that good government was no substitute for self-government.

In its military doctrine, Fenianism sought to compensate for its disadvantages in regard to weapons and resources, by secret organisation and choosing a time of attack when Britain was embroiled with other conflicts. England's difficulty is Ireland's opportunity was very much its dic-

33. Ibid., p. 156.
34. See Beckett, *The Making of Modern Ireland*, p. 359.
35. See J. Lee, *The Modernisation of Irish Society 1848-1918* (Dublin: Gill and Macmillan, 1973), pp. 53-59. Lee refers to a 'loosely defined commitment to agrarian reform' (p.54). An agrarian radicalism is suggested by the fact that the proclamation issued at the time of the failed 1867 rising, envisaged that the new democratic republic would pursue a policy of land redistribution. See K. B. Nowlan, 'The Fenian Rising of 1867' in T. Moody, ed., *The Fenian Movement* (Cork: Mercier Press, 1968), pp. 23-35 (30).

tum. When the American Civil War ended, a number of officers came to Ireland. Strained relations between Britain and the United States seemed to afford a favourable opportunity in 1865. In the event a rising was delayed until 1867, and British infiltration and adverse weather conditions brought a swift end to the insurgents' efforts.

The Fenian movement derived its primary importance through its influence upon public opinion, not least in the burgeoning Irish diaspora in the United States and Britain. Financial support from America furnished significant funds, while in Ireland and among the Irish living in Britain, widespread sympathy was evoked by Fenian trials, speeches from the dock and imprisonments. A wave of emotion was produced by the Manchester executions of three Irishmen following the ambush of a police wagon transporting Fenian prisoners, when a policeman had been killed by a shot fired to break a lock. In Britain – despite outrage at the more extreme Fenian operations – the feeling that something must be done to address conditions in Ireland gained ground.[36]

The emotional intensity which Fenianism was able to summon in support of patriotic feeling was to remain a potent factor in Irish politics, as is well illustrated by the oration of Patrick Pearse in 1915 at the graveside of O'Donovan Rossa:

> Life springs from death; and from the graves of patriot men and women spring living nations. The defenders of the Realm have worked well in secret and in the open. They think that they have pacified Ireland. They think that they have purchased half of us and intimidated the other half. They think they have foreseen everything, think that they have provided against everything; but the fools, the fools, the fools! – they have left us our Fenian dead, and while Ireland holds these graves, Ireland unfree shall never be at peace.[37]

CHURCHES IN TRANSITION: PRESBYTERIANISM, CARDINAL CULLEN'S ROMAN REFORMS AND ANGLICAN DISESTABLISHMENT

Before continuing to survey wider political developments, it will be instructive at this juncture to look at some of the changes in ecclesial life as

---

36. See Beckett, *The Making of Modern Ireland*, pp. 361f.
37. Patrick Pearse, *Political Writings and Speeches* (Dublin: The Talbot Press, 1952), pp. 136f.

the nineteenth century unfolded.

The difficulties O'Connell's campaign had experienced in Ulster should be seen in the context of the fact that from the 1820s Ulster Presbyterianism had become much more variegated. The fundamentalism of Henry Cooke, which was firmly wedded to support for the Union, stood in marked contrast to the self-confident liberal Presbyterianism of the 1790s. Protestantism throughout the island had become steadily more favourably disposed towards the Union in response to what Oliver Mac-Donagh describes as the 'rising tide of catholic assertion, and the growing realisation that the union was not threatening but shoring up protestant (even presbyterian) privilege'.[38] Rapid industrial development in and around Belfast had undoubtedly brought greater prosperity to many Presbyterians and more divergent class interests now told against older more radical alliances. With the consolidation of the Union and free trade, Presbyterians were increasingly more inclined to look to the industrial towns of Britain. Moreover, many Protestants who came from the country to work in Belfast had not been exposed to the republican politics for which the town had been so renowned in the 1790s. The other important factor was a resurgent Orange Order fostering anti-Catholic feeling easily aggravated by competition in the workplace.[39]

In short, the religious cleavages and sectarianism that had already proved damaging in the period of the United Irish Rebellion, had become an even more pronounced feature of the political landscape.

The ecclesial culture within the two other main denominations also underwent considerable evolution, especially during the second half of the century.

In the Roman Catholic Church the success of the Emancipation struggle was followed by Paul Cullen's arrival in Ireland midway through the century, with the Synod of Thurles in 1850 ushering in a series of reforms under his direction.[40] Cullen was successively Archbishop of Armagh (1849-52) and then Dublin (1852-78), becoming the first Irish

38. 'The Age of O'Connell, 1830-45', in Vaughan, *A New History of Ireland*, pp. 158-168 (166).
39. For a discussion of Presbyterianism, Orangeism and other Protestant groups in this period see Foster, *Modern Ireland 1600-1972*, pp. 303ff.
40. I have drawn below closely upon Hoppen, *Ireland since 1800: Conflict and Conformity*, pp. 143ff.

bishop to be made a Cardinal in 1866. Having spent most of his earlier career in Rome, Cullen was a fervent devotee of the Holy See, and favoured stricter Roman discipline and greater clerical control. The general movement had in fact been in this direction for some time, most notably with Archbishop Troy and the foundation of Maynooth College in 1795, and Cullen's influence should not be overstated.[41]

One of the means by which Cullen was assisted in ensuring that the priesthood increasingly conformed to his ultramontane views and conservative vision of Irish Catholicism was through control of the seminaries by insisting on loyalty oaths from the staff. Emigration and the Famine also meant that there were, in relative terms, more clergy, and as the century progressed the number increased and they became a good deal more wealthy. Church building, liturgical reform and the encouragement of more regular observance among the laity, all made their contribution to consolidating a stricter adherence to the Church's teaching and a greater uniformity of practice. The decline of the Gaelic language would have also told against older forms of popular ritual.[42]

Cullen's high profile defence of Catholic interests and readiness to take a strong line on issues like mixed marriages, proved effective in strengthening a distinctive Catholic ethos. He looked to Rome far too much to ever get seriously embroiled with Irish nationalism and was an ardent opponent of the Fenians, whom he saw as impious extremists exercising a detrimental influence upon the faithful. More moderate and constitutional demands, consistent with what he perceived to be the interests of 'Catholic Ireland' could, though, count on his enthusiastic support. In the 1860s he joined with Liberal politicians in founding the National Association of Ireland, which championed constitutional reform in opposition to Fenianism.[43]

Cullen's policies and his use of the power and theatre of ritual, furthered the process whereby a formerly marginalised Church had become

---

41.   See S. J. Connolly, *Religion and Society in Nineteenth-Century Ireland* (Dundalk: Dundalgan Press, 1985), pp. 12-15; and on Troy see Dáire Keogh, *The French Disease: The Catholic Church and Irish Radicalism, 1790-1800* (Dublin: Four Courts Press, 1993), especially pp. 1-26.

42.   This is emphasised by Seán Mac Réamoinn in 'With the Past, in the Present, for the Future' in D. Carroll, ed., *Religion in Ireland: Past, Present and Future* (Dublin: Columba, 1999), pp. 96-126 (112).

43.   See Norman, *A History of Modern Ireland*, pp. 173ff.

a powerful institution. The native experience and traditions of a more indigenous Church that had a greater affinity with dispossession, had been receding over the previous century, and with Cullen the hierarchy often seemed more concerned with immediate ecclesial interests than addressing social disadvantage. The energies from 'below', that had been the motor for many of the political and economic advances earlier in the century, were now invited to be channeled in more conservative directions. The vitality of later political struggles would suggest that in political terms at least, the experiment was only a partial success. For example, Roman censure of the later Land Campaign had little domestic impact and the hierarchy itself bowed to popular pressure.[44]

Within the Established Church major changes were also on the way.[45] By the 1830s the privileges of the Church of Ireland clergy had become in the 'Tithe War' the subject of great resentment and agitation for political change. The legislation on tithes may have reduced the sense of grievance, but made little dent in the wealth of the Established Church. During the Emancipation struggle and Tithe War, the possibility of partially endowing the Roman Catholic Church had been mooted by the Government. It was resisted as an unacceptable encroachment upon the independence of the Church, and opposition to the injustice of an endowed established Church gained ground. The National Association in which Cardinal Cullen was closely involved, campaigned vigorously on the issue. Along with Irish Roman Catholic and nationalist disdain, liberal opinion in Britain pressed for disestablishment. Gladstone made the point that while he could understand the case for the endowment of the Church of the majority, or even the Church of the poorest in society, the endowment of a small already privileged minority had little justification. Disestablishment took centre stage during the election of November 1868, which gave the Liberals a majority of 112 seats.

The Bill implementing the disestablishment policies of the newly elected governemnt vested a new Representative Church Body with corporate rights over church buildings and clerical residences. It also made available the Church of Ireland's historic resources to compensate exist-

44. See S. J. Connolly, *Religion and Society*, p. 14.
45. In the discussion below I have drawn upon K. Nowlan 'Disestablishment: 1800-1869' in M. Hurley, ed., *Irish Anglicanism 1869-1969* (Dublin: Allen Figgis and Co., 1970), pp. 1-22.

ing clerical holders of office or transfer capital sums by way of commuta-
tion to the Representative Church Body who would then pay the clerical
stipend. Nearly half the historic resources were released for dispersal by
the Government for the relief of distress and educational and social initiatives. On the 1st January 1871 the Church of Ireland was no longer
the Established Church and a long-running grievance had been settled.
The old Ascendancy interest still commanded significant political and
economic power, but it had lost an important constitutional bulwark.

CHARLES START PARNELL: LAND AND CONSTITUTIONAL
AGITATION, AND THE ORIGINS OF MODERN UNIONISM

If Fenianism – except in an *ad hoc* manner – failed to root its strategy in
the smouldering discontent of rural Ireland, the same cannot be said of
Parnellism. The extraordinary success of Parnell's political leadership
lay in his skill in bringing together a coalition of constitutional, social
and revolutionary forces that would shake the foundations of Irish and
British society.

As a member of the Protestant gentry, a minor career in politics was
the natural complement to what might have otherwise been a rather
reclusive life. Surprisingly, for one who did so much to shape events,
Parnell knew very little about Irish history. The same can be said of politics, at least at the theoretical level; it held little attraction for him. Accordingly, there are no political treatises in which we can examine
Parnell's ideas and we must confine ourselves to accepting his career for
what it was: a remarkable triumph of political instinct and campaigning
ability.

The Home Rule movement, with which Parnell is primarily associated, was in fact established in 1870 by Isaac Butt, a lawyer and Tory
member of Parliament. Butt had become convinced that Irish affairs
were grossly mismanaged. His legal defence of Fenians had impressed
upon him the urgency of the situation and his idea of Home Rule was
conceived as a remedy to Ireland's ills which was preferable to the excesses of revolutionary politics. 'It is equally essential,' he wrote, 'to the
safety of England and to the happiness and tranquillity of Ireland, that
the right of self-government should be restored to this country'.[46] An

---

46. Beckett, *The Making of Modern Ireland*, p. 377.

Irish Parliament adopting progressive measures should be entrusted with administering domestic Irish affairs and containing dissent. Enough interest was expressed among landlords and members of the middle classes to secure the founding of a non-party Home Government Association in 1870. Support for Gladstone's Liberals was not easily detached, and it was only when Home Rule was linked with land reform that – despite defections by some Tory Home Rulers – wider support was forthcoming. In 1873 the Home Rule League was formed, with members elected in the 1874 election constituting a distinct party in parliament. With some vigour Butt argued the case for Home Rule in the Tory-dominated parliament. It was, however, those who engaged in the obstructionist tactics initiated by Joseph Bigger who caught the public imagination back in Ireland. Parnell, who was returned as the member for Meath at a by-election in 1875, quickly established himself as a master of this particular art, and given his public utterances showing sympathy with Fenian sentiment, he was soon perceived as a more menacing advocate of Irish interests than Butt could ever be.

The times were propitious for Parnell. Chronic economic depression and increased competition in the agricultural sector had reduced the value of Ireland's agricultural exports.[47] This loss, which bore harshly on tenant farmers, exacerbated the conflict with the landlords and brought the land question into sharp relief. New political energies had come into play, and sensing this, a number of leading Fenians, impressed by Parnell's work in parliament, were now ready to revise their attitude to constitutionalism, if it was linked to the land issue. Michael Davitt formed the Land League in 1879 and invited Parnell to become President. In what was known as 'the New Departure', Fenianism, the land agitation and the parliamentary struggle were drawn into a powerful alliance. By this time Butt had died; the Parliamentary party elected William Shaw in his place, however, and Parnell had to wait for the leadership until after the general election in 1880.

Even with Gladstone's return to power in April 1880, entrenched opposition from powerful interests meant land reform was by no means a

---

47. See Strauss, *Irish Nationalism and British Democracy*, pp. 170ff. Strauss writes that 'Ireland's agricultural output declined from £72 million in 1866-70 to only £54 million in 1884-8' (p. 172).

foregone conclusion. Parnell's message in Ireland was that 'the measure of the land bill of next session will be the measure of your activity and energy this winter'.[48] The Act was passed but did not pacify the Irish tenantry. The authorities decided to use the Coercion Act, and, taking a dim view of Parnell's speeches on the matter, had him imprisoned at Kilmainham. The conflict escalated and it was soon clear that this situation was neither in the interests of Parnell nor of the government. In 1882 an agreement was reached (the 'Kilmainham treaty') that the Land Act should be amended and that for his part Parnell should do his best to win acceptance for the new Act. This did not present him with too many difficulties since his alliance with social revolutionaries like Davitt had been tactical and for him the land agitation was a means to wider political objectives. His natural sympathies were with the interests of the Irish middle class and he was not sorry to see the left wing of the Land League weakened by acceptance of the new Act.[49]

Gladstone's legislation was to have far-reaching consequences; it represented the first stage in a process that was to transform rural Ireland through the settlement of the land question by tenant ownership.[50] At the time though, Parnell's compromise was widely regarded as a sell-out and his standing was at some risk. It was only the obvious sincerity of his condemnation of the murders of Lord Cavendish and his Under-Secretary, combined with his spirited opposition to the subsequent introduction of a new Coercion Bill, which retrieved his prestige as a national leader.[51]

Gladstone's government was defeated in June 1885, Parnell voting with the opposition, and Salisbury formed a Tory administration. Prior to the November 1885 election, Gladstone had been convinced that the Liberals were not ready to accept Home Rule and Parnell was tempted into a brief alliance with the Tories who had made overtures in his direction. In the event, the Tories were unwilling to support Home Rule, and the electoral arithmetic after the November election was once again in

---

48. Beckett, *The Making of Modern Ireland*, p. 389.
49. Davitt was a socialist and favoured land nationalisation and cooperative industry. See Desmond Fennell, 'Irish Socialist Thought', in Richard Kearney, ed., *The Irish Mind: Exploring Intellectual Traditions* (Dublin: Wolfhound, 1985), pp. 188-208 (195-7).
50. Beckett, *The Making of Modern Ireland*, pp. 390ff.
51. Ibid., p. 393.

the Liberals' favour. Gladstone decided to enlist Parnell's support on the basis of preparing a bill for Home Rule.

In opposing Home Rule the Tories could enlist powerful religious and economic interests and they hoped to sway public opinion through manipulating anti-Irish feeling. Despite the fact that some Home Rule Members of Parliament were Protestant, Irish Protestants generally were dismayed at the prospect of a Dublin parliament and executive, which was seen as raising the spectre of a Roman Catholic ascendancy, with the support of the Roman Catholic hierarchy fuelling fears that 'Home Rule' might mean 'Rome Rule'.[52] The old religious cleavages were revived, especially in Ulster, where the Orange Order organised opposition across class boundaries. This was the context in which much of the iconongraphy of orangeism was created. Banners celebrating the settler past and victory at the Boyne identified the struggles of loyal Protestant subjects with the people of Israel.

As Unionism emerged as an organised political body, former political allegiances were replaced and through an alliance with popular orangeism and loyalism a powerful cross-class coalition in support of the maintenance of the Union was created. The threat of violence was never far away and incitement in this direction was given by Lord Randolph Churchill, who after a visit to Belfast said: 'Ulster will fight; Ulster will be right'.[53] From 1885 onwards the home rule movement under the auspices of the Nationalist League began to assume a more 'nationalist' hue with more overt clerical backing, and the polarisation of Irish politics upon Catholic Nationalist and Protestant Unionist lines which was to characterise the political scene for years to come was to become the dominant feature of the political landscape.[54]

The opposition to Home Rule was undoubtedly closely intertwined with British imperial interests and it is in this period that modern Unionism as a distinct ideology has its roots. Increased economic rivalry between the major economic powers and protectionist measures had meant

52. Ibid., pp. 398ff. E. Norman points out that the Home Rule Party repudiated Papal interference in Irish affairs during the tenants 'Plan of Campaign' in 1888 (*A History of Modern Ireland*, p. 217).
53. Beckett, *The Making of Modern Ireland*, p. 400.
54. See Brian Walker, 'The 1885 and 1886 General Elections – A Milestone in Irish History' in his *Dancing to History's Tune: History, Myth and Politics in Ireland* (Belfast: Institute of Irish Studies, 1996), pp. 15-33.

that the markets of Empire were perceived as more crucial than ever. In the popular literature of the period, the industrial success of the North-East was contrasted with the backwardness of the rural economy of the South. Parnell – against the advice of Michael Davitt – had linked Home Rule with protectionist policies for Ireland. This would have been widely seen as likely to have dire economic consequences for the industrial North-East and prove damaging to British business interests. In such circumstances religious bigotry had in economic self-interest found a powerful ally.[55] Although unionism opposed the granting of Home Rule to any part of Ireland, from its inception as an organised political force it also marked the birth of an Ulster separatism that was at a later date to prove intensely pragmatic when it came to defining boundaries.

To pass his Bill Gladstone had to carry the bulk of his own party. In the event, at the end of a protracted parliamentary struggle the Bill was defeated. The general election that followed only served to underline the defeat.

The story of Parnell's demise, and of the risks he took for the woman he loved, is well known. In the first instance the Roman Catholic hierarchy remained loyal to him and it is sometimes forgotten that it was only when under pressure from the Liberals that he was disowned and pilloried. In the closing months of his life he tried to revive his political fortunes. He again played the Fenian card, but having lost the support of the Parliamentary Party, his electoral efforts proved forlorn. His health broke and he died in 1891 aged forty-four.

Parnell had always envisaged Home Rule as a stage in a process rather than an end in itself. He had no wish to set limits upon the prospects for Ireland's nationhood:

> No man has a right to fix the boundary of the march of a nation. No man has a right to say 'Thus far shalt thou go, and no further'; and we have never attempted to fix the *ne plus ultra* to the progress of Ireland's nationhood, and we never shall.[56]

In linking Home Rule to protectionist domestic policies, Parnell had tried to march too quickly and lacked the sagacity he had shown on so

55. See Strauss, *Irish Nationalism and British Democracy*, pp. 174ff.
56. From a speech given in 1885 and quoted in Pearse, *Political Writings and Speeches*, p. 242.

many other occasions.

THE NATIONALIST MOVEMENT AFTER PARNELL

For the generation after Parnell, Irish parliamentary politics was to re-volve around the prospects of an alliance with the Liberals that might achieve Home Rule. After the failure of a second Bill in 1893, a third opportunity presented itself under Asquith in 1912 and on this occasion the Lords' veto could only delay the legislation. Opposition from Ulster Protestants and within the British political establishment once again proved vociferous, and the eventual outcome of the general crisis this precipitated was to be the foundation of an Irish State and Partition.

The intervening period had seen attempts to revive the Irish language and Gaelic culture through bodies such as the Gaelic League and the Gaelic Athletic Association. The disillusionment with constitutional poli-tics after the fall of Parnell had been widely felt, and, in addition to their general cultural interest, these organisations undoubtedly provided an outlet for nationalist sentiment. Co-founded by the Protestant, Douglas Hyde, the Gaelic League was intended to be non-political in character. It succeeded in attracting both Protestants and Catholics and secured a following in Ulster, though the League's implicit narrowing of cultural horizons in regard to what might be considered 'Irish', would not have commended it to many Ulster Protestants.[57] Despite its non-political ori-gins, the Gaelic League did undoubtedly interest the more politically minded, and like the Gaelic Athletic Association, it became a focus for the fostering of a separatist nationalist consciousness. The path from a cultural to a political nationalism was to be traversed by many activists in the Gaelic revival. Looking back in 1913 at his own participation in the Gaelic League, Patrick Pearse acknowledged its contribution to the emer-gence of revolutionary politics in Ireland.[58]

Another major development during this period was the Anglo-Irish literary and dramatic movement, which we associate primarily with the

---

57. See Campbell, *The Dissenting Voice*, p. 339, and Beckett, *The Making of Modern Ireland, 1603-1923* (London: Faber, 1969), p. 417.
58. See Pearse, *Political Writings and Speeches*, pp. 94f. Pearse claimed: 'For if there is one thing that has become plainer than another it is that when the seven men met in O'Connell Street to found the Gaelic league, they were commencing, had there been a Liancourt there to make the epigram, not a revolt, but a revolution.'

romantic nationalism of W. B. Yeats. In contrast with much of the Gaelic revival, this did suggest a more inclusive nationalism. Evocative plays like Yeats' *Cathleen ní Houlihan*, however, which called Ireland's sons to patriotic sacrifice, were scarcely likely to appeal to more moderate opinion or to encourage a wider identification with nationalist aspirations.

The formation of Sinn Féin ('We Ourselves') in 1905 by Arthur Griffith provided one political outlet for the heightened nationalist consciousness that now existed. The Sinn Féin programme was scarcely a radical one. Although Irish Members of Parliament were asked to stay away from Westminster and meet in Dublin, the link with the Crown was to be maintained. Protectionist policies to assist domestic industrial expansion were advocated, and Griffith's economic thinking, which was inspired by the German economist Frederick List, was strongly pro-capitalist. He had no sympathies for the trade unions and was a stalwart opponent of socialism.

These multifarious strands of nationalist resurgence did not as yet alter the political landscape by way of challenging the dominance of the Irish Parliamentary Party, led by John Redmond. It was the Home Rule crisis which transformed the situation. Protestants in the North were ready to resist by force if necessary and many a political speech from the Gladstone era was dusted down to remind unionists that Home Rule would mean Rome Rule. After the formation of the Ulster Volunteers with financial backing from unionist businessmen, a provisional government was formed in September 1913 ready to take office should the Home Rule Bill become law. Although Edward Carson had argued in defence of the Union as such, it was Ulster which Protestants sought to defend.

In direct response to these dramatic developments, the National Volunteers was formed in the South, and Ireland edged towards conflict. The European war provided a respite, and most of the 188,000 National Volunteers followed Redmond in support of the war effort, though 13,000 left to form the Irish Volunteers.[59] The Irish Republican Brotherhood, fortified by the thought that England's difficulty might be Ireland's op-

59. Numbers taken from J. Lee, *Ireland 1912-1985: Politics and Society* (Cambridge: Cambridge U. P., 1989), p. 22. For a discussion of this period see F. X. Martin, 'Eoin MacNéill and the Rising: Preparations' in F. X. Martin, ed., *The Easter Rising, 1916 and University College, Dublin* (Dublin: Browne and Nolan, 1966), pp. 3-31.

portunity, was intent on using the crisis to effect a rising, and successfully infiltrated the Irish Volunteers. Old-style Fenian conspiratorial politics was given the added twist provided by Patrick Pearse's poetic incitements to defend Ireland's cause by force of arms and his belief in the purifying qualities of patriotic conflict.

Easter Week 1916 was chosen as the time to act. Surprisingly, given the limited forces at their disposal, the insurgents held out for a week. The British, for their part, inflamed public opinion by the series of executions after the Rising, followed by an ill-advised Conscription Bill in 1917, and managed to secure greater sympathy for the nationalist cause by these deeply unpopular measures. Arthur Griffith's Sinn Féin, which had met with little success until 1917, was now to undergo a metamorphosis. With the support of the Irish Republican Brotherhood, Sinn Féin adopted a Republican constitution in October 1917, and was soon regarded as the only viable alternative to the Redmondite Home Rulers. The more militant and separatist outlook that characterised the nationalist resurgence in the period after Parnell now found powerful political expression.

In the general election of 1918 Sinn Féin won seventy-three seats and routed the Home Rulers who were left with just six.[60] A policy of parliamentary abstentionism, the forming of a rival administration by Sinn Féin and a military campaign by the Irish Volunteers (now reconstituted as the Irish Republican Army) eventually brought the British to the negotiating table. Michael Collins' legendary capacity to avoid arrest and his successful infiltration of the Dublin Castle intelligence network proved particularly damaging to the British. His undoubted skill was accompanied by a ferocious ruthlessness. On both sides, it has to be said, horrendous things were done during this period. The atrocities of the Black and Tans left particularly deep scars. No side wanted a return to war, and after the Treaty negotiations with Lloyd George, Southern Ireland achieved its independence and an Irish Free State was created in 1922.

CONCLUSION

In retrospect, the nineteenth and early-twentieth centuries can be seen as a protracted struggle for the same goals that had been envisaged as

60. Lee, *Ireland 1912-1985*, p. 40.

achievable in one mighty upheaval by the radicals of the 1790s. The Tithe War, the Emancipation struggle, the Repeal movement, Anglican disestablishment, the Land agitation, the Home Rule campaign, the 1916 Rising and War of Independence, meant that through this period the Protestant Ascendancy structure and British rule were contested and gradually dismantled. Throughout the nineteenth century internal social arrangements had been transformed and this undoubtedly helped prepare the way for later developments that finally led to independence. As we have seen, it was largely the energy and dynamism of popular discontent when harnessed effectively which transformed the social and political order.

The role of the Churches in this political process was not without importance and yet in each instance it was fraught with ambiguity. The Established Church may have been the religion of the ruling Ascendancy interest, but it also produced figures like William Sharman Crawford, Thomas Davis, Isaac Butt and Charles Stuart Parnell. Roman Catholicism likewise did much to sustain many of the political struggles of the century through leaders like Daniel O'Connell, and Gavin Duffy of Young Ireland, and yet Cardinal Cullen's policies and reforms had undoubtedly made Catholicism a socially conservative and sometimes reactionary influence. Presbyterianism for its part largely abandoned the radicalism of the previous century, identified positively with the Union and became much more conservative in its theology. And yet it also produced figures like Henry Montgomery who supported Catholic Emancipation, and James Armour of Ballymoney who favoured land reform, Home Rule and sought to separate Protestantism from unionism.[61]

Finally, it should be noted that this chapter has not treated of the Great Famine, which merits a special attention of its own. If the nineteenth century had seen a process of social and political advance, the Famine is a reminder of just how precarious, limited and fragile that process was. By and large, it was those at the very bottom of the social ladder, the cottier class, who had no vote or economic foothold, which suffered the worst fatalities.

61. See Campbell, *The Dissenting Voice*, pp. 137ff. and 343ff. Also Denis Carroll on 'Armour of Ballymoney', *Unusual Suspects: Twelve Radical Clergy* (Dublin, The Columba Press: 1998), pp. 175ff.

CHAPTER THREE

Religion and the Nationalist Cause in the Thought of Patrick Pearse

O Wise men, riddle me this: what if the dream come true?
What if the dream come true? and if millions unborn shall dwell
In the house that I shaped in my heart, the noble house of my thought?

'The Fool', Patrick Pearse

RELIGION AND NATIONALISM: THE HISTORICAL CONTEXT

In Western culture religion and nationalism have been closely intertwined. The idea of a chosen people or holy nation has its roots within the Judaeo-Christian tradition. This status was specifically ascribed to Israel, though not without qualification, especially in the prophetic literature with its strong ethical concern and more universal sympathies. In the New Testament Jewish particularlism was displaced in favour of the universal mission to the Gentiles, and thus nationalism gave way to internationalism. It was not long, though, before the Christian missionary endeavour entered a more conservative phase and was to spawn a whole series of religious forms of nationalism, as Christianity baptised, first, the Imperial Roman Empire, and then the various kingdoms and principalities of Christendom. This process occurred as Christianity after Constan-tine largely jettisoned its social utopianism, and increasingly assumed the role of a 'political religion' of existing society.[1]

In the modern period we find religion and nationalism again allied, though this time in opposition to the prevailing order, in the republicanism of both the English Civil War and the American Revolution. It is only with the Enlightenment that nationalism assumed a more secular form, closely associated with the bourgeois and democratic revolutions, which, with the aid of the armies of revolutionary France, shook the foundations of the old feudal order in Europe. Strictly speaking, it is

---

1. See Conor Cruise O'Brien, *God Land: Reflections on Religion and Nationalism* (Cambridge, MA: Harvard University Press, 1988), pp. 11ff. For a discussion of 'political religions of society' see Jürgen Moltmann, *The Experiment Hope* (London: SCM, 1975), pp. 101-118.

misleading to speak of 'nationalism' prior to this period, since it was at this time that the idea of 'the nation' was specifically used to express the sovereignty of the people

In this connection it is interesting to note that even in the phase of the French Revolution when the monarchy was still retained, a constitutional change of enormous significance had occurred. 'The King', writes Eric Hobsbawm, 'was no longer Louis, by the Grace of God, King of France and Navarre, but Louis, by the Grace of God and the constitutional law of the state, King of the French.'[2] In many ways during this period nationalism was beginning to take the place of religion. The nation itself was given an exalted status and became the supreme focus for people's loyalties (a process which carried its own dangers should the nation forget the principles of liberty and democracy upon which it had been founded).

In the nineteenth century, the romantic reaction to the rather too austere Enlightenment rationalism, produced with J. G. Herder a cultural German nationalism which again involved a union between religious sentiment and nationalism. This romantic form of nationalism was to prove widely influential throughout the century and beyond. Its celebration of cultural and ethnic roots undoubtedly gave it a strong emotional appeal, but it did not always combine this with the inclusiveness and democratic sympathies of earlier republicanism. The danger with this form of nationalism was that it lacked a corrective, should what was perceived to be the nation's interests, conflict with other values such as justice or individual liberty.

Like its European counterparts Irish nationalism has been a highly variegated phenomenon. With each generation there have been significant changes of emphasis and sometimes sharp discontinuities. The political ideas of Wolfe Tone and the United Irish movement are best seen as a version of the democratic nationalism of the Enlightenment, albeit with an often strong religious undercurrent. By the second half of the 1790s this movement had become radically republican and separatist as regards the British connection. In contrast, Daniel O'Connell – who waded into Kingstown harbour to meet George IV and described Queen Victoria as his 'darlin' Queen – would have been content with greater

2. *The Age of Revolution 1789-1848* (New York: Mentor, 1962), p. 81.

independence for Ireland under the Crown.[3] Young Ireland took its inspiration from the same springs as European romantic nationalism, and despite its earlier support for Repeal, was more separatist in outlook and ready to countenance physical force. Parnell used constitutional methods in an effort to secure tenant rights and achieve Home Rule within the Empire. The Fenian movement and the nationalism associated with the later stages of the Gaelic revival were militantly separatist.

Unquestionably the two most significant figures among the leaders of the 1916 generation were Patrick Pearse and James Connolly. Their distinctive contribution to the extraordinary political ferment during the years leading up to the Rising, means that they both merit a prominent place in any understanding of the modern nationalist tradition. Connolly's innovative exploration of the relationship between socialism and nationalism, along with his treatment of religion, will be considered after the present chapter which concerns itself with Pearse's fusion of different strands within the nationalist tradition and his use of religious imagery in the cultivation of nationalist self-consciousness.

PEARSE: MODERNISER AND MYSTIC,
DEMOCRAT AND ROMANTIC NATIONALIST

In his work as poet, dramatist and essayist, Pearse embodied the romantic spirit of nationalist Ireland. There was, however, a pragmatic and modernising side to Pearse's character. As an educationalist his enthusiasm for Gaelic custom was consistent with the fact that he held advanced views informed by the latest European thinking. As his tastes developed and broadened, the same can be said of his literary interests. His social and economic thinking was similarly progressive [4] – he favoured universal suffrage and towards the end of his life had come to believe in the

---

3. On O'Connell's loyalty to the British Crown see Maurice O'Connell, *Daniel O'Connell: The Man and his Politics* (Dublin: The Irish Academic Press, 1990), pp. 41ff., and E. Norman, *A History of Modern Ireland* (London: Penquin, 1971), pp. 57f.

4. See Patrick Pearse, *Political Writings and Speeches* (Dublin: The Talbot Press, 1952), especially pp. 5ff. and 180. The main biography of Pearse is Ruth Dudley Edwards, *Patrick Pearse: The Triumph of Failure* (London: Faber and Faber, 1979). See also J. Lee, 'In Search of Patrick Pearse', in M. Ní Dhonnachadha and T. Dorgan, eds., *Revising the Rising* (Derry: Field Day, 1991), pp. 122-38; J. Lee, *The Modernisation of Irish Society 1848-1918* (Dublin: Gill and Macmillan, 1973), pp. 141ff.; and Francis Shaw's highly critical 'The Canon of Irish History – A Challenge', *Studies*, Vol. 61, No.242 (Summer 1972), pp. 117-53.

need for state intervention to secure economic improvement.

It is of course Pearse the romantic nationalist summoning up legends of Cuchulain the warrior hero who is best known: the seer and mystic whose language at times had an almost apocalyptic fury. This more forbidding side of Pearse's temperament has been stressed in more recent years, as interest has swung from an uncritical reverence in the early years of the State, towards an equally unhelpful revisionist disenchantment. A recovery of balance in studies of Pearse is needed if justice is to be done to his complex and enigmatic character, and some account taken of the evolution and maturation of his political ideas. Critics who question Pearse's motives and reject his political ideology, invariably reject their own caricature of Pearse, whether it be the failed artist desiring fame or an emotionally crippled figure seeking resolution of some inner crisis.[5]

It should come as no surprise to find that two main strands can be discerned in Pearse's mature political thinking. First, he was a radical democrat in the Enlightenment tradition of Wolfe Tone. This committed Pearse to a conception of nationalism which is recognisably modern. Pearse saw national freedom as essentially an expression of the rights of the individual:

> If we accept the definition of Irish freedom as 'the Rights of Man in Ireland' we shall find it difficult to imagine an apostle of Irish freedom who is not a democrat. One loves the freedom of men because one loves men. There is therefore a deep humanism in every nationalist. There was a deep humanism in Tone.[6]

Although Pearse's passion for things Gaelic sometimes gives the impression that he equated Irishness with Gaelic culture, the following passage indicates that this was not the case:

> I challenge again the Irish psychology of the man who stands up the

---

5. The former interpretation is held by Dudley Edwards, *Patrick Pearse: The Triumph of Failure* and William Irwin Thompson, *The Imagination of an Insurrection: Dublin, Easter 1916* (New York: Oxford University Press, 1967), while the latter has been recently advanced by Seán Farrell Moran in *Patrick Pearse and the Politics of Redemption: The Mind of the Easter Rising, 1916* (Washington: The Catholic University of America Press, 1994).

6. Pearse, *Political Writings and Speeches*, p. 326.

Gael and the Palesman as opposing forces, with conflicting outlooks. We are all Irish, Leinster-reared or Connaught-reared; your native Irish speaker of Iveragh or Erris is more fully in touch with the spiritual past of Ireland than your Wexfordman or your Kildareman, but your Wexfordman or your Kildareman has other Irish traditions which your Iveraghman or your Errisman has lost.

Directly echoing the sentiments of Tone, Pearse continued:

I propose also that we substitute for the denominations Gael, Gall and Gall-Gael the common name of Irishman.[7]

The second and certainly the stronger strand in Pearse's nationalism stemmed from the romantic nationalism of Young Ireland. This is evident whenever Pearse is pressed to defend Ireland's right to nationhood. 'I believe that there is really a spiritual tradition which is the soul of Ireland, the thing which makes Ireland a living nation.'[8] It is significant that Pearse identified as his four 'voices' or 'fathers' of Irish nationalism, Wolfe Tone, Thomas Davis, James Fintan Lalor and John Mitchel.[9] He gave pride of place to Tone, but the latter three were all associated with Young Ireland, and this tells us quite a lot about Pearse's own outlook. In Pearse, the democratic republicanism of the Enlightenment is uneasily combined with the romantic nationalist tradition, which, in part at least, arose as a reaction to the Enlightenment. With some success Thomas Davis had sought to incorporate the Gaelic and Anglo-Irish in his cultural conception of nationalism. Not all who followed in the romantic nationalist tradition retained the same breadth of vision and purpose, and the uncritical celebration of nationalist sentiment in later romantic nationalism carried its dangers especially if it became too narrowly focused.

The strong romantic element in Pearse's nationalism helps explain what is one of its more disturbing features: its elevation of the ideal of national freedom to religious heights. This tendency is evident in an oration given at Wolfe Tone's grave, where Pearse declared: 'We stand in the holiest place in Ireland, for it must be that the holiest sod of a na-

7. Ibid., pp. 105f.
8. Ibid., p. 301.
9. Ibid., pp. 223ff. (especially pp. 240 and 246).

tion's soil is the sod where the greatest of her dead lies buried.'[10] It is again apparent when Pearse specifically described patriotism in religious terms as a

> faith which in some of us has been in our flesh and bone since we were moulded in our mothers' wombs, and which in others of us has at some definite moment of our later lives been kindled flaming as if by the miraculous word of God; a faith which is of the same nature as religious faith and is one of the eternal witnesses in the heart of man to the truth that we are of divine kindred.[11]

This uncritical attachment of religious aura to nationalist sentiment is one of the principal faults with some romantic forms of nationalism. Although Francis Shaw goes too far in saying that Pearse regarded patriotism and holiness as 'convertible concepts', he has put his finger on a real difficulty.[12] Patriotism may have a genuinely religious dimension, as indeed do other spheres of human life and culture, but this does not mean that patriotic feeling should always be given an unqualified religious approval.

Religious motifs in fact run through Pearse's nationalism. He never shrunk from making identifications which others might think ill-advised:

> ... I am not sure that there will be any visible and personal Messiah in this redemption: the people itself will perhaps be its own Messiah, the labouring people, scourged, crowned with thorns, agonizing and dying, to rise again immortal and impassible. For peoples are divine and are the only things that can properly be spoken of under figures drawn from the divine epos.[13]

This is a serious point, which acknowledges humanity's participation in the redemptive process. Unfortunately though, in the absence of any note of qualification, does not the language Pearse uses run the danger of raising that participation to idolatrous proportions? That humanity has a sacredness is a central Christian conviction. This belief is rooted in an understanding of our createdness in the image of God, and in the

10. Ibid., p. 54.
11. Ibid, p. 65.
12. Shaw, 'The Canon of Irish History – A Challenge', p. 122.
13. Pearse, *Political Writings and Speeches*, pp. 91f.

doctrine of the Incarnation which teaches that it is in Christ's perfect humanity that divinity itself is made manifest. But this does not mean that the 'people' should be idealised, much less deified. Sometimes human liberation struggles take a wrong turn and the oppressed in turn become oppressors. The possibility exists that an uncritical and sentimental reverence for the people might give a religious sanction to a destructive assertion of national identity. Indeed, something of this nature has in fact happened in the use which has been made of Pearse by sections of the nationalist movement in Northern Ireland, where religious mysticism was used to support the Provisional IRA campaign of violence by portraying prisoners on hunger strike as martyrs.

Pearse's fusion of republicanism and romantic nationalism can perhaps be viewed in more favourable light if the claims he wished to make for the nationalist cause are understood as a natural extension and expression of fundamental democratic rights. In other words, Pearse is not so much extolling the virtue of the assertion of national self-identity, which, as we know, can easily degenerate into the self-aggrandisement of nations, as celebrating the freedom and sovereignty of the people. There is nothing wrong with deploying some of the emotional force of romanticism to this end, provided it is done in such a way that it underwrites human freedom and democratic rights. In his nationalism Pearse surely saw himself as not in any way coming to contradict or abolish the democratic tradition, but to fulfil it. The point is evident in the following passage:

> Freedom is so splendid a thing that one cannot worthily state it in the terms of a definition; one has to write it in some flaming symbol or to sing it in music riotous with the uproar of heaven. A Danton and a Mitchel can speak more adequately of freedom than a Voltaire and a Burke, for they have drunk more deeply of that wine with which God inebriates the votaries of vision.[14]

In practice, though, Pearse sometimes makes the move from democratic freedom to national freedom and then on to national assertion, with such rapidity that the latter becomes almost an end in itself to which everything must be subordinated. A measure of romantic fervour and

14. Ibid., pp. 261f.

gaiety may be a very fine thing, but without the calming balm of moral reason, the 'votaries of vision' often lose their way. John Mitchel certainly did. His emotional intoxication with the nationalist cause did not lead him to question the betrayal of human freedom entailed in his support for slavery. This is quite a contrast with the opposition to slavery from members of the United Irish Society of the 1790s such as Thomas Russell, who when he dined would not take his sweet lest it contained sugar. Pearse may not have known the full details of Mitchel's chequered career, though this was not the only occasion he showed a lack of discrimination. Like many nationalists of the period, Pearse admired Napoleon – not everyone's idea of an apostle of human freedom.

The energy and vitality of romantic nationalism is of value provided it does not lead to an exclusive association of nationality with a specific ethnic or cultural identity which thereby excludes some members of the nation; the pursuit of nationhood should never be allowed to contradict democratic principle. Pearse's nationalism might have fared better if Tone, Parnell, Davis and Lalor had been his four 'voices'. The replacement of Mitchel by Parnell would have provided an improved balance between the democratic and romantic traditions he endeavoured to combine, and thereby guarded against the inherent dangers of romantic nationalism. Pearse had a high regard for Parnell's achievements as a constitutional politician and accepted that in the right circumstances Home Rule might become a stepping-stone to full nationhood. It was Parnell's constitutional successors who had sold Ireland short. Pearse in fact readily acknowledged that if he were to add a fifth 'voice', it would have to be Parnell.[15]

PEARSE ON VIOLENCE AND WARFARE

Although regarded by his contemporaries as a quiet and indeed a remarkably gentle person, Pearse in his writings certainly did not always convey that impression. In 1913, in the context of the growing militarisation in the North during the Home Rule crisis, he wrote: 'bloodshed is a cleansing and a sanctifying thing, and the nation which regards it as the final horror has lost its manhood. There are many things more hor-

15. Ibid., pp. 241ff.

rible than bloodshed; and slavery is one of them.'[16] In 1915, his glorification of the violence of the First World War used appalling language.

> The last sixteen months have been the most glorious in the history of Europe. Heroism has come back to the earth. On whichever side the men who rule the peoples have marshalled them, whether with England to uphold her tyranny of the seas, or with Germany to break that tyranny, the people themselves have gone into battle because to each the old voice that speaks out of the soil of a nation has spoken anew. Each fights for the fatherland. It is policy that moves the governments; it is patriotism that stirs the peoples. Belgium defending her soil is heroic, and so is Turkey fighting with her back to Constantinople.
>
> It is good for the world that such things should be done. The old heart of the earth needed to be warmed with the red wine of the battlefields. Such august homage was never offered to God as this, the homage of millions of lives given gladly for the love of country.[17]

Pearse was by no means alone in his willingness to contemplate the sacrifice of human life in the cause of national freedom. The Solemn League and Covenant in Ulster had done precisely this, and throughout Europe patriotism and war were enthusiastically embraced by romanticist poets and seen as providing a sense of purpose and possibilities for cultural renewal. It is also true that it was only comparatively late in his career that Pearse came to advocate violence and that he took the view that 'if a nation can obtain its freedom without bloodshed, it is its duty so to obtain it.'[18] Nonetheless, even when such allowances are made, Pearse's view of the redemptive value of bloodshed is difficult at the best of times and, when applied to the First World War, repellent and grotesque. James Connolly's response to Pearse was suitably blunt: 'We are sick and the world is sick of this teaching.'[19]

Some attempt should however be made to try and understand the thinking and motivation that lay behind Pearse's outlook. Pearse felt acutely the need to rouse Ireland from its slumbers. People had become so used to oppression that they were in danger of losing the will to resist.

16. Ibid., p. 99.
17. Ibid., p. 216.
18. Ibid., p. 323.
19. K. Allen, *The Politics of James Connolly* (London: Pluto, 1990), p. 151.

'There comes to the slave' he wrote in June 1913, 'as there comes to a tortured child or a tortured animal, a time when stripes seem normal and it is easier to endure than to protest.' Pearse was no doubt conscious of the need to counter O'Connell's view that 'liberty is too dearly purchased at the price of a single drop of blood.'[20] If Home Rule was obstructed, then a 'passionate assertion of nationality' would be needed, and Pearse's rather chilling rhetoric needs to be seen in the context of his desire to instil a fighting spirit in people.[21]

The reference to the purifying qualities of bloodshed makes use of religious imagery in what would seem to be a poetic allusion to the stirring effects conflict would have on a quiescent people – the lesson of Fenian defiance was never lost on Pearse. Pearse was sensitive to the way the oppressed not only accept their lot but internalise the values of the oppressor. This was indeed insightful, and Pearse's response anticipates the need for what Latin American liberation theologians have described as a process of 'conscientization'.[22] Pearse's summoning up of subversive counter-images – like that of 'a Risen People' – should be seen in these terms, as creative ways of enlisting the energies of the oppressed and excluded in order to produce political change.

In his essays and speeches Pearse primarily sought to address the plight of a subject nation which lacked the will to assert itself. Extending his rhetoric to less innocent belligerents and endorsing the glorification of nationhood in any circumstances was another matter altogether. The fact that Pearse slipped into doing this points to a weakness in his romantic celebration of nationhood that has already been highlighted. As to blood warming the battlefields, this might perhaps be viewed as an instance of what Pearse once called 'the *divina insania* of the poets',[23] though even poets have to take responsibility for what they say. Although at the time he was writing less was known of the carnage of the trenches, and, as Joseph Lee puts it, the war was still being reported as a 'knightly joust', a large dose of Connolly's realism would have done Pearse good.[24]

20. Pearse, *Political Writings and Speeches*, pp. 147 and 240f.
21. Ibid., p. 155.
22. The term was first used by Paulo Freire in his *Pedagogy for the Oppressed* (New York: Herder and Herder, 1970).
23. Pearse, *Political Writings and Speeches*, p. 165.
24. See Lee, 'In search of Patrick Pearse', p. 133.

Pearse should have had the wit to realise the use to which patriotic rhetoric about defending the nation's soil was being put by rival imperialist
powers, but his own romanticist emotionalism and political naïvety
blinded him.

Pearse's religious view of nationalism placed much too high a pre-
mium on a political aspiration and ideal, and this carried the attendant
danger that in the pursuit of such an objective unacceptable measures
might be considered. The democratic right to self-determination may
be inalienable, but the manner in which this ideal is striven for must be
subject to moral restraint. Wolfe Tone conceded the point when at his
trial he indicated his shock at the horrors of the civil carnage in 1798
and stated that he had only sought an open and honourable conflict.[25]
Pearse would not have denied that moral considerations have their claim.
In 1914 he wrote: 'It is a terrible responsibility to be cast upon a man,
that of bidding the cannon speak and the grapeshot pour.'[26] Indeed
Pearse often stated that it was precisely because of moral concerns that
war might in fact be necessary.

> There can be no peace between right and wrong, between truth and
> falsehood, between justice and oppression, between freedom and tyr-
> anny. Between them it is eternal war until the wrong is righted, until
> the true thing is established, until justice is accomplished, until free-
> dom is won.[27]

This still leaves the difficulty of those passages where we find Pearse
glorifying violence, even that of the Great War, though it could be claimed
that some of the extravagance of his language might betray self-doubt.
His writings often included an element of self-analysis and a rather too
anxious attempt to vindicate his viewpoint. Like most of the leaders of
the 1916 Rising, Pearse showed a refreshing quality of self-doubt throughout the whole terrible business – this contrasts sharply with the dogmatism and certitude which characterised much of the Provisional IRA's
campaign of violence in the North.

25. M. Elliott, *Wolfe Tone: Prophet of Irish Independence* (New Haven and London: Yale Uni-
    versity Press, 1989), p. 383.
26. Pearse, *Political Writings and Speeches*, p. 209.
27. Ibid., p. 77.

PEARSE'S JUSTIFICATION OF THE RISING

Pearse justified recourse to arms as a last resort and as a direct response to the Ulster Unionist's intention to resist Home Rule by rebellion.[28] The democratic will of the people had been subverted and should be affirmed in arms. In this respect F. X. Martin's comment on Eoin MacNéill's interpretation of the events leading up to the Rising is relevant: 'On more than one occasion in later life MacNéill declared that the revolution in modern Ireland was brought about mainly by Edward Carson and the Orangemen.'[29]

But the problem remains that Pearse went a good deal further than arguing his case on the basis of an appeal to democratic rights. He often seemed too ready to absolutise the nationalist ideal by giving it unqualified religious sanction. When this is done there is a real danger that moral considerations may be neglected in the pursuit of national freedom. British troops may have been thinner on the ground in Easter Week, but by unabashedly planning a Rising for Easter Sunday itself the insurgents showed little awareness that they perhaps implied too close an identification with the Christian vision of passion and resurrection, which suggested an unqualified divine sanction for their cause. MacNéill opposed the Rising, and due to his countermanding order issued to the Volunteers, the Rising was delayed until Easter Monday. In the event, having an insurrection on this day pointed to an arguably more defensible theological position, since it suggested a religious sanction which gave their cause a penultimate and not an ultimate status! Democracy and the fundamental right to self-determination may indeed have justified such a stance if the view is taken that a viable mandate for such action existed and the chances of success were high. This very question was debated within the Irish Republican Brotherhood and by the Volunteer leadership, and it is to the credit of Pearse and MacNéill that although they took different views, after the Rising they both showed respect for each other's actions.

Pearse's mysticism served to make good any deficiency which he may

28. Ibid., pp. 147, 155 and 185ff. Joseph Lee writes that 'Pearse's elaboration of the moral right of rebellion can only be understood as a response to the Orange appeal to Violence'. (Lee, *The Modernisation of Irish Society*, p. 145.)

29. 'Eoin MacNéill and the Rising: Preparations' in F. X. Martin, ed., *The Easter Rising, 1916 and University College, Dublin* (Dublin: Browne and Nolan, 1966), pp. 3-31 (10).

have felt remained in his rationale for the Rising. At times, he seemed to identify himself, as well as the people, with Christ. In his 1915 play *The Singer*, the central character says:

> One man can free a people as one Man redeemed the world. I will take no pike. I will go into the battle with bare hands. I will stand up before the Gall as Christ hung naked before men on the tree.[30]

It is often claimed that Pearse viewed the Easter Rising solely in terms of 'blood sacrifice'. This cannot be substantiated. Although Pearse's reflections on Tone and Emmet, his poetry and his plays, all show that he believed in the value of such a sacrifice in defending national honour and keeping alive the will to resist, he clearly saw the Rising as more than a gesture. The elaborate preparations and military strategy alone indicate that the Rising was serious in intent. Pearse himself had hoped for success, and cited the loss of the German guns from the *Aud* as part of the reason for failure. It was only after defeat and the executions that followed, that the 'blood sacrifice' interpretation of the events in Easter week established itself.[31]

Pearse's recourse to the language of blood sacrifice and his identification with Christ are best seen as romantic excess. His poetry and plays were written in order to invite others to embrace the same course of action – he would have had no objection to a thousand Cuchulains. Although Yeats was right that Pearse had 'the vertigo of self-sacrifice',[32] he should not be charged with *hubris*, still less blasphemy. In 1916 Pearse, at thirty-seven, was still a relatively young man who retained the idealism and passion of youth. He was also in his own way a religiously devout person. Loyal to his Catholicism, he understandably sought ways to root his nationalism in religious imagery, but this did not always make for good theology.

Pearse's fatal error of judgement was to become too dedicated to a cause he had come perilously close to regarding as in itself holy. This is where some sort of theological assessment was badly needed. Although nationalist aspirations can be a channel for much that is positive in hu-

---

30. P. Pearse, *'The Singer' and Other Plays* (Dublin: Maunsell & Co., 1918). p. 44.
31. See J. Lee, *Ireland 1912-1985: Politics and Society* (Cambridge: Cambridge U. P., 1989), pp. 24ff.
32. Dudley Edwards, *Patrick Pearse: The Triumph of Failure*, p. 335.

man society, if the cause of the nation is elevated above all other human
values, then Christian theology must give expression to what Paul Tillich
described as 'the divine and human protest against any absolute claim
made for a relative reality'.[33] Patriotism may be a noble virtue, but true
patriotism is not the same as saying 'my country above all else', still less
'my country right or wrong'.

In Jewish monotheism, the interests of the nation always remain subordinated to the demand of justice. Love for the land and the people is
provisional and remains subject to the ethical obligation of the divine
command. The real interests of the nation cannot prosper if the poor
and the widow are not protected and the foreigner and stranger not
afforded every hospitality. In continuity with this tradition, in his proclamation of the coming reign of the Kingdom of God, Christ does not
appear as a zealot for the national cause, but as the one who turns towards the downtrodden and excluded. He tells the poor that God de-
sires their liberty from oppression; he speaks to the Samaritan woman of
the way of salvation; he helps the Roman centurion who is a foreigner
and commends him for his faith; he readily meets with lepers whom
society has shunned.

Pearse recognised that the national question should in fact be linked
with wider questions of human obligation. At the time of the lockout in
Dublin during 1913 he railed against the injustice and poverty in Ireland, and set the struggle for national freedom in the wider context of
the transformation of social conditions.[34] His enthusiasm for James Fintan
Lalor – one of his four 'voices' or 'gospels' – was because of the way Lalor
had recognised that the land issue was central to the cause of Irish freedom. Lalor, wrote Pearse,

> held in substance that Separation from England would be valueless
> unless it put the people – the actual people and not merely certain
> rich men – of Ireland in effectual ownership and possession of the
> soil of Ireland.[35]

Pearse was not especially successful at translating such sentiments into

---

33. *The Protestant Era*, abridged ed. (Chicago: University of Chicago Press, 1957), p. 163.
34. Pearse, *Political Writings and Speeches*, pp. 171ff.
35. Ibid., p. 350.

a viable programme to command public support. Although there is every indication that his views on economic matters were taking a radical direction – largely due to Connolly's influence – he did not have the ability to think on a broader canvass in the way that Connolly could.[36] The firing squad ensured that Pearse never faced the task of state-building, and so we can only guess at what his 'dream' would have been like in reality. It was a dream that was not without promise in a whole variety of ways. Ireland does well to mourn his loss and honour him in memory.

---

36. Pearse read Connolly's *Labour in Irish History* several times. See Dudley Edwards, *Patrick Pearse: The Triumph of Failure*, p. 244.

CHAPTER FOUR

Socialism, Nationalism and Religion: James Connolly

Political and Social freedom are not two separate and unrelated ideas, but are two sides of the one great principle, each being incomplete without the other.

James Connolly

Widely acknowledged as the most formidable intellect among the leaders of the 1916 Rising, James Connolly has been accorded a place of honour by the Irish State. His socialist belief, however, has made him a contentious figure, and he is often remembered with a certain discomfort, even among those who share his socialist outlook. His decision to lead a small band of Irish socialists as junior partners in a nationalist insurrection posed acute questions at the time, and arguably proved to be damaging to the socialist cause in Ireland.

Born in 1868 to Irish Catholic emigrants in working-class Edinburgh, Connolly left school at an early age. After a series of poorly paid jobs, at fourteen he falsified his papers and took the 'King's shilling'. Army service allowed him to meet his appetite for reading, and brought him to Ireland, where he met his future wife, Lillie Reynolds. When his father died in 1889 Connolly deserted and eventually found manual work in Edinburgh, where he was to make the most of the lively culture of socialist political education and where he engaged in a disciplined study of Marxist theory.

During this period Connolly also began to address Irish issues. Influenced by John Leslie, the secretary of the Scottish Socialist Federation, he argued that the Home Rule alliance with the land agitation was essentially opportunist and that continued cooperation with the Liberals would be neither in the interests of British nor Irish labour: in both countries what the workers needed was independent representation.

Despite his growing stature as a socialist campaigner, Connolly still needed to earn a living, and the loss of his job threw him and his family into crisis. John Leslie intervened, placing an appeal in the socialist journal, *Justice*, which elicited a response from the Dublin Socialist Club offering to employ him as an organiser.

THE RELATIONSHIP BETWEEN SOCIALISM, NATIONALISM AND RELIGION

Soon after his arrival in Dublin, Connolly founded the Irish Socialist Republican Party (ISRP). He was convinced that, in an Irish context, socialism must be closely tied to the national question.

In this respect Connolly's approach to Marxism was refreshingly undogmatic. He realised that the internationalism of socialism does not obviate the need to relate socialist aspirations to the specific political and cultural conditions of a given national context. Accordingly he argued

> that the two currents of revolutionary thought in Ireland, the socialist and the national, were not antagonistic but complementary … that the Irish question was at bottom an economic question, and that the economic struggle must first be able to function nationally before it could function internationally, and as socialists were opposed to all oppression, so should they ever be foremost in the daily battle against all its manifestations, social and political.[1]

In 1898 Connolly launched the ISRP paper, *Workers' Republic*. The first issue denounced sectarianism and declared its intention to 'unite the workers and to bury, in one common grave, the religious hatreds, the provincial jealousies and the mutual distrusts upon which oppression has so long depended for security.'[2] On 17 June 1899, Connolly used the paper to warn against the dangers of allying socialist belief with either atheism or a particular religious viewpoint:

> To identify Socialism and Religion would be to abandon at once that universal, non-sectarian character which to-day we find indispensable

---

1. Quoted by Ruth Dudley Edwards in *James Connolly* (Dublin: Gill and Macmillan, 1981), p. 18. Other important works on Connolly include: Owen Dudley Edwards, *The Mind of an Activist – James Connolly* (Dublin: Gill and Macmillan, 1971); K. Allen, *The Politics of James Connolly* (London: Pluto, 1990); C. Desmond Greaves, *The Life and Times of James Connolly* (London: Lawrence and Wishart, 1972); S. Levenson, *James Connolly: A Biography* (London: Quartet, 1977); A. Morgan, *James Connolly: A Political Biography* (Manchester: Manchester UP, 1988); B. Ransom, *Connolly's Marxism* (London: Pluto, 1980).
2. *Workers' Republic*, 13 August 1898.

to working-class unity, as it would mean that our members would be required to conform to one religious creed ... Socialism, as a party, bases itself upon its knowledge of facts, of economic truths, and leaves the building of religious ideals or faiths to the outside public, or to its individual members if they so will. It is neither Freethinker nor Christian, Turk nor Jew, Buddhist nor Idolater, Mahommedan nor Parsee – it is only HUMAN.[3]

If Connolly was open-minded with regard to the national question and religion, the same cannot be said of his attitude to cross-class alliances. Although he was ready to co-operate with individuals from other social classes, he regarded the notion of national unity as a dangerous myth. When the ISRP sent delegates to the First International, they took the minority line and opposed co-operation with bourgeois parties.[4] During this period Connolly was strongly influenced by the syndicalist views of the American Daniel De Leon, which made industrial unionism rather than social reform its chief strategy. The American Socialist Labour Party (SLP) sought to organise workers into one big union, believing the route to state power to be via the workplace.

Financial support from his Dublin colleagues had always been precarious and Connolly had a difficult time obtaining other employment. A successful trip to the United States only served to underline his frustrations with the ISRP, not all members of which were enamoured by his new emphasis on industrial unionism. This combination of economic necessity and disillusionment induced Connolly to emigrate to the United States in 1903. By 1905 the Industrial Workers of the World (IWW) had been formed and he was employed as organiser for one of the New York sections. Connolly's relations with De Leon by this stage were less than cordial, and he became distinctly uncomfortable with the narrowness of the political stance of his American colleagues. He eventually left the SLP for the more politically heterogeneous Socialist Party of America (SPA), who appointed him as one of their national organisers.

During his time in America Connolly involved himself closely with

3. The article, entitled, 'Socialism and Religion', is included in the collection by Owen Dudley Edwards and Bernard Ransom, eds., *James Connolly: Selected Political Writings* (London: Jonathan Cape, 1973), pp. 195-8 (197f.).
4. R. Dudley Edwards, *James Connolly*, p. 36.

Italian and Irish workers, publishing a newspaper, the *Harp*, which serial-ised his later book *Labour in Irish History*. Connolly's publications were not without impact on the movement in Dublin, and some members, at least, wanted him back. His American experience had taught him that socialist thinking should always be rooted in a wider involvement in the labour movement and had given him a healthy distrust of the emphasis which some socialists place on doctrinal purity. Perhaps even more sig-nificantly, we now find Connolly ready to see the positive elements in a non-socialist body like Arthur Griffith's Sinn Féin.

In July 1910 Connolly returned to Ireland. Arrangements were made for the *Harp* to be transferred to Dublin, and shortly after his arrival *Labour, Nationality and Religion* and *Labour in Irish History*, both of which had been written in America, were published. The former work, written at the prompting of Dublin colleagues shortly before his return to Ire-land, was a reply to a series of Lenten lectures from the leading Jesuit, Father Robert Kane. The lectures were a forthright attack upon social-ism as an irreligious creed which was incompatible with adherence to the Catholic faith.

In his reply Connolly pointed out that the official condemnation of socialism must be seen in the light of what history has shown of the par-tiality of the hierarchy's political judgements in the past. Had not the Catholic Church defended the conquest of Ireland, condemned the American War of Independence, the 1798 rebellion, and attempts to repeal the Act of Union? Again adroitly turning the tables on his oppo-nent, Connolly asks whether in its complete rejection of socialism the Catholic Church is not endorsing capitalist values which are incompat-ible with the social teachings of Christianity? A series of quotations from the early Fathers are marshalled to make the point that 'socialist agita-tors are soft and conservative' by comparison. For example, he could quote St Clement: 'The use of all things that is found in this world ought to be common to all men. Only the most manifest iniquity makes one say to the other, "This belongs to me, that to you." *Hence the origin of conten-tion among men.*'[5]

Connolly's argument carried weight where it mattered, among Catholic

5. P. Berresford Ellis, ed., *James Connolly: Selected Writings* (Harmondsworth: Penguin, 1973), p. 83.

workers, who could see that his case was based not on a rejection of their religious allegiance since it invoked the underlying principles of the Christian religion.

In addition to the charge which equated socialism with atheism, Connolly found it necessary to counter the claim that socialists rejected the institution of marriage – another perception which was likely to prove damaging in an Irish context. Socialism, Connolly insisted, was an economic doctrine, which did not entail particular views on religious matters or marriage. Thus his reply to Father Kane stated:

> Socialists are bound as Socialists only to the acceptance of one great principle – *the ownership and control of the wealth-producing power by the state*, and that therefore totally antagonistic interpretations of the Bible or of prophecy and revelation, theories of marriage, and of history, may be held by Socialists ... [6]

Connolly himself considered monogamous marriage to be conducive to the progress of civilization and saw close parallels between family life and socialist values. In an article in January 1916, he wrote:

> We accept the family as the true type of human society. We say that as in the family the resources of the entire household are at the service of each, as in the family the strong does not prey upon the weak, as in the family the least gifted mentally and the weakest physically share equally the common store of all with the most gifted and the physically strongest, as in the family the true economy consists in utilizing and conserving the heritage of all for the good of all, so in like manner the nation should act and be administered.[7]

As we have seen, Connolly's attempt to define the relationship between socialism and religion sometimes led him to show the convergence between socialism and Christian social teaching. How well did this sit with his insistence elsewhere that socialism was an exclusively economic doctrine? In its concern with economic justice socialism does give practical expression to the moral values with which Christianity is concerned. However, by confining its interests to the economic realm, socialism does

6. Ibid., p. 68.
7. Printed in L. McKenna, *The Social Teachings of James Connolly* (Dublin: Veritas, 1991), pp. 85-7 (86). See also T. Morrissey's introduction, especially pp. 14f. and 24f.

not consider the import of many of the issues which traditionally religion has sought to respond to.

Socialism does not give due regard to the fact that there exist other forms of human alienation beside those arising in the social and economic domain. In the realm of individual life, there is existential anxiety. Then there are questions of moral obligation in inter-personal and familial relations. Sometimes there is the need to cope with grievous personal loss and tragedy. Religion concerns itself with areas of individual subjective human experience which socialism as an economic and political doctrine does not even attempt to address.

Socialism is similarly disinterested with regard to the whole question of evil and suffering, which has been a primary interest of religion. What consolation does the prospect of human freedom and fulfilment for future generations provide for the victims and maimed of the past? Should citizens in a future Ireland largely freed from the injustices of the past forget the dead of 1798 or the Famine? To pose such questions is to answer them. Arguing for a reassessment of this issue one socialist writer maintains:

> The evils of prehistory may have been overcome, but they will linger on in the collective *anamnesis* of liberated mankind … To pretend that these ancestral shadows have no place in the sun-lit world of solidarity is to be unkind, inhuman.[8]

The remembrance and solidarity which is spoken of here is certainly important, but is not hope also required? Is this not where the Christian belief in the resurrection of the dead in which God will wipe away every tear finds its relevance?

Connolly's insistence that religious faith is consistent with a socialist commitment was complemented by his own sensitivity to the fact that there are many matters with which socialism does not treat. It would be quite wrong to dismiss Connolly's interventions concerning the relationship between religion and socialism as purely tactical. His decision to receive Communion before his execution was thus a perfectly intellectually consistent one, even if he may not have always done his duty Sunday

8. Christian Lenhardt, 'Anamnestic Solidarity: The Proletariat and its *Manes*', *Telos*, Vol. 25 (1975), pp. 133-54 (138).

by Sunday. It need not be viewed as motivated by political rather than religious conviction as has sometimes been suggested.[9]

SOCIALISM, NATIONAL CULTURE AND DEMOCRACY

Although Connolly's position on the religious question was no matter of narrow political calculation, it was informed by his strategic conception of the need to relate socialism to the specific cultural determinants of the given national context. If socialism was to prove meaningful it must become more than an abstract set of ideals: there must be a process whereby socialism finds expression within existing cultural forms. Here Connolly was remarkably prescient, since it was precisely the failure to do this which so marred the work of socialist parties of his and later generations – an inadequacy that was to be addressed by the theoretical innovation of Antonio Gramsci's emphasis upon the necessity of socialism achieving cultural hegemony prior to the attempt to achieve state power.[10] It is perhaps significant that this development occurred in a largely Catholic country like Italy where the hold of religion on the masses posed similar issues to the questions facing socialism in Ireland.

Connolly's most important literary effort, *Labour in Irish History*, should be seen in the light of his concern to place socialist aspirations in a wider cultural and historical context. In this ambitious work, Connolly sought to interpret the struggle for Irish freedom in social and economic terms, and thereby relate it to the socialist cause. He also identified in the early socialism of William Thompson in the 1820s, the communitarian experiments at Ralahine and the social radicalism of Young Ireland, indigenous antecedents for the socialism of his own generation. Connolly's endeavour to articulate the national question in a socialist framework offered both a serious effort to hibernicise Marxism[11] and a significant advance

9. C.f. Levenson's treatment of this question in *James Connolly: a Biography*, pp. 321f.
10 . See Jack Lindsay's discussion of Gramsci in *The Crisis in Marxism* (Bradford-on-Avon: Moonraker Press, 1981).
11. 'Each country requires,' Connolly maintained, 'a local or native literature and spoken propaganda translating and explaining its past history and present political developments in the light of the knowledge derived from a study of Socialist classics. Any country which is content to depend solely upon these great Socialist classics will never have a Socialist movement of the working class; it may have a socialist sect of a few true believers, but it cannot hope for the adhesion of the great mass of the toilers.' (In 'A Forgotten Chapter of Irish History', *Forward*, 9th August, 1913).

on the treatment of the national question by Marx himself.

Marx's starting point had been that the emancipation of the working class was primarily an international issue: workers of all nationalities are subject to capital and have more in common with each other than their respective bourgeoisies. He did, however, generally favour the formation of larger nation states on the basis that this facilitated capitalism's development of the productive forces. Exceptions were made when smaller nationalist movements assisted the international struggle for socialism. Thus Irish independence was supported because it would weaken the main capitalist power and assist the workers' struggle in Britain. The difficulty with this outlook was that it was much too instrumentalist. Although Marx thought workers should strive for the extension of formal democratic rights, he did not do sufficient to make this struggle for political freedoms a major criterion in a socialist assessment of national movements.[12]

In contrast, Connolly's attempt to relate the national and social question had the merit of approaching the issue in a way which brought into sharp relief the intimate relation between political liberty and economic justice. It also opened the way for enlisting the energies of ordinary working people behind the struggle for national freedom in ways that made the links with their day-to-day fight for better conditions. Bearing in mind the modest level of independent labour representation in this period, this was important. The crucial linkages Connolly felt able to make are evident in an essay on 'Socialism and Irish Nationalism' in 1897, where he described the national struggle in terms of the extension of democracy. 'Representative bodies in Ireland', he argued, 'would express more directly the will of the Irish people than when those bodies reside in England.' When political liberty had been won it should be used 'as a means of social redemption'. The achievement of national freedom thus in its turn paves the way for socialist advance: 'An Irish Republic would then be the natural depository of popular power; the weapon of popular emancipation'.[13] A democratic form of nationalism of this kind is perfectly compatible with international proletarian solidarity, as Connolly's

---

12. See John Schwarzmantel's discussion of Marx's views on nationalism in *Socialism and the Idea of the Nation* (Hertfordshire: Harvester Wheatsheaf, 1991), pp. 59ff.

13. In *Socialism and Nationalism: A Selection from the Writings of James Connolly*, introduction by D. Ryan (Dublin: Three Candles, 1948), pp. 33-38 (33 and 36).

own record of opposition to the First World War showed.

The difficulties Connolly faced in translating such a project into effective practical action were undoubtedly formidable. The nationalist tradition in Ireland was closely associated with the middle classes. Catholic Emancipation, Repeal, Home Rule, the radical separatism of the Fenians and the resurgent nationalism of the early twentieth century, were all consistent with a bourgeois social hegemony. In 1916, Arthur Griffith and the IRB leadership may have thought Connolly's small Citizen Army would swell the ranks of the insurgents, but they did not share Connolly's vision for a Workers' Republic. The high water mark of socialism in Ireland had been the industrial troubles in 1913, when under James Larkin and Connolly, an immense social struggle had been waged in Dublin in defence of the rights of labour. But with only weak support from the British TUC, defeat was inevitable. The other notable failure of this period was the inability to sustain an independent labour interest in Belfast. Religious cleavages proved stronger than class differences, and the Protestant working class in the North was largely incorporated into Orangeism and reaction.

It is frequently asserted that Irish labour did not behave according to Connolly's socialist theory. This is not quite fair, since his Marxism readily acknowledged the role of religious and nationalist sentiment. Events may have shown him to have been far too sanguine, but did not necessarily contradict his theoretical analysis. The Unionist enthusiasm for God and Empire was, after all, but one more variant of the extreme nationalism sweeping through Europe, and the Protestant working class was only behaving like its European counterparts in rallying to the flag rather than proletarian solidarity.

To some extent the enthusiasm for maintaining the Union with Britain reflected the distinct industrial profile of Ulster, and it is surprising that as a student of Marx Connolly did not give this more weight.[14] However, Connolly's failure was primarily one of judgement: the socialist cause in Ireland was too weak and isolated in both Dublin and Belfast and in such circumstances an alliance with militant nationalism carried far too many risks. Better to preserve strength for another day and more favour-

---

14. See P. Bew, et al, *The State in Northern Ireland 1921-72: Political Forces and Social Classes* (Manchester: Manchester U. P., 1979), p. 8.

able terrain. Connolly was not, of course, naï0ve about the more limited
and socially conservative objectives of the IRB and Sinn Féin. Before the
Rising he told his Citizen Army:

> In the event of victory, hold on to your rifles, as those with whom we
> are fighting may stop before our goal is reached. We are out for eco-
> nomic as well as political liberty.[15]

EASTER 1916: FAILURE OR SUCCESS?

It was Connolly's hope that the Rising would touch off a wider social
upheaval with possible implications for the continental war – not a wholly
improbable scenario bearing in mind the repercussions of the Russian
Revolution in 1917. Events proved otherwise. The 1916 Rising and the
War of Independence which followed produced a democratic Free State,
but also left the ambiguous legacy of Partition and a predominantly Roman Catholic dominated Irish State in which socialist politics have been
largely excluded by the party allegiances stemming from the Civil War.
Connolly's prediction back in 1914 that if Partition was conceded it would
lead to 'a carnival of reaction both North and South', had proved quite
correct.[16]

After the First World War British imperialism was in steep decline.
Indeed, imperialism itself was giving way to more subtle forms of economic domination with the United States as the main hegemonic power.
It would, admittedly, have been difficult to have fully appreciated these
trends at the time. But if in such a context Irish nationalism had used
methods of popular agitation short of violence and concentrated on re-
defining itself in more inclusive and culturally expansive terms, it is ar-
guable that the War of Independence, the subsequent Civil War and Partition might all have been avoided. Having said this, it still remains the
case that the primary moral responsibility for the 1916 Rising lies on the
British side. The failure throughout the preceding generation to introduce a programme of democratic reforms in Ireland, and – more immediately – the connivance of the Conservative Party with the Unionist willingness to defeat Home Rule by unconstitutional means, had done much

15. R. Dudley Edwards, *James Connolly*, p. 145.
16. In *Socialism and Nationalism: A Selection from the Writings of James Connolly*, p. 111.

to diminish still further the legitimacy of the British mandate to rule Ireland and thereby create the conditions whereby recourse to insurrection became more acceptable.[17]

It must have been known, however, that the prospects of a successful rising in 1916 were not great, and this alone must raise the question of whether the insurrectionary route was justified. At the time the intellectual and moral case against the Rising was made by Eoin MacNéill the leader of the Irish Volunteers, who argued that a more defensive posture by the Volunteer movement might produce better dividends.[18] Venturing a judgement on this kind of question is fraught with difficulty. Even the advantage of hindsight still leaves us with a series of questions which it would be difficult to settle. Without the events of Easter 1916 how much longer would it have taken to achieve independence? To what extent did the Rising exercise a positive or negative influence upon the future development of Ireland? Did Ireland's Rising – functioning as myth as well as history – assist anti-colonial struggles in other countries such as India?

One conclusion can perhaps be safely drawn. Despite his undoubted intellectual calibre and moral stature, Connolly made a tragic error of judgement when he made the fateful decision to join the insurgents. His untimely death was an immense loss to the nationalist and socialist causes in Ireland. The presence of someone as articulate as Connolly would very likely have had a decisive impact in the critical debates during the early days of the formation of the Irish State. He certainly would not have stood silent in the face of the kind of patriotic humbug which neglects a concern for social justice. The following quotation aptly serves as Connolly's political testament.

17. See T. Garvin, 'The Rising and Irish Democracy' in M. Ní Dhonnachadha and T. Dorgan, eds., *Revising the Rising* (Derry: Field Day, 1991), pp. 21-28.
18. Joseph Lee has argued that MacNéill's own position was not superior to that of Pearse, but he fails to give sufficient weight to the crucial moral distinction between initiating violence and legitimate defensive action. (See J. Lee, *Ireland 1912-1985: Politics and Society* (Cambridge: Cambridge U. P., 1989), pp. 24-28). MacNéill was the victim of deception and his actions immediately prior to the Rising were both consistent and honourable, and almost certainly prevented greater bloodshed. MacNéill's arguments and role are discussed by J. C. Beckett in *The Making of Modern Ireland, 1603-1923* (London: Faber, 1966), pp. 436-9. For the important documents see F. X. Martin, 'Eoin MacNéill on the 1916 Rising', *Irish Historical Studies*, 12 (1961), pp. 226-71.

Ireland without her people is nothing to me, and the man who is bubbling over with love and enthusiasm for 'Ireland', and can yet pass unmoved through our streets and witness all the wrong and the suffering, the shame and the degradation wrought on the people of Ireland, aye, wrought by Irishmen upon Irishmen and women, without burning to end it, is, in my opinion, a fraud and a liar in his heart, no matter how he loves that combination of chemical elements which he is pleased to call 'Ireland'.[19]

19. 'The Coming Generation' (1900) in O. Dudley Edwards and B. Ransom, *James Connolly: Selected Political Writings*, pp. 363-5 (364).

CHAPTER FIVE

Ireland: Gaelic and Catholic?

This chapter sets out to explore the developing ethos of the Irish State following independence. The degree to which there emerged a lack of sufficient pluralism that has only been addressed in more recent times, should not obscure the fact that, given the background of colonial rule, the War of Independence and the Civil War, the maintenance of political institutions and stable democracy in the early years of the Irish State was a considerable achievement.

NATIONALISM IN THE FREE STATE AND IRISH REPUBLIC

The provisions of the Anglo-Irish Treaty of 1921 made mandatory continued membership of the British Empire, the availability of British access to Irish ports and an oath of allegiance to the Crown from deputies in the Dáil. These terms proved unacceptable to many who wanted a fully republican constitution and the fledgling Free State was plunged into civil war.

During this period large parts of Ireland were under the control of anti-treaty forces. Protestants had fears as to how far they would be welcome in the new state whoever was the victor. These fears were by no means without foundation, and in those areas not under full government control, there were assassinations and many Protestant country houses were raided and sometimes burned down.

Winston Churchill had in fact written to the Irish Cabinet on the 5th of April 1922, expressing his concern for the 300,000 Protestants living in the twenty-six counties and stating that 'their position may become very grave.'[1] In May anxious Protestants sent representatives to Dublin to find out the Government's policy and were quickly given assurances that as soon as things were under control they would get proper protection. The delegation that met Collins and Cosgrave asked

> for assurances that the Government was desirous of retaining them, or whether, in the alternative, it was desired that they should leave the country.

1. D. Kennedy, *The Widening Gulf* (Belfast: Blackstaff Press, 1988), p. 116.

To which Collins responded, saying that

> the Government would protect its citizens, ensure civil and religious liberty, and restore homes and property to any that had been deprived of them.[2]

Throughout this period some Protestants left Ireland and felt they had little choice in the matter. In the fifteen years from 1911 to 1926 the Protestant population declined by more than 100,000 (32 per cent). Although land reforms resulting in emigration and the loss of life in the Great War made a significant contribution to this decline, political turmoil and instability would have induced some to leave mainly for Northern Ireland and Britain.[3] The 220,723 who remained at the time of the census of 1926[4] had withstood the more testing times and looked to better fortunes.

Consistent with the promises and assurances that had been made, the new Free State gave leading Protestants seats in the Senate and courteous negotiations on Protestant interests in education and health took place. The constitution that had been agreed in the Treaty negotiations had been non-sectarian and liberal in character. Many Protestants continued their influential business interests, held prominent roles especially in the civil service and journalism, and remained well represented in other top professions. Despite the respect accorded to them both as individuals and collectively, there was an understandable tendency among Protestants to keep a low profile. The following sentiment captures something of prevailing attitude:

> if anyone does not intend to be a loyal subject of the lawful and recognized government of the country, let him leave it and not jeopardise the position of the thousands who must remain and who intend to work for the common good.[5]

Being a 'loyal subject' here would seem to imply staying well away from political controversy, and that is generally what Protestants did. This

2. Ibid., pp. 119 and 123.
3. Ibid., p. 127.
4. T. P. Coogan, *Ireland Since the Rising* (London: Pall Mall Press, 1966), p. 248.
5. Quoted in P. Buckland, *Irish Unionism 1: The Anglo Irish and the New Ireland 1885 to 1922* (Dublin: Gill and Macmillan, 1972), p. 274.

meant that while Protestants had full political rights and were accorded every respect, apart from some notable exceptions they did not take an active part in shaping the new state.

Given that a large majority of the population was Roman Catholic, this compounded the danger that Irish political culture might evolve in the direction of a confessional state. This is in fact what did happen. In the years following independence the Irish State conceived its national identity in terms of a predominantly Gaelic and Catholic cultural ethos. Without wanting unduly to simplify a complex historical process, it is possible to adduce a number of factors which contributed to the formation of such a perspective: the increasingly Catholic popular constituency of the nationalist movement in the preceding century; the influence of the Gaelic revival upon militant nationalists in the period immediately prior to independence; an understandable mental proclivity to jump from the Gaelic period to the Free State given that the intervening period was seen as one of settlement and incursion; and finally the removal by partition of the necessity of attempting to reconcile culturally divergent traditions. It became an almost sub-conscious assumption that a primary objective of state policy should be the fostering of a Gaelic and Catholic identity. All this was quite consistent with the fact that the Protestant minority was shown every courtesy. Indeed, in at least some respects, the State could afford to be generous to Protestants as individuals and as a section of the community, precisely because they were a minority and therefore posed no threat.

The ethos of the new Free State quickly began to encroach on its inherited liberal constitutional framework. Although the Treaty of 1921 had ensured the new Irish Free State would fully respect religious freedom and that its constitution would be that of a secular state,[6] in practice things were to work out rather differently. From an early stage the Cosgrave government saw the approval of the Roman Catholic hierarchy as an essential means of augmenting its own authority in the context of the recent trauma of civil war.[7]

While genuinely concerned to avoid measures that would alienate Protestants, Cosgrave responded to pressure from the Catholic bishops

---

6. See Conor Cruise O'Brien, *States of Ireland* (London: Hutchinson, 1972), pp. 111ff.
7. See R. Fanning, *Independent Ireland* (Dublin: Helicon, 1983), pp. 18ff. and 53ff.

to ensure there would be no provision whatsoever for divorce in the Free State. Yeats told the Senate that it was 'tragic that within three years of this country gaining its independence we should be discussing a measure which a minority of this nation considers to be grossly oppressive.'[8] Protestants who held a different view to Roman Catholics no longer had the option to divorce and remarry in circumstances where they felt at liberty of conscience to do so. There may not have been many who would have wanted to, but the right was denied. The government's handling of the divorce issue was all of a piece with the deferential attitude to ecclesial pressure shown over a range of matters, and not least on censorship.[9] Along with Yeats there were other writers in the early years of the State, such as Sean O'Casey, who expressed unease at the way Irish nationalism was developing.

Because of his involvement with the anti-treaty forces, Eamon de Valera had been frequently singled out for clerical condemnation. Nonetheless, from its inception in 1926, Fianna Fáil courted the approval of the ecclesiastical authorities and did its best to show even more zeal than Cosgrave's government on such cherished issues as censorship.[10] Shortly after his election in 1932, the Eucharistic Congress provided de Valera with the opportunity to confirm his own status as a loyal Roman Catholic and publicly demonstrate that the rift between Republicanism and Catholicism had been healed.[11]

Although de Valera did not wish to see an established Church, when he set about writing a new constitution, the privileged position of the Roman Catholic Church was given formal recognition. Article 44 of the 1937 Constitution accorded to the Catholic Church a 'special position ... as the guardian of the faith professed by the great majority of the citizens.'[12]

Legislation to allow the dissolution of marriages was now forbidden by the Constitution itself (Article 41). This was not a position that would commend itself to Christians (or atheists), who did not owe any allegiance to the social and moral teachings of the Roman Catholic Com-

8. Ibid., p. 56.
9. J. Lee, *Ireland 1912-1985: Politics and Society* (Cambridge: Cambridge U. P., 1989), pp. 157ff.
10. Ibid., pp. 160f.
11. Ibid., p. 177.
12. R. Foster, *Modern Ireland 1600-1972* (London: Penguin, 1988), p. 544.

munion. The whole tenor of the Constitution seemed to belie its specific reassurance that 'the state shall not impose any disabilities or make discrimination on the grounds of religious profession, belief or status.'[13] This was surely precisely what was being done by infringing the civil liberties of the minority and making the exercise of such liberties unconstitutional. De Valera's own later public references to Ireland as 'a Catholic nation' would not have calmed these fears.[14]

The Constitution also gave expression to a rather paternalist view of marriage and the family in Article 41, which stated that the State shall 'endeavour to ensure that mothers shall not be obliged by economic necessity to engage in labour to the neglect of their duties in the home.'[15]

Articles 2 and 3, which claimed the right to jurisdiction over the whole of Ireland, would scarcely have been well received by Northern Protestants, and were very different in tone from seeing a united Ireland as an aspiration which would not be imposed against the will of the majority in Northern Ireland.

The Constitution was adopted by referendum and this in itself was significant. How could a constitution purporting to be for the whole of Ireland be valid when only citizens in the twenty-six counties were consulted? Did not the whole exercise reveal a less than generous conception of the nature of democracy, which did not take proper account of the need to safeguard individual rights and minority interests? What had happened to the inclusive nationalism of Wolfe Tone, which sought to unite Catholic, Protestant and Dissenter? It was this latter question that drew from Conor Cruise O'Brien the following rather caustic remarks in his perception of the general outlook that shaped de Valera's thinking:

> The nation is felt to be the Gaelic nation, Catholic by religion. Protestants are welcome to join this nation. If they do, they may or may not retain their religious profession, but they become, as it were, Catholics by nationality. Recognising, as they must, at least the overwhelming primacy and predominance of the Gaelic and Catholic compo-

13. Lee, *Ireland 1912-1985*, pp. 201ff. (203).
14. Ibid., p. 206
15. See Mary Robinson, 'Women and the New Irish State' in M. MacCurtain and D. Ó'Corráin in *Women in Irish Society: The Historical Dimension* (Dublin: The Women's Press, 1978), pp. 58-70 (60).

nent of the nation, they are not expected to quibble or jib at such an expression as 'We are a Catholic Nation'.[16]

There is undoubtedly some substance in this assessment, though it should not be accepted if it is taken to imply that Irish nationalism is incapable of breaking out of such a mould. That would be to abandon the high ground through acquiescing in a narrow reading of nationalism and by extension regarding Ireland as an irredeemably sectarian society.

Constitutional politics had not always been de Valera's *forte* and in such circumstances producing a new constitution was undoubtedly a triumph for political presentation that helped confirm Fianna Fáil's newly established status. The process of constitutional development was to be continued when the post-war Fine Gael led coalition formally declared Ireland a Republic in 1949.

Although by 1937 Fianna Fáil can be said to have arrived as a constitutional party, there nonetheless lingered a certain ambivalence regarding its loyalties. De Valera certainly showed that he was as ready as Cosgrave had been to move against the IRA, but not all the members of Fianna Fáil were above fanning the militant republican flames. There was an echo of this in the furore over alleged ministerial involvement in gun running during the emergence of the Troubles in Northern Ireland, which showed that at least some elements in Fianna Fáil were ready to place what Roy Foster describes as 'an each-way bet on force'.[17] Moreover, the earlier aggressiveness shown by Fianna Fáil in the anti-partition campaign of the 1950s has been described as 'a cold war', and scarcely helped in a situation where the possibility of resort to violence was never far away.

What was needed was a policy more in tune with democratic instincts and committed to the articulation of a more inclusive and culturally heterogeneous nationalism. To his lasting credit Seán Lemass recognised this when he insisted that Ulster Protestantism was a vital component of Irish culture. He rejected the idea that Northern Protestants should be

---

16. O'Brien, *States of Ireland*, p. 121. O'Brien makes these remarks in the context of his discussion of the inconsistency of de Valera's idea of Ireland as a Catholic nation with the Irish Republican tradition.
17. Foster, *Modern Ireland 1600-1972*, p. 592. See also Conor Cruise O'Brien's view of the ambivalence of Fianna Fáil in this respect in his *States of Ireland*, pp. 209ff. and 247ff.

coerced into a united Ireland, and argued that 'unity has got to be thought of as a spiritual development which will be brought about by peaceful, persuasive means'.[18]

There were significant Protestant voices, like the essayist and Protestant Republican, Hubert Butler, who lamented the narrowness of some of the prevailing conceptions of nationalism. Butler, informed by his experience from the Balkans, instituted the influential Kilkenny debates that sought to promote a more inclusive and pluralist nationalism and from the 1940s onwards sounded an important note of dissent.[19] W. B. Stanford, a Classicist at Trinity, issued a number of pamphlets during the forties calling for more comprehensive visions of both nationalism and unionism. He also urged the Church of Ireland to be more robust in its interventions in public affairs. Addressing the Dublin Diocesan Youth Conference in November 1943, he said:

> Having our principles, we must protest when they are publically infringed, whether the infringement is against ourselves personally or against any citizen. The policy of *lying low* and *saying nothing*, which many of our elders have advocated for our Church, is neither honourable nor good for ourselves or our country.[20]

Although Protestant clergy in the Free State and Republic had generally kept a low profile, there were notable exceptions like Victor Griffin.[21] Griffin had spent twenty years in Derry, where he was a stalwart critic of the Stormont Government and Derry Corporation, and had supported the ecumenical movement in an effort to counter the 'unholy alliance' of religion and politics in the North. When he came back to the Republic as Dean of St Patrick's Cathedral, his anger at the prevalent assumption that to be Irish was to be Roman Catholic, Gaelic and anti-British, was only matched by his frustration at the acquiescence of Southern Protestants and their failure to call for a more pluralist state. Griffin very effectively used the constitutional amendment debates on

18. See J. Lee, 'Seán Lemass' in J. Lee, ed., *Ireland 1945-70* (Dublin: Gill and Macmillan, 1979), pp. 16-26 (23).
19. See his *Escape From the Anthill* (Mullingar: Lilliput, 1986).
20. *A Recognised Church: The Church of Ireland in Éire* (Dublin and Belfast: APCK, 1944), p. 25. For his views on nationalism and unionism see *Faith and Fiction in Ireland Now* (Dublin and Belfast: APCK, 1946).
21. See his autobiography *Mark of Protest* (Dublin: Gill and Macmillan, 1993).

abortion and divorce during the 1980s to join with liberal Roman Catholics in support of the campaign for a greater pluralism in Irish society.

Isolated as intellectuals like Butler and Stanford, and a doughty campaigner like Dean Griffin, must have often felt, the case for a greater pluralism and for shedding the trappings of a confessional state was increasingly accepted. The removal by referendum in 1972 of the clause granting the Roman Catholic Church a 'special position' marked the beginning of a process of constitutional revision which has continued apace. The commitment of the Irish Republic to the Sunningdale Agreement of 1973 also represented an important milestone, insofar as it formally acknowledged the rights of unionists when it stated 'that there could be no change in the status of Northern Ireland until a majority of the people of Northern Ireland desired a change in that status'.[22] The Anglo-Irish Agreement of 1985 and more recent Joint Declaration and Good Friday Agreement reaffirmed this commitment by the Republic.

Rulings from the Supreme Court and the European Court have also made significant contributions in promoting civil rights and a greater pluralism. History has shown that Garret Fitzgerald had been right to campaign for a 'constitutional crusade', and although the referendum on divorce was lost in 1986, his political leadership, if only indirectly, paved the way for some of the more encouraging developments of the 1990s, including the outcome of the 1995 divorce referendum.

Perhaps the most significant portent for the future is the accelerating pace of secularisation in the Republic. There is often a critical juncture in this process of change which in the longer-term proves decisive. The narrow victory in the 1995 divorce referendum would seem to fall into this category. The divorce debate touches directly on major issues such as the relationship between Church and State, the claims of pluralism and the place of civil rights in a democratic society.[23] There are signs that the Churches are adapting to the new climate, and it is to be welcomed that there is now an increasing recognition that in a pluralist and democratic society, when the churches wish to give a lead, the emphasis should be on seeking to imbue society with religious insights and values rather than trying to impose them.

22. Fanning, *Independent Ireland*, pp. 211f.
23 . I have discussed these issues in J. Marsden, 'Divorce, Remarriage and Civil Rights in a Pluralist Society', *The Furrow*, 47 (9) (1996), pp.480-88.

CHAPTER SIX

Social Inequality
in Modern Ireland:

Retrospect and Prospect

In the preceding chapter, the deficit of an insufficient pluralism in the earlier years of the State following independence was identified and the ways in which this has changed in more recent times strongly welcomed. An examination of Ireland's record on social inequality reveals a similar deficit and throws into sharp relief the need for further social as well as democratic advance within Irish society. This applies to both jurisdictions and whilst the resources at the disposal of governments were no doubt meagre and the problems faced considerable, this alone does not explain the marked inequality that has persisted in Irish society.

IRELAND: FREE STATE AND REPUBLIC

The 1916 Proclamation had included the promise 'to pursue the happiness and prosperity of the whole nation and of all its parts, cherishing all the children of the nation equally'.[1] This reference to the social responsibilities of the new Republic reflected primarily the concerns of Connolly and Pearse.[2] More generally, the coalition of literary figures and Irish Republican Brotherhood members who planned the events of Easter Week, was chiefly preoccupied with the achievement of national freedom. In any event, the vacuum in political leadership resulting from the Rising, was soon to be filled by the then socially conservative Sinn Féin. The loss of more socially advanced nationalists – most notably Connolly and Pearse – now had damaging repercussions for the labour interest

1. The Easter Proclamation is included as an appendix in R. Foster, *Modern Ireland 1600-1972* (London: Penguin, 1988), pp. 597f.
2. In January 1914 Pearse wrote: 'Parnell, as leader of the Irish in their struggle for nationhood, would not have been justified in devoting one hour of his time or one penny of his funds to the land war except as a means to an end.' However, by March 1916, Pearse's enthusiasm for Lalor in *The Sovereign People* shows that he thought that the national question should be more integrally linked with the land issue and social rights. See Patrick Pearse, *Political Writings and Speeches* (Dublin: The Talbot Press, 1952), pp. 105 and 346ff.

within the nationalist movement.[3]

Although after the December 1918 election the more socially radical elements within the Volunteers and IRB did succeed in getting the first Dáil in 1919 to adopt a programme of social reform, this occurred when many Sinn Féin members were imprisoned. With the conclusion of the Anglo-Irish War and the death of Michael Collins in the Civil War that followed, Sinn Féin's conservatism again reasserted itself.

The primary motive behind the decision of the anti-treaty forces to plunge the fledgling Free State into civil war had been the subordination of all else to an uncompromising interpretation of the ideal of national freedom. The real sticking point was not Partition or the social direction of the new Irish State, but the inclusion of the oath which

> prescribed allegiance first to the constitution of the Irish Free State, secondly to the crown in virtue of the common citizenship between the two countries and the association of Ireland with the Commonwealth of Nations.[4]

Had de Valera's advanced notion of 'external association' been accepted in London, it would not have satisfied the purists, whose adherence to an unyielding interpretation of the republican ideal was now elevated above the expression of the democratic will of the people. To his credit Michael Collins – the military man *par excellence* – had the sagacity to throw his weight behind the Treaty. He also had the good sense to accept that the North should not be coerced into a united Ireland. Collins espoused a progressive social policy, insisting that national unity, economic concerns and social interests were all integrally related. 'A prosperous Ireland will mean a united Ireland', he maintained, condemning 'the destitution of poverty at one end, and at the other an excess of riches in possession of a few individuals.'[5]

The Cosgrave administration of Cumann na nGaedheal was to steer

3. See P. Lynch, 'The Social Revolution That Never Was' in D. Williams, ed., *The Irish Struggle 1916-26* (London: Routledge and Kegan Paul, 1966) pp. 41-54 (especially pp. 45ff.).

4. Quoted in J. Lee, *Ireland 1912-1985: Politics and Society* (Cambridge: Cambridge U. P., 1989), p. 50. See also R. Fanning, *Independent Ireland* (Dublin: Helicon, 1983), p. 24, where he concludes: 'the treaty split was not about unity but about sovereignty: about how much independence independent Ireland should have, not about how nationalist Ireland should be re-united with unionist Ireland.'

5. See J. Lee, *Ireland 1912-85*, pp. 60ff. (64).

the ship of state in a somewhat different direction. It took the advice of civil servants who had served under the British administration and regarded the classical *laissez faire* tradition as the accepted wisdom in economic matters, and a stringent economic policy was pursued.[6] Ernest Blythe's Finance Department cut public expenditure from £42 million to £24 million in its first three years. The more vulnerable sections of society soon found themselves hit by these economies, while at the same time reductions in income tax favoured the better off. Fiscal correctness was underlined by the decision to follow Britain and rejoin the gold standard in 1925. Industry was generally regarded as a poor relation to agriculture and the notion that government might have some responsibility for the high level of unemployment did not gain much of a hearing. While Cosgrave must be credited with maintaining political stability after the trauma of the Civil War, in a rather harsh verdict Joseph Lee notes the irony of some at least of his policy:

> [Cosgrave's] cabinet waged a coherent campaign against the weaker elements in the community. The poor, the aged, and the unemployed must all feel the lash of the liberators.[7]

The situation was scarcely helped by the fact that with Sinn Féin deputies unwilling to take their seats there was no effective opposition in the Dáil, though all this was to change when in 1926 de Valera launched Fianna Fáil and the June 1927 election confirmed the new party as the main opposition. Having failed to get a referendum on the oath, the mental dexterity de Valera had shown with his constitutional innovation of 'external association', was now applied to the vexed question of the oath: deputies would sign with the Bible (faced downwards) covering the wording![8]

Cosgrave still clung to his social and fiscal conservatism during the years of the Great Depression and lost the 1932 election. Fianna Fáil, with Labour support, formed an administration, which promised dra-

---

6. See K. Kennedy, et al, *The Economic Development of Ireland in the Twentieth Century* (London and New York: Routledge, 1988), pp. 34ff. Kennedy stresses the way in which priority was given to agriculture.

7. Lee, *Ireland 1912-1985*, pp. 105ff. (124). K. Theodore Hoppen makes a similar assessment in *Ireland Since 1800: Conflict and Conformity* (London and New York: Longman, 1989), pp. 209f.

8. Lee, *Ireland 1912-1985*, pp. 150ff.

matic changes in social and economic policy. The new government pursued a drive towards industrialisation in adverse conditions under the energetic direction of Seán Lemass. Given the previous neglect of industry, it would have been surprising if domestic planning and regulation did not yield some benefits. Moreover, Fianna Fáil did begin to honour pledges in social policy, with the result that the economy was given the added boost of a house-building programme and measures on pensions and unemployment assistance. The industrialisation policy was however fundamentally flawed in its reliance on self-sufficiency and protection. To contract out of the international economy and rely on the home market for as much industrial production as possible was inefficient and particularly ill-advised for a country the size of Ireland. De Valera's trade war with Britain over land annuity payments confirmed Ireland's status as a siege economy.[9] A policy of selective protection to build up industries with strong potential in home and export markets would have been a different matter altogether, but this was not the way in which the policy was applied.

The ideology of self-sufficiency was de Valera's fixation; his largely rural Gaelic utopia would supply the people's frugal needs through domestic agriculture and industry.[10] Social spending might have a limited role in ensuring some of the bare necessities, but must be kept within responsible bounds. In practice this meant that fiscal conservatism continued to dominate the social and economic agenda. To his credit Seán Lemass fought hard and long for concessions with the Finance Department.[11] His expansionist instincts were again to be thwarted during the wartime administration. Debate was joined on Keynes, Beveridge and full employment, but it was fiscal parsimony that prevailed.[12] The process whereby British society was soon to be transformed by the creation of a welfare state had only the faintest of parallels in Ireland. Even the introduction of modest child allowances was fiercely contested.[13]

The 1948 Fine Gael-led coalition benefited from Marshall Aid and

9. Ibid., pp. 175ff. Also Hoppen, *Ireland Since 1800: Conflict and Conformity*, pp. 211ff., and K. Kennedy, et al, *The Economic Development of Ireland in the Twentieth Century*, pp. 40ff.
10. Lee, *Ireland 1912-1985*, pp. 186f.
11. Ibid., p. 189.
12. Ibid., pp. 226ff.
13. Ibid., pp. 280ff.

initially looked more promising. Its policy included the creation of the Industrial Development Authority, a house-building drive and a health programme. The new government, however, lacked the internal cohesion, skill and determination, requisite to the challenge it faced. The fiasco over the apparent ecclesial interference in the 'Mother and Child Scheme', which sought to extend the provision of free medical care, heralded its demise.

The succeeding de Valera administration steered a cautious line on health policy, though the 1953 Health Act did widen eligibility for free hospital treatment. Social welfare provision was also slightly improved. In the economic sphere, Seán MacEntee's sustained deflationary response to balance of payments difficulties proved disastrous. The Fine Gael-led coalition of 1954-7 repeated this fiscal exercise. The consequence of all this was while the rest of Europe benefited from the economic growth resulting from Keynesian economic management, the 1950s were for Ireland years of stagnation and massive emigration.[14]

The first four decades of the Irish State was thus characterised by high unemployment and poor social provision, with emigration acting as the safety valve. Regrettably, whilst the Roman Catholic Church undertook valuable social responsibilities in the absence of a welfare state, the State's socially conservative economic policy went largely uncontested by the Roman Catholic hierarchy, which frequently issued dire warnings against the threat of atheistic socialism and communism. Although the social teaching of the Roman Catholic Church enshrined in encyclicals from *Rerum Novarum* (1891) was critical of *laissez faire* capitalism, in Ireland socialist ideas raised the uncomfortable spectre of the secularism associated with the French and Russia revolutions. Whatever the precise role of the hierarchy in the 'Mother and Child Scheme', it can scarcely be denied that it had little enthusiasm for socially progressive legislation.

Protestantism in the Free State and Republic proved little better and remained rather disengaged from matters of public policy. Its primary objective in relation to the State was to safeguard its interests in the spheres of education, medicine and other matters of direct concern to itself. In contrast with Britain where, stemming from F.D. Maurice, a strong tradi-

14. Ibid., pp. 321ff. On welfare improvements see also Foster, *Modern Ireland 1600-1972*, pp. 572ff.

tion of Christian Socialism had influenced Church leaders like Archbishop William Temple, there was insufficient recognition of the need
to articulate an effective social critique of prevailing conditions.[15]

After winning the 1957 election, de Valera was at last more wary of
pursuing a deflationary course and did not appoint McEntee to Finance.
This considerably strengthened Seán Lemass' already strong position
and when de Valera became President in 1959 Lemass succeeded him as
Taoiseach. Lemass had learned his lessons too. This time his industrial
strategy would be unencumbered by protectionist measures. He was also
undoubtedly aided by the new thinking among civil servants, most notably the influential T. K. Whitaker, Secretary of the Finance Department,
who was a keen advocate of free trade and the need for 'productive'
investment. Under Lemass, Fianna Fáil succeeded in shifting economic
policy in the direction of industrialisation, free trade and greater integration with the international economy. The policy resulted in increased
economic growth, a marked rise in living standards, employment levels
in industry that soon outstripped those in agriculture, and a rapid expansion of education at second and third levels.[16]

Internationally, the 1960s was a period of rapid economic growth and
some commentators have argued that Ireland's success owed more to
this than to changes in domestic policy. But the fact remains that Ireland
had not participated in the high growth of the 1950s and that the
reorientation of Irish economy towards free trade and expansion – in
admittedly favourable conditions – had a markedly beneficial effect. Increased prosperity made possible improvements in social welfare and
health care, though Ireland still lagged behind European standards.

Lemass and Whitaker were moderate Keynesians, and, in addition to
arguing for increased demand, they had placed a strong emphasis upon

15. The Church of Ireland's Ascendancy background and degree of support for the North-
    ern state would no doubt have inhibited a more generous treatment of social ques-
    tions. More research needs to be done in this area, beginning perhaps with the biog-
    raphies of the Church of Ireland Archbishops. For a more positive assessment than I
    have felt able to give see R. B. McDowell, *The Church of Ireland 1869-1969* (London:
    Routledge, 1975), pp. 136f. Some notable individual Protestant voices who did call
    for a greater involvement in public affairs and were ready to contest narrower read-
    ings of nationalism are mentioned in Chapter 5, pp. 96f.
16. Lee, *Ireland 1912-1985*, pp. 341ff. and 359ff. Also Hoppen, *Ireland Since 1800: Conflict
    and Conformity*, pp. 218ff.; Foster, *Modern Ireland 1600-1972*, pp. 577ff.; and Fanning,
    Independent Ireland, pp. 193ff.

the need for productive investment and trade liberalisation. Future Irish governments, which were a good deal less discriminating, ran into two difficulties. First, with the end of the long boom at the time of the 1973 oil crisis, international conditions were much less favourable. Second, flushed by earlier successes, public borrowing was allowed to rise to unsustainably high levels. By the 1980s the Irish economy was blighted by stagnation and mass unemployment, and even when fiscal profligacy was corrected and growth resumed at the end of the decade, unemployment stayed persistently high. 'No other economy in the whole of Europe', Joseph Lee complained in 1986, 'appears to have experienced remotely so slow a growth of its total gross national product'.[17]

This assessment has been disputed and is perhaps too negative[18], but it can scarcely be denied that serious errors were made and opportunities therefore missed. Moreover, not having created a welfare infrastructure in the early post-war years, Ireland noticeably lagged behind other European countries in public health care and efforts to redistribute wealth and alleviate poverty. Although welfare levels did improve in the 1960s and 1970s, there is evidence that in relative terms there had still been 'a shift from the poor to those at the top of the economic scale'.[19] Provision in health care, education and welfare support remain poor by European standards – a point which is cited in the literature explaining the reasons for Ireland's high allocation of structural funds in the mid 1990s.[20] In 1989 K. Theodore Hoppen concluded his discussion of Irish economic and social history with the following observation:

The fact that the Republic has failed to fulfil the pledges of the 1916 Declaration of Independence, the Democratic Programme of 1919, and Article 45 of the Constitution of 1937 to cherish all the children

---

17. 'Whither Ireland? The Next Twenty-Five Years!' in K. Kennedy, ed., *Ireland in Transition: Economic and Social Change since 1960* (Cork and Dublin: Mercier Press, 1986), pp. 152-66 (153f).

18. Kieran Kennedy takes a less extreme view than Lee, but describes the performance of the Irish economy as 'mediocre' in Kennedy, *The Economic Development of Ireland in the Twentieth Century*, pp. 121f. David Johnson and Liam Kennedy take a more positive view in a recent study 'The Two Economies of Ireland in the Twentieth Century' in J. R. Hill, ed., A *New History of Ireland*, Vol VII, *Ireland 1921-84* (Oxford: Oxford UP, 2003).

19. Hoppen, *Ireland since 1800: Conflict and Conformity*, p. 228.

20. *Commission of the European Communities: Community Support Framework 1994-99* (Brussels: E.U. Commission, 1994).

of the nation equally and provide for their physical, mental, and spiritual well-being is hardly surprising. Subsequent realities rarely match initial promises. But that so little relative progress has been made, that the handicap of weights carried by individuals have been distributed hardly at all, that, by western standards, Ireland remains not only a highly unequal society but one in which inequality is generally apportioned by accident rather than ability, adds up to at best a poignant and at worst a melancholy commentary upon almost seven decades of self-rule.[21]

The 1990s saw a resumption of growth, which gathered pace and reached high levels by the end of the decade. Before considering some of the reasons for this expansion, it should be acknowledged that combating social exclusion still remains a major priority in the Republic.

Ireland's failure with the marginalised is a more notable example of a wider trend in Western industrialized societies, whereby the relatively affluent majority have of late shown a remarkable capacity to acquiesce with conditions of social deprivation which mean a sizeable proportion of society are, in economic terms, relatively excluded. In this regard John Kenneth Galbraith has rightly warned of the dangers of what he calls 'the culture of contentment', whereby the economically successful ignore the needs of others.[22] In the more automated society of the future a choice will need to be made between a two-tier society and one which spreads wealth and the opportunity to work more equitably.

A comprehensive identification of inequality would no doubt require elucidating a whole series of categories of social exclusion such as class, gender, the low paid, unemployed, carers, disabled and travellers. In many instances these categories intersect and the incidence of social deprivation is therefore compounded by several factors. Thus women are often low paid, while unskilled manual workers are much more likely to be unemployed.

One important study [23] has criticised the way in which in Ireland the

---

21. Hoppen, *Ireland since 1800: Conflict and Conformity*, p. 229.
22. *The Culture of Contentment* (London: Sinclair-Stevenson, 1992).
23. R. Breen, et al, *Understanding Contemporary Ireland: State, Class and Development in the Republic of Ireland* (Dublin: Gill and Macmillan, 1990), pp. 70ff. I have drawn on this fascinating empirical study which examines the role of the State in shaping the social structure in the discussion immediately below.

cost of social expenditure has been disproportionately borne by the less well-off who too quickly enter the tax net, and has pointed to the decline in revenue from property, inheritance and corporation taxes. Tax cuts have too often been focussed on the relatively affluent, which squanders the opportunity to use tax revenues to redistribute resources, without which economic growth only serves to heighten existing disparities in wealth and opportunity. If progress is to be made in reducing taxation for people on low incomes, while at the same funding initiatives to improve the life chances of the marginalised and excluded, then more must be expected from both the wealthier in society and the business community – including the transnationals who have too readily been granted major exemptions. In the Economic and Social Research Institute's Medium Term Review 2001-2007, John Fitzgerald maintained that there was scope for raising corporation tax without frightening off the multinationals.[24]

Through its taxation policy, over the longer term, the State can exercise a profound influence on the social structure of society by adopting measures that redistribute wealth and opportunity.

Education would be a prime example where the State must deploy resources generously. More than anything else it has been improved second and third level educational provision that has in recent years assisted economic growth by providing an attractive skills base. More remains to be done since participation rates at third level are still unacceptably low for poorer-income groups. Initiatives are needed to rekindle hope among deprived communities and disrupt the vicious circle whereby the experience of unemployment and unsatisfactory social conditions is passed down from one generation to the next. Imaginative social engineering could do much to redress the situation where third level education would no longer be an unheard of dream – as it is at the moment – for some sections of Irish society.

This emphasis upon the role of the State is relevant when we look at the other factors which have assisted economic growth in the 1990s which include: the correction of previous indiscipline in the control of public finances; the moderate pay agreements agreed through National Partnership forums; increased participation especially of women in the

24 . See *The Irish Times*, 28 September 2001.

workforce; the large injection of EU Structural Funds; and the encouragement of the inflow of US high-tech companies.[25] As we have seen with education, these other factors point to the critical role of the State, and this should caution against too great a reliance on a market-orientated ethos when looking to the future of the Irish economy.

Much more could undoubtedly be achieved if more enlightened social policies were adopted. Despite improved economic conditions it is salutary to be reminded that a United Nations Report in July 2001 found that 'proportionately more people live in poverty in Ireland than in any other industrialised nation outside the US.' With 15.3% of its population living in poverty, Ireland ranked sixteenth out of seventeen western countries. In the same year the annual report of the Combat Poverty Agency (funded by the Government and the EU) pointed out that Ireland has the highest rate of child poverty in the EU and called for increased investment in health, education and housing services.[26] 'The last decade has seen unprecedented economic success,' Martin Mansergh rightly notes, 'which gives us an equally unprecedented opportunity and resources to deal with the main outstanding social problems'.[27] The record on these matters of the Justice Commission of the Conference of Religious of Ireland (CORI) testifies to a much keener awareness in the Churches today of the need to challenge state policy when important social needs are not being properly addressed.[28]

These issues need to be put in a historical context. With its two main political parties representing a wide coalition of interests and having divisions rooted in the Civil War, Ireland has in consequence lacked a strong social democratic tradition. In the case of Fianna Fáil an articulation of the nationalist project that would secure a large popular appeal was certainly sought and more corporatist policies frequently pursued, though this was always balanced by more conservative rural interests and its ties with business. The Labour Party may have assiduously cultivated its work-

25 . See K. Kennedy, 'The Irish Economy Transformed', *Studies*, Vol. 87, No. 345 (Spring 1998), pp. 33-42.

26 . *The Irish Times* 10 and 31 July 2001.

27 . 'Republicanism in a Christian Country – Past, Present and Future', *Studies*, Vol 89, No 355 (Autumn 2000), pp. 247-66 (259).

28 . See Chapters Ten and Twelve in James Mackey and Enda McDonagh (editors), *Religion and Politics in Ireland at the Turn of the Millennium* (Dublin: The Columba Press, 2003).

ing class roots but its centre of gravity remained more 'integrative' with respect to diverse social constituencies, and policy often reflected a coalition context. Fine Gael, although historically tied to more conservative interests, did have luminaries like Garret Fitzgerald who attempted to steer the party in a more social democratic direction. Regrettably, difficult international conditions severely curtailed this development which proved short lived.[29] All this contrasts with the British and European experience, where strong social democratic parties helped sustain a political culture that has been lacking in Ireland.

This has led to too great a subservience to the market, with the false assumption that *laissez faire* somehow automatically results in optimal activity. The market economy should not be treated as though it was a morally free zone, since aggregate market outcomes are evident and foreseeable and moral responsibility by society therefore attaches to them. The market is a human institution and should be subject to a political framework where decisions about its efficient operation and appropriate measures of redistribution can be deliberated upon.[30] As we have already observed, the role of the State remains crucial both for economic development and in the achievement of social objectives. The relatively low levels of government expenditure in Ireland as a proportion of GDP, when compared with other European countries, suggests that there is indeed scope for increased spending on public services and policies to redistribute wealth.[31] Chronic under-investment in health and education warrants additional efficiently applied resources. The reaction to the national debt difficulties of the 1980s has gone too far and in the name of economic efficiency and social justice a renewal of social democratic vision is urgently needed. Here the Churches have a vital contribution to make in forging a more generous social consensus by speaking more prophetically and being less defensively pre-occupied.

29. For a detailed discussion of successive government and party policies see Paul Bew, et al, *The Dynamics of Irish Politics* (London: Lawrence and Wishart, 1989).
30. For a useful treatment of these issues see R. Plant, *Politics, Theology and History* (Cambridge: Cambridge U.P., 2001), pp. 177ff and 196ff.
31. Pertinent in this regard is the submission by the Conference of Religious of Ireland (CORI) to a plenary meeting at Dublin Castle of Social Partners and Government on 24 October 2003. Fr Sean Healy pointed to the very low level of spending on social provision in Ireland as a proportion of GDP (Ireland's 14.7% GDP, compared with 26.6% in the UK and 29.6% in Germany).

Perhaps the most poignant indication of the way in which Irish society is still so marred by social injustice is the scandal of the conditions forced upon the Traveller population. The treatment of the Travellers is an extreme example of the ugly politics of exclusion that has consigned such a large section of the community to hopelessness and despair. Irish Travellers can trace their origins to economic displacement, with families forced to take to the road because of a lack of demand for their skills. More recent changes since the 1960s has restricted the scope of the traditional role they had acquired, and this has resulted in migration to the outskirts of urban areas. Local authorities are obliged to provide sites and housing, but have been ineffective in doing so. Although some Travellers may not wish to settle, survey and census information shows that the majority would prefer standard housing, and that three out of four of those housed continue in their new homes. One of the main features of Traveller families is high birth rates and short life spans. The combination of poor living conditions, low income, lack of adequate primary health care and interrupted schooling for children can prove very destructive. Citing some Travellers' anti-social patterns of behaviour, people often dismiss them as a public nuisance and see them as being responsible for their own plight.

One study describes the Travellers' predicament as being 'caught in a classic vicious cycle. The more squalid and insanitary their living conditions, the more despised and outcast they become.' After examining the available evidence this study concludes its findings: 'the circumstances of the Irish Travelling people are intolerable. No humane and decent society, once made aware of such circumstances, could permit them to persist.'[32] And yet this is precisely what has been allowed to happen by the inaction of local authorities, failure of central government, and the prejudice and lack of generosity of spirit of the public at large. The frequent malnourishment among the children of Traveller families, evident from their stunted growth, is an offence to the 1916 Proclamation's call to cherish 'all the children of the nation equally'.

32. D. Rottman, A. Dale Tussing and M. Wiley, *The Population Structure and Living Circumstances of Irish Travellers: Results from the 1981 Census of Traveller Families*, Economic and Social Research Institute, Paper no 131, (Dublin: 1986), especially pp. 59-74 (60 and 73). See also *Report of the Task Force on the Travelling Community: Executive Summary*, Department of Equality and Law Reform (Dublin: Stationery Office, 1995).

NORTHERN IRELAND: SECTARIANISM AND SOCIAL INEQUALITY

Northern Ireland's first Prime Minister, James Craig, inherited a difficult economic position. The traditional industries of shipbuilding and linen were particularly vulnerable to the depressed state of the world economy in the 1920s and 1930s, and unemployment levels remained high. Conditions would have been worse if Craig had adopted a tight fiscal policy. Although no friend of organised labour, he recognised that the maintenance of the unionist cross-class alliance imposed its own constraints and with the encouragement of some of his ministers fought hard to ensure that Northern Ireland should have the same social welfare arrangements as Britain.[33] This undoubtedly benefited both sides of the religious divide, though Roman Catholics too often faced discrimination in political representation, employment and other fields. This disadvantage was sanctioned by the government which, with the aid of the Orange Order, unabashedly sought to maintain Protestant dominance in the Northern State. Craig put the position succinctly in 1934:

> I have always said that I am an Orangeman first and a politician and member of parliament afterwards ... All I boast is that we have a Protestant parliament and a Protestant state.[34]

The situation was no doubt compounded by the refusal of many nationalists to recognise the Northern State or participate in its political institutions.

World War II and the subsequent welfare measures introduced by the Attlee government, transformed economic conditions in Northern Ireland. Unemployment, which had made the inter-war years so bleak, was dramatically reduced. Living standards rose sharply, both in absolute terms and relative to the rest of the United Kingdom. The trend continued throughout the years of the post-war boom, with income per capita rising to 84 per cent of the level in Britain. Although remaining below 10 per cent, unemployment was by British standards high. More worryingly, the rate was disproportionately higher among Catholics.[35]

33. Lee, *Ireland 1912-1985*, pp. 139f. John Andrews made a particularly important contribution in this matter (See David Richardson, *The Career of John Miller Andrews, 1871-1956*, PhD Thesis, Queens University Belfast, 1998).

34. See M. Farrell, *Northern Ireland: The Orange State*, 2nd ed., (London: Pluto Press, 1980), especially pp. 81ff. (I have used Farrell's quotation of Craig on p. 92).

35. Lee, *Ireland 1912-1985*, pp. 256 and 411ff.

When Terence O'Neill became Prime Minister in 1963 modest reforms were pursued to ensure economic development and conciliation across the religious divide.[36] His economic policy met with some initial success and secured a higher growth rate than the rest of the United Kingdom. Discrimination was certainly reduced in the newer industries, though with the decline of traditional industries the net gain in jobs did not make much impact on unemployment. Moreover, efforts at economic rejuvenation favoured the more affluent, predominantly Protestant, eastern part of Northern Ireland – a situation which was hardly helped by the decision to site a new university at Coleraine instead of Derry. O'Neill's other social initiatives failed to satisfy a much more confident and articulate Catholic populace, which wanted more vigorous attempts to reverse inequalities.

The growth of the civil rights movement in the late 1960s, and the response to it by the RUC and vigilante groups, was to result in open sectarian conflict and rioting. Despite intense pressure from Westminster on unionists to adopt more enlightened measures, O'Neill was replaced by a more conservative unionist leadership that was reluctant to countenance reform of the Northern State. The deployment of troops and a series of major errors in British policy, most notably internment, resulted in an increased level of paramilitary violence.[37]

The most important initiative after the introduction of direct rule was the 1973 power-sharing executive and Sunningdale Agreement. This attempt at reform was blocked by the intransigence of more extreme unionists and the militancy of the rank and file.[38] Things might have worked out differently if the Labour Government had acted more firmly, which it should have done given the issues at stake. The failure to democratise the Northern State along the lines of the Sunningdale Agreement resulted in the stalemate of continued direct rule. Throughout the 1970s and 1980s the marked slow down in world growth resulted in a return of

36. See Lee, *Ireland 1912-1985*, pp. 414ff. and M. Farrell, *Northern Ireland: The Orange State*, pp. 229ff. and 240ff. The emphasis should be on the word 'modest' when considering O'Neill's reforms (see R. Foster's comments on O'Neill's '*démarche* towards liberalism' in his *Modern Ireland 1600-1972*, p. 585).
37. See Lee, *Ireland 1912-1985*, pp. 418ff., and Foster, *Modern Ireland 1600-1972*, pp. 587ff. Foster says that for Protestants 'civil rights demonstrations meant that the republican fifth column was on the march again.' (p.588).
38. For a detailed account see Farrell, *Northern Ireland: The Orange State*, pp. 306ff.

high unemployment, bearing disproportionately heavily on Catholics.

It is doubtful if the Troubles would have sustained themselves in quite the way they did if sectarian conflict did not have some underlying economic foundation. Indeed, the salient economic factors that have provided such powerful sustenance to extremist nationalist and unionist ideologies can be readily identified. If we take unemployment, we find that not only has it been disturbingly high in Northern Ireland, but that it has been concentrated in particular locations and also unevenly distributed between Catholics and Protestants.[39] For example, in 1993 Catholic male unemployment stood at 23 per cent, over twice the level of Protestant male unemployment (11 per cent). Although unemployment levels have fallen since the early 1990s the black spots and uneven distribution by religion persist.[40]

Throughout the Troubles disparities were also reflected in other areas of economic life. Using information from the Northern Ireland Family Expenditure Survey, Inez McCormack states that in 1993 'average gross weekly income for Protestants was 17 per cent higher than for Catholics.'[41] As regards access to better paid jobs, the efforts made to redress these inequalities by the Fair Employment Commission are to be welcomed, but inequalities persist. In the context of such inequality it is not surprising that the sense of grievance and injustice experienced by Catholics, and the economic insecurity felt by Protestants especially those in poorer districts, have fuelled political conflict. The absence of constructive channels for democratic participation prior to the Good Friday Agreement, makes discernible the process whereby the most threatened sections of the community – the Catholic and Protestant ghettos – became

39. See *1993 Labour Force Survey: Religion Report.* A Government Statistical Publication, PPRU Monitor 2/94, December 1994. Also Gerard Quinn, 'Northern Ireland: Social Policy and Economic Privilege', *Studies*, Vol. 81, No. 322 (Summer 1992), pp. 191-202. Quinn's article draws heavily on work by Bob Rowthorn, especially B. Rowthorn and N. Wayne, *Northern Ireland: The Political Economy of Conflict* (Cambridge: Polity Press, 1988). In Chapter 7, Rowthorn and Wayne give detailed breakdowns of the regional distribution of unemployment and comparisons with other depressed parts of United Kingdom which show the marked severity of unemployment among Catholics in Northern Ireland.

40. Northern Ireland Statistics and Research Agency. *Annual Labour Force Survey 1990-2000.* In 2000 Roman Catholic unemployment stood at 8.8% and Protestant at 5.2%. See also Measures of Deprivation (by areas) at www.nisra.gov.uk.

41. 'A View from The North' in M. D'Arcy and T. Dickson, ed., *Border Crossings: Developing Ireland's Island Economy* (Dublin: Gill and Macmillan, 1995), pp. 145-53 (148).

such a fertile recruiting ground for paramilitary organisations.

Given that Northern Ireland has for so long been one of the more depressed regions in the United Kingdom, the case must be sustained for more concerted governmental action to stimulate new investment, help redistribute wealth, provide greater equality of opportunity and, perhaps most important of all, address the problems of areas with unacceptably high levels of unemployment. If such a policy was adopted the socio-economic basis of sectarian discontent would no longer be such a potent factor.[42] Appeals for mutual tolerance, political dialogue and inter-governmental initiatives, are not enough on their own. Action needs to be taken to create the economic conditions that might facilitate and underpin a political solution.

The costs of economic regeneration are quite manageable when seen in a British and European context. It has only to be pointed out that the population of Northern Ireland is 2.5 per cent of the total in the United Kingdom to realise that, in fiscal terms at least, the options are there to cover the cost of social reconstruction required to achieve economic development.[43] This is already happening through capital transfers from the United Kingdom, but more substantial and better targeted funding that addresses social disadvantage is required. What is needed is not merely a question of throwing more money at the problem, and care would need to be taken not to produce distortions or reduce competitiveness in the economy in a way that might prove counter-productive.

An effective strategy would require the provision of greater technical and managerial expertise, the brokering of international marketing agreements, policies to widen the skills-base and measures to assist the long-term unemployed who are in danger of being effectively excluded from

42. The importance of stronger legislation on equal opportunities and the widespread neglect of this issue by politicians is the main theme of Gerard Quinn's article 'Northern Ireland: Social Policy and Economic Privilege'.

43. Rowthorn and Wayne have rejected such a policy, saying: 'Compulsory direction of investment into Northern Ireland is impractical. There are both political and economic limits to the effectiveness of government aid as a stimulus to private investment in the province.' (See Rowthorn and Wayne, *Northern Ireland: The Political Economy of Conflict*, p. 124). There are, however, historical precedents on a far grander scale than Northern Ireland that would surely question such a judgement. It may be true that continued disorder on a large scale always poses a threat to economic development, and spending would need to be avoided that might produce distortions or impair competitiveness, but it would be a counsel of despair not to take judicious initiatives as circumstances permit along the lines suggested below.

participating in the market economy. The good will that is there internationally would make it possible to construct an impressive package of
public and private investment and trade agreements to underwrite the
continuing search for a lasting peace.

In the early 1990s the British Government announced that Targeting
Social Need (TSN) was to become a part of its spending priority. The
extension of such initiatives would do much to improve the position of
both the poorest Catholics and the poorest Protestants, and Inez
McCormack has rightly argued that tackling disadvantage needs to be
made the centre-piece of a viable and effective economic strategy. Advocating a more 'integrated' approach to the allocation of government
expenditure, she maintains:

> targeting disadvantage at the heart of economic policy and in part-
> nership with the communities themselves, could make a dramatic dif-
> ference to the future, to provide sustainable and reasonably well-paid
> jobs for those who have been on the periphery.[44]

Despite progress being at times faltering, the ceasefires, peace process and commitment flowing from the Good Friday Agreement to try to
make parity of esteem, power-sharing and new democratic institutions
an effective reality have all undoubtedly helped stimulate a resurgence
in business activity. Between North and South, cross-border institutions
have an important role to play in securing economic regeneration, since
there is clearly no justification for continuing the economic fragmenta-
tion of this island.[45] Infrastructural investment, not least in transport, is
urgently needed to facilitate trade, which in its turn, can play no small
part in creating mutual understanding. Peter Sutherland, former Direc-
tor-General of the World Trade Organisation, has rightly commented:

> The staggering communication deficit between Belfast and Dublin,
> whether by air or road, speaks volumes for the indifference of succes-
> sive administrations, particularly on the southern side of the border.

---

44. 'A View from the North', in D'Arcy and Dickson, *Border Crossings: Developing Ireland's Island Economy,* pp. 145-53 (152).
45. See J. Bradley, 'The Two Economies of Ireland: An Analysis' in D'Arcy and Dickson, *Border Crossings: Developing Ireland's Island Economy*, pp. 38-52. Bradley discusses the changing industrial profile of Ireland both North and South since the 1920s and the implications this has for a less fragmented island economy.

Perhaps closed minds and fantasies could be removed if we developed better economic relations. Ireland could be then be presented as a paradigm for others in demonstrating that economics and peace are inextricably bound together ... As the political parties involve themselves in the search for agreement, it is important, I believe, not to lose sight of the economic and trade dimension so cruelly undermined by the years of violence. Ireland, North and South, shares the problem of high unemployment. If we are to tackle this scourge we can best do it together in co-operation, not only through trade with each other but also in co-operating to sell into the global market.[46]

With transformed economic circumstances, greater social cohesion and more viable democratic structures, there is a real prospect that the religious divide will become much less pronounced. A more open, and increasingly pluralist society might then approach the question of wider political relationships and sovereignty with the pragmatism and good sense it deserves. Whatever difficulties may doggedly beset the political process, parity of esteem, power sharing, new institutions and a new executive, have rightly been identified as the essential ingredients of a political settlement leading to the democratisation of the Northern State in a constitutional form that would preclude the domination of one religious tradition by another.

Statecraft, vision and a renewal of the political culture, will also undoubtedly be needed to sustain the break with the many injustices of the past that have so marred Irish society – both North and South. Maureen Gaffney is therefore quite right when she concludes:

The achievement of peace in Northern Ireland signals more than an end to hostilities. A historic opportunity now presents itself to both parts of this divided island to articulate a vision of what kind of society we want to live in and what civic and moral values we subscribe to, and to mount an energetic and positive challenge to the economic and social problems that have historically bedevilled both societies.[47]

---

46. 'Letter from Geneva', in D'Arcy and Dickson, *Border Crossings: Developing Ireland's Island Economy*, pp. 8-18 (17f.).
47. 'A View from the South' in D'Arcy and Dickson, *Border Crossings: Developing Ireland's Island Economy*, pp. 154-61 (154).

CHAPTER SEVEN

Redemption and the Recovery of the People as Subject in Irish History

The revolutionary desire to achieve the Kingdom of God is the beginning of modern history.
                                                            – Friedrich Schlegel

Once man has comprehended himself and has established his own domain in real democracy, without depersonalization and alienation, something arises in the world which all men have glimpsed in childhood: a place and a state in which no one has yet been. And the name of this something is home or homeland.
                                                            – Ernst Bloch

The attempt to venture a theological reading of Irish history is admittedly ambitious, both as an exercise in historical interpretation and because it will need to be set in the context of more universal themes in politics and theology. Democratic and social emancipatory aspirations have the widest of provenance, but connections can be made which locate all that is best in the struggle for freedom in Ireland with the larger human story.

THE ROOTS OF MODERN DEMOCRATIC POLITICS

Political thought in the West has been decisively shaped by the treatments of what might constitute the ideal form of the State in Plato's *Republic* and in Aristotle's *The Politics*. Here we find an acceptance of the ideal of justice, albeit variously defined, as central to the ordering of human society. The incipient utopianism which the classical tradition introduced had its counterpart in the strong current of prophetic literature and millenarian thinking within the Judaeo-Christian tradition.

It is against this background that we must view the burgeoning aspirations of Renaissance humanism, with its vigorous confidence in the human subject as the measure of all things, that gave rise to a body of literature which became the seed-bed for the future development of modern democratic thinking and politics. Two interconnected strands can be discerned within this body of writing: Political Utopianism and Republicanism.

With the former the possibility of thinking in wholly new ways about the political order drew upon both the renewed interest in the classical political corpus and influences that can be traced to the millenarian thinking of Joachim of Floris and the radical Franciscans.[1] It was Thomas More who first introduced the word 'Utopia' meaning 'no place', from the Greek *ou* and *topos*. The poet laureate of the island of Utopia said it deserved to be called 'Eutopia', meaning good or ideal place.[2] This highlights the moral purpose behind More's literary endeavour, which was an attempt to give expression to the social and political ideals of renaissance humanism that form the background to political thinking in the modern period and the marked aspirations for greater human freedom by which it has been characterised.

The new republicanism of this period took a wide variety of forms, ranging from Machiavelli's artful reflections on the exercise of political power to the eventual emergence of social contract theory. The revival of interest in the classical republic generated an impressive vocabulary of political discourse that was to prove widely influential. James Harrington's defence of the English Commonwealth, in his *Oceanna* of 1656, was especially important for the dissemination of this republican lexicon and tradition (sometimes referred to as 'civic humanism') in the English-speaking world. Themes such as the opposition of virtue and corruption, the idea of the public good and responsible citizenship, were articulated and adapted by Harrington in the context of the turbulent years following the English Civil War.[3] Considerations of this kind in turn formed the setting in which the principle of government by consent and social contract could be advocated.

1. The influence of Christian eschatology via the Franciscan-Joachimite tradition on Rennaissance views of history and utopianism is stressed by Reinhold Niebuhr in *The Nature and Destiny of Man*, Vol 2, *Human Destiny* (New York: Scribners, 1964), pp. 160ff.
2. See T. More, *Utopia*, trans. P. Turner, (Harmondsworth: Penguin, 1965) (Rep. 1970), p. 27, and F.E. Manuel and F.P. Manuel, *Utopian Thought in the Western World* (Oxford: Blackwell, 1979), pp. 1ff and 117ff.
3. On 'Civic humanism' see J. Pocock, *The Machiavellian Moment: Florentine Political Thought and the Atlantic Republican Tradition* (Princeton: Princeton, 1975) and also *Virtue, Commerce, and History: Essays on Political Thought and History, Chiefly in the Eighteenth Century* (Cambridge: Cambridge U. P., 1985), especially Chapter 2.

The response during the Enlightenment to the perennial question of the ideal form of the State was to oppose all manifestations of political absolutism in the name of popular sovereignty and democracy. The year 1789 saw the appearance of the *Declaration of the Rights of Man and the Citizen,* the famous proclamation of political liberty that for many marked the birth of modern democracy. A moment of intoxication which Wordsworth captured saying: 'Bliss was it in that dawn to be alive'.[4]

The alternatives of a constitutional republicanism or radical Jacobinism still set wide parameters for those opposed to absolutism. The value of a Painite assertion of the rights tradition in a country like Ireland which denied the majority political rights, still left the question of the excesses of the French experiment in liberty, which understandably led many to seek shelter in a conservative liberalism. Edmund Burke was as offended as anybody else by the suppression of the rights of Catholics, but saw this as fully consistent with his pointing to the danger of sweeping away all countervailing influences to executive power, and the importance of tradition and constitutional safeguards.[5]

There are other respects besides its limited success in creating a sustainable democratic culture, in which the French experiment can be said to have promised more than it delivered. Democratic rights and formal liberties are a necessary but not a sufficient condition for real human freedom. Reformist socialist thinkers like Ernst Bloch, who resisted Soviet orthodoxy, are therefore right to remind us that a healthy democracy requires social as well as political equality. As long as social and economic power is not controlled in the interests of the whole community, there may exist a formal political equality, but this freedom remains too abstract and limited. It was for this reason that socialism sought to give more substantial expression to the ideals of the French Revolution by insisting that genuine democracy requires a greater measure of social equality. Thus although socialism identified itself with the democratic ideals of the Enlightenment, it rejected the private monopoly of ownership and the new economic individualism, articulating a powerful

4. M. Arnold, ed., *Poems of Wordsworth* (London: Macmillan, 1879), p. 252.
5. See his *Reflections on the Revolution in France* (1790) (Harmondsworth: Penguin, 1968). For a treatment of some of the nuances of Burke's liberalism see Seamus Deane, 'Edmund Burke and the Idelogy of Irish Liberalism', in Richard Kearney, ed., *The Irish Mind: Exploring Intellectual Traditions* (Dublin: Wolfhound, 1985), pp. 141-156.

protest against inequality and injustice.

The failure of totalitarian communist states in the twentieth century has undoubtedly muted the socialist protest against capitalism's often unbridled individualism and subjection of the social order to the requirements of the market. The disastrous democratic deficiencies of these collectivist states do not, however, justify the equating of Stalinist totalitarianism with Marxism, still less Socialism – a procedure which is often used to inhibit any questioning of the prevailing economic order. Such questioning is justified since it still remains the case that capitalist societies have not eliminated the profound injustices that effectively exclude so many from a fully participatory citizenship. There may be a wide range of views among socialists concerning the scope and limits of the market, but the commitment to at least some degree of intervention to secure social objectives and greater equality retains its relevance.

LIBERTY AND JUSTICE IN THE JUDAEO-CHRISTIAN TRADITION

When democracy is viewed in the broader perspective which includes a concern for social equality, the contribution of the Judaeo-Christian tradition is brought into sharp relief. In Israelite religion the work of redemption had a predominantly social *locus*. This is evident when we look at Israel's experience of the Exodus – the event which more than anything else gave Israel its self-identity. Thus the writer of the Book of Deuteronomy records: 'The Lord heard our voice, and saw our misery, our toil, and our oppression; and the Lord brought us out of Egypt with a mighty hand and an outstretched arm'. (Deuteronomy 26:7-8) The understanding of Israel's deliverance as act of political liberation has been a central theme in recent liberation theology. Alfredo Fierro says of the Exodus: 'It was a liberative revolution in the strict sense, a socially subversive act comparable to slave rebellions or other struggles of oppressed peoples against imperialism.' [6]

Israel was, as we know, a rebellious people, perfectly capable of oppressing others in its turn and then projecting its self-aggrandisement onto Yahweh. Moreover, when Israel entered the promised land and embarked upon a settled agricultural form of social organisation, there

6 A. Fierro, *The Militant Gospel: An Analysis of Contemporary Political Theologies* (London: SCM, 1977), p. 141.

quickly emerged a sharp polarisation between rich and poor. It is in this context that the prophets appeared thundering against injustice. The prophets remained faithful to the tradition of Yahweh as the God of the poor, and upheld the cause of the dispossessed and exploited. Their exhortation to act justly is linked with the memory of Yahweh's redemptive act in the Exodus. The denunciation of apostasy took on its special significance from the way it represented the struggle between Yahweh, the God of the poor, and Baal, the God of the expropriators. At the height of the prophetic tradition following the Babylonian Exile, the prophetic message becomes more universal in scope, and we find the literature filled with utopian visions of a future reign of justice that Yahweh will bring for all the nations.[7]

This current of social utopianism was brought to powerful expression in Christ's proclamation of the Kingdom of God. When Christ used the metaphor of Kingdom, such was his largeness of vision that he managed to both subvert it and to expand it at one and the same time. He subverted it through a different notion of power in line with the radical self-emptying of the incarnation, whereby he came not to lord it over others, but to serve in vulnerability and openness through the power of a love ready to embrace suffering. The expansion of the Kingdom theme is evident in the way Christ pushed aside boundaries through an all-inclusive sense of Kingdom, open to people of all races and one that especially welcomed the excluded and downtrodden. In all this Jesus was a religious reformer preaching in the very best traditions of Israel. Situating himself in line with Jewish prophetic expectation, his message, with its far-reaching implications, was essentially an announcement of the coming of a new social order characterised by justice, love and social harmony.

With the publication of Albert Schweitzer's *The Quest of the Historical Jesus* in 1911, the twentieth century saw a rediscovery of the eschatological dimension of Christ's message. Coming to terms with this interpretation of Christian origins has become one of the most central tasks for contemporary theology. Schweitzer regarded eschatology as the key to the whole of Jesus' ministry. Understanding himself as the agent of the

---

7 . Here I am drawing upon the work of Ernst Bloch discussed at greater length in J. Marsden, *Marxian and Christian Utopianism: Toward a Socialist Political Theology* (New York: Monthly Review Press, 1991), pp. 96ff

end times, Christ had sought to bring in the Kingdom of God on earth.
Schweitzer described the situation thus:

> There is silence all around. The Baptist appears and cries: 'Repent,
> for the Kingdom of Heaven is at hand'. Soon after that comes Jesus,
> and in the knowledge that He is the coming Son of Man lays hold of
> the wheel of the world to set it moving on that last revolution which is
> to bring all ordinary history to a close.[8]

It is of interest in passing to note that a year ahead of Schweitzer in
1910, James Connolly, responding to the Lenten lectures of a leading
Dublin Jesuit, showed a lively awareness of the socially subversive and
transformative dimension of Christ's eschatological preaching:

> All but the merest dabblers in Scriptural history know that the eco-
> nomic oppression of the Jewish people was so great immediately be-
> fore the coming of Christ that the whole nation had been praying and
> hoping for the promised Redeemer, and it was just at the psychologi-
> cal moment of their bondage as a nation and their slavery as a race
> that Christ appeared ... Roman and Jewish historians alike speak con-
> temptuously of early Christianity as a religion of slaves and labourers.
> These early Christians had been socially enslaved. Christ and His dis-
> ciples spoke to them of redemption, of freedom. They interpreted,
> rightly or wrongly, the words to mean an earthly redemption, a free-
> dom here and now as a prelude possibly to the freedom hereafter;
> and hence they joined with enthusiasm the sect hated by their oppres-
> sors.[9]

Jesus' conviction concerning the imminent reign of God on earth,
most readily evident in the synoptic Gospels, was soon modified by early
Christianity. This process was inevitable, given the disaster of the cross.
Although hope was rekindled through the proclamation of the resurrection, Jesus' eschatological message was now increasingly relaxed and to a
degree individualised. Thus it is that Ernst Bloch has argued that in
Pauline theology the call for a new social order was gradually replaced

---

8. See J. Moltmann, *Theology of Hope: On the Ground and the Implications of a Christian Eschatology*, trans. J. W. Leitch, (London: SCM, 1967), p. 39.
9. 'Labour, Nationality and Religion' in P. Berresford Ellis, ed., *James Connolly: Selected Writings* (Harmondsworth: Penguin, 1973), pp. 57-117 (97f.)

by a concentration on inwardness and belief in a beyond: 'Instead of a radical renewal of this world, an institute of the beyond appeared – the Church – and interpreted the Christian social utopia as referring to itself.'[10] A similar process would seem to be evident in John's Gospel, where the expectation for the Kingdom of God is in danger of being absorbed within a transcendentalism which owes more to Hellenism than Jewish prophetism. Here the Kingdom of God refers more to the eternally present realm of God than the eschatological order at the end of history.[11]

This assessment must not of course be taken too far since the Pauline and Johannine eschatology have vitally important elements in respect of both realised and future eschatology. The theme of light and darkness in John's Gospel, for example, presents the Christian hope in way that offers a profound appreciation of the tragic element in human existence whilst holding out the prospect of the ultimate fulfillment the purposes of the divine love. Moreover, despite the attenuation of Christian eschatology traceable within the New Testament itself, the Book of Revelation with its teaching of the millennium is testimony to the persistence of hopes for the Kingdom of God upon earth.

The writings of the early Fathers show that this teaching remained influential in the early Church.[12] Papias (c.60-130) spoke of a millennium of perfect felicity where the fertility of the earth would abound. Justin Martyr (+165) taught that Christ's coming in humiliation would be followed by a triumphant return, where he would reign on earth for one thousand years in a Kingdom of peace and prosperity which would fulfil the hopes of Old Testament prophecy. Justin's teaching encompassed a radical social message:

We who once took most pleasure in accumulating wealth and property now bring what we have in a common fund and share with everyone in need; we who hated and killed one another and would not

10. E. Bloch, *Man on His Own* (anthology), trans. by E. B. Ashton, (New York: Herder, 1970), p. 126.

11. Seán Freyne touches on some of these issues in his 'The Early Christians and Jewish Messianic Ideas' in *Concilium*, 1993/1, *Messianism Through History*, ed. by W. Beuken, S. Freyne and A. Weiler, pp. 30-41.

12. For a treatment of millenarianism in the Patristic period see B. Daley, *The Hope of the Early Church: A Handbook of Patristic Eschatology* (Cambridge: Cambridge U. P., 1991).

associate with men of different tribes because of their different customs, now, since the coming of Christ, live familiarly with them ... [13]

Perhaps the most articulate theological defence of millenarianism was given by Irenaeus (c.125-200). His main concern had been to defend the faith against Gnostic dualism, which was marked by an extremely pessimistic view of the created order. Here creation was seen as the work of a lesser deity – the Demiurge – as distinct from the unknowable supreme God. Irenaeus countered this teaching through insisting that the world is created by God the Almighty out of nothing. 'All things were made through Him and Without Him was nothing made.' With these few words Irenaeus successfully affirmed the essential goodness of creation and combated the dualistic notion that matter is eternal, intractable and probably therefore unredeemable. If God the Creator and God the Redeemer are one and the same, and the material creation is essentially good, then it follows that it should be included within the scope of the divine saving purpose. The prophetic teaching concerning the material restoration of creation in a future period of unparalleled peace and prosperity should not therefore be subject to a false spiritualisation, and Irenaeus accepted the biblical teaching of a future resplendent earthly kingdom.[14]

Thus there is in the writings of the early Fathers an impressive defence of millenarianism. Despite this, the pressures to moderate the Christian eschatological hope under Hellenic and Latin influences remained considerable. Origen (184-254) reduced the second coming of Christ into something occurring in the soul of the individual believer, and chastised those who held millenarian beliefs for interpreting scripture 'in a Jewish sense'.[15]

The really decisive development in millenarian thinking in the Patristic period, however, took place with Augustine (354-430). Interpreting Revelation 20 in allegorical terms, Augustine identified the 1000 year reign of Christ and the saints with the Church, thereby laying the foundations

13. See P. Phan, *Message of the Fathers of the Church: Social Thought* (Delaware: Michael Glazier, 1984), p. 56.
14. J. Kelly, *Early Christian Doctrines*, fifth edition, (London: A. and C. Black, 1977), pp. 86f and 468f. For a useful introduction to Irenaeus' theology see D. Minns, *Irenaeus* (London: Geoffrey Chapman, 1994), esp pp. 122ff.
15. Daley, *The Hope of the Early Church*, p. 49.

for what was to become the dominant interpretation throughout the Christian era. In large measure the decline of millenarian belief reflected the incorporation of Christianity into the imperial system. A religion that was no longer predominantly one of oppressed slaves is less interested in changing the world.

The efforts of the Church authorities to suppress the millenarian impulse were not a complete success, and throughout Christian history the idea of a third or final stage of history remained influential. Joachim of Floris' prophecy of the age of the Spirit, the radical sects of the Reformation and the dissenters of the English Revolution all kept this interpretation of history alive. Ernst Bloch refers enthusiastically to Joachim's 'complete transfer of the kingdom of light *from the beyond, from the consolation of hoping for the beyond, into history'*. Joachim's eschatology was accompanied by a passionate social critique of the Church: 'Altars are trimmed, and the poor suffer the bitter pangs of hunger.'[16]

To survey millenarian doctrines and movements is of more than antiquarian interest and has a direct bearing on a Christian understanding of modern political developments. The birth of modern democracy and socialism in the period following the French revolution constituted a critical moment in universal history. The dynamic that lay behind the millennial movements which convulsed the medieval Church – the prospect of a new era of genuine human freedom and justice – had at last become a concern no longer confined to enthusiastic sects on the margins of society. In the Enlightenment's audacious faith in human perfectibility and progress, millenarian hopes may have assumed a more secular form, but, as scholars like Carl Becker have insisted, the connections with earlier Christian modes of discourse can scarcely be denied.[17]

Although the social and democratic advances of the last two centuries have been considerable, what Ernst Bloch has described in his utopian philosophy as the '*regnum humanum*', remains as an unfinished agenda in our modern world. Bloch was forced to leave Eastern Germany because of his conviction that there is no such thing as socialism without democracy. 'Humanitarianism finds a place where democracy has been

16. Bloch, *Man On His Own*, pp. 135 and 140.
17 . C. L. Becker, *The Heavenly City and the Eighteenth Century Philosophers* (New Haven and London: Yale University Press, 1932).

made really possible', he insisted, 'for true democracy is the first really
human domicile.'[18] But Bloch's humanist utopianism was an indictment
not just of the Soviet Union but of the capitalist West as well. Free-market capitalism must be subject to democratic restraint in the interests of
the whole community if we are to achieve greater social justice and a
more truly democratic polity. This is not an impossible ideal; and in the
second half of the twentieth century, Keynesianism, with its commitment
to maintaining full employment and using the State finances to maintain more optimal levels of economic activity, was successfully used by
social democratic parties to provide public services and a degree of redistribution of wealth. Social democratic policies, when suitably re-envi-
sioned for the present context of a more inter-dependent and globalised
economy, hold out a much better prospect for human flourishing than
exclusively market-orientated alternatives.

The need to respond to the political and social ideals stemming from
the upheavals of the French Revolution and its aftermath has been the
inspiration behind the recovery of a strong sense of eschatological hope
in the modern era. The Religious Socialist Movement that blossomed in
Switzerland and Germany in the earlier part of the twentieth century
and the 'political theology' of the 1960s, were both responsible for a
renewed interest in eschatology. It is also no accident that the liberation
theologies which have emerged in the context of the political struggles
of the poorer countries have in recent times led the way in this respect.

Welcome as these developments may be, undoubtedly much Christian theology, especially in the Northern hemisphere, has a lot of catch-
ing up to do if it is to be faithful to its roots as a socially liberative creed.
Theology cannot afford to be disinterested in the current world-histori-
cal endeavour to achieve social and democratic freedoms. The way in
which a good deal of recent theology in Europe and the United States
has allowed itself to become preoccupied with the post-modernist agenda,
when the predominant experience in the world is surely still pre-mod-
ern, is an indication that this challenge is still not being faced in many
quarters. That is not of course to say that the Enlightenment itself, or
indeed the political thinking associated with it, is beyond criticism. It is
merely to insist that there should be no going back on the commitment

18. *On Karl Marx* (anthology), translated by J. Maxwell (New York: Herder, 1971), p. 23.

to human liberty, which was an essential part of the revolutionary ferment of that period. There is no warrant for replacing the, at times, overweening optimism of the Enlightenment, which showed insufficient appreciation of the tragic dimension of human existence, with an unre-
lenting pessimism. There needs to be a critique of modernity, as has
always been recognised: the question is whether, when purged of an instrumental rationality, sufficient confidence in human reason can be
retained to continue the endeavour to attempt to order society according to rational and humane principles and ideals. Despite all the set-
backs, disappointments and lessons to be learned (particularly with regard to respect for cultural diversity), there surely remains a meta-narra-
tive in the goal of universal human emancipation.[19] However incomplete such emancipation may still be, to deny that would be a denial of
redemptive hope for the *polis* that runs counter to the affirmation of the
essential goodness of the created order from Irenaeus onwards.

POLITICAL LIBERTY AND MILLENARIAN HOPE IN IRELAND

We have already referred to the burgeoning republicanism and 'civic
humanism' stemming from the Renaissance. James Harrington's seven-
teenth-century republicanism – albeit purged of its anti-monarchial elements – was not without its supporters in Ireland. Two of the leading
figures in this regard were Robert, Viscount Molesworth, and the Deist
and free-thinker, John Toland. Although little is known about the
Molesworth circle, it is likely that it was through Molesworth that Francis
Hutcheson (who was to exercise a seminal influence on future developments) was introduced to Harringtonian ideas.

Hutcheson taught at a Dissenting academy in Dublin in the 1720s and
later became Professor of Moral Philosophy at Glasgow. It was largely
through Hutcheson that the civic humanist tradition of classical republicanism was mediated to the Presbyterian clergy and educated classes.
Much of the language and culture of opposition in the later Volunteer
and United Irish movements can thus be traced to Hutcheson; as indeed

19. *Pace* J. F. Lyotard, *The Post-Modern Condition: A Report on Knowledge* (Manchester: Man-
    chester U.P., 1984). Lyotard would be a prime example of recent thinkers who main-
    tain that the 'great meta-narratives' of modern society have broken down. For an
    account and critique of post-modernism see T. Eagleton, *The Illusions of Post-Modern-
    ism* (Oxford: Blackwell, 1996).

can a social contract theory of government which defended the right to resistance in certain circumstances.[20]

When the shock waves produced by the French Revolution began to shake the foundations of European society, Ireland already had a strong native republican tradition and proved particularly receptive to the new political thinking. Thomas Paine's *The Rights of Man*, regarded by many as the key radical text was particularly widely circulated.[21] The United Irish Society, which began as a movement seeking parliamentary reform, represented a wide coalition of interests. It was only when war broke out with France and Pitt introduced a policy of repression that it became separatist and more avowedly republican. The movement was now committed to a wider extension of democratic rights and sought to create a republic along French lines. It was also ready to countenance bolder measures of social amelioration and act in alliance with oppositional groups like the Defenders which gave expression to agrarian discontent and were themselves beginning to respond to the new political thinking.[22]

It would have been a basic tenet of the more ideologically committed members of United Irish movement that nothing should limit or circumscribe liberty. Mary Ann McCracken's observations concerning the extension of citizenship for women are but one instance where the championing of political liberty was seen as having far-reaching implications. Aligning herself with Mary Wollstonecraft, McCracken wrote:

> I hope the present Era will produce some women of sufficient talents to inspire the rest with a genuine love of Liberty … I think the reign of prejudice is nearly at an end, and that the truth and justice of our cause alone is sufficient to support it, as there can be no argument produced in favour of the slavery of women that has not been used in favour of general slavery.[23]

20. See I. McBride, 'The School of Virtue: Francis Hutcheson, Irish Presbyterians and the Scottish Enlightenment' in D. George Boyce, et al, *Political Thought in Ireland since the Seventeenth Century* (London and New York: Routledge, 1993), pp. 73-99.
21. See David Dickson, 'Paine and Ireland', in D. Dickson, D. Keogh and K. Whelan, eds, *The United Irishmen: Republicanism, Radicalism and Rebellion* (Dublin, Lilliput Press: 1993), pp. 135-150.
22 . See Chapter 1.
23. Quoted in Mary McNeill, *The Life and Times of Mary Ann McCracken 1770-1866: A Belfast Panorama* (Dublin: Allen Figgis, 1960), p. 127. On women's role in the United

The more advanced thinkers in the United Irish Society recognised that political reform would need to be accompanied by social measures to redress the imbalance of power between different sections of society. Although their social-radicalism reflected the more agrarian social conditions of the times, much might still be learned from their insights concerning the interrelation between political liberty and social justice, and the manner in which they rooted their thinking in egalitarian principle. The United Irish Society was certainly possessed of a healthy outlook when it countered criticisms of measures of amelioration with the laconic rejoinder: 'Nothing, we hope, is impossible that is just.'[24]

Within the United Irish Society the struggle for democracy and social justice often involved an expression of the republican ideal that seems to have incorporated utopian and millenarian themes. A definite millenarian tone is particularly evident in the preaching of many of the Presbyterian clergy associated with the United Irish movement. The victory of liberty in France and Ireland's subjection to tyranny are seen as part of the same titanic struggle in which ultimate victory is assured. 'We must think that the final overthrow of the Beast, or opposing power, is almost at the door,' declared Ledlie Birch, 'a prelude to the peaceful reign of a 1000 years.' Taking the Book of Revelation as his text, Samuel Barber extolled the French Revolution:

> Seated in the midst of Europe like a lily on a hill to shed light, Liberty and humanity all around. Happy Country! where the rights of man are sacred, no Bastille to imprison the body, nor religious establishment to shackle the soul. Every citizen free as the thoughts of man.

William Staveley, similarly enthused by the French example, spoke of 'that millennium state', soon approaching, 'when men will cast off the chains of slavery'.[25]

A millenarian perspective on Irish history was not confined to Presby-

---

Irish Society see Mary Cullen, 'Partners in Struggle: The Women of 1798', in Cathal Póirtéir, ed., *The Great Irish Rebellion of 1798* (Dublin: Mercier Pr, 1998), pp. 146-159.

24. T. Moody, 'The Political Ideas of the United Irishmen', *Ireland Today*, Vol. III, Dublin, 1938, pp. 15-28 (16).

25. See essays by Pieter Tesch and Kevin Whelan in Dickson, Keogh and Whelan, *The United Irishmen: Republicanism, Radicalism and Rebellion*, pp. 33-48 (46f.) and 269-296 (282).

terians in the North. Thomas Russell (who at one stage considered entering the Anglican priesthood) was an avid reader of millenarian texts.
Russell linked the biblical hope for a 'new age' with his republican faith
in the impending triumph over despotism of justice, liberty and virtue.
His keen advocacy of the right of the poor to self-governance was rooted
in his understanding of how they were endowed equal passions, reason,
and capacity for virtue, and therefore had the same rights to political
liberty. Ireland's struggle for liberty was part of the wider struggle of
mankind for the overthrow of tyranny that would usher in a new dawn.
When he asked for the short stay of execution, it had been to write a
brief work discussing Francis Dobbs' application of biblical prophecies
to Ireland, which he thought might prove 'some advantage to the world'.
The request was regrettably denied.[26]

This millenarian speculation was not necessarily at variance with the
Enlightenment principles that the United Irish movement sought to apply
to Irish society. The principles enshrined in this philosophical *credo* included a belief in the innate goodness and perfectibility of human nature and consequent malleability of civil society; a confidence in the triumph of reason over ignorance and arbitrary oppression; and a conviction that the end of life is to be found on earth and not reserved for a
heavenly afterlife. Although in a European context these ideals assumed
a more secular form, there is no reason why many aspects of this audacious faith in the possibilities of totally reshaping the social order should
not re-connect with and be reinforced by a Christian millenarianism.[27]
This seems to have been precisely what happened in Ireland, where the
reception of the Enlightenment was particularly strong among Presbyterians. Although some members of the United Irish Society were more
rationalist and deist in outlook, and therefore nearer their continental

26. *A Letter to the People of Ireland* (Belfast, 1796). See also D. Carroll, *The Man From God
     Knows Where: Thomas Russell 1767-1803* (Dublin: Gartan, 1995), pp. 220ff. and John
     Gray, 'Millenial Vision: Thomas Russell Reassessed' in *Linen Hall Review*, Vol 6, no 1
     (Spring 1989), pp. 5-9 (9). James Quinn has produced a useful biography *Soul on Fire:
     a life of Thomas Russell* (Dublin: Irish Academic Press, 2002), though he does not make
     the connections with the earlier republicanism of Francis Hutcheson.
27. On the links between millenarianism and Enlightenment ideas of utopia and progress
     see E. L. Tuveson, *Millennium and Utopia: A Study in the Background of the Idea of Progress*
     (Berkeley: University of California Press, 1949), and C. L. Becker, *The Heavenly City
     and the Eighteenth Century Philosophers* (New Haven and London: Yale University Press,
     1932).

neighbours, many others sought to find a Christian basis for their political ideals. Thomas Russell, for example, claimed: 'The only true basis of liberty is morality, and the only stable basis of morality is religion'.

In addition to the often strong millenarian sentiment, a most pronounced feature of the thinking of so many of the United Irish leaders was the manner in which their political idealism was rooted in a devout sense of divine providence. During his incarceration in Fort George in Scotland, Thomas Russell wrote: 'Providence orders all things for the best. *I am sure the people will never abandon the cause; I am equally sure it will succeed.*' [28]

Like Russell, Robert Emmet exemplifies the combination of a radical republicanism with the conviction that both the fitness and the fortunes of the cause of liberty must be lodged with the Almighty. Emmet's primary objective was the realisation of those social and political liberties which he said at his trial were denied by 'superinhuman oppression' and 'that perfidious Government which upholds its domination by blasphemy of the Most High'. Roy Foster's caricature of Emmet as motivated by an 'élite separatism' overlooks the fact that for Emmet independence from England was but the necessary corollary of the advance of liberty in Ireland. Against the charge of treason and the calumny that he acted as an emissary of France, Emmet looked to the verdict of posterity:

> Let no man write my epitaph; for as no man who knows my motives dare now vindicate them, let not prejudice or ignorance asperse them. Let them and me rest in obscurity and peace, and my tomb remain uninscribed, and my memory in oblivion, until other times and other men do justice to my character. When my country takes her place among the nations of the earth, *then, and not till then*, let my epitaph be written. I have done.[29]

These words, which have a definite millenarian ring, reflect the confidence in the perfectibility of human society that was so characteristic of the Enlightenment. Emmet drew his consolation from the assurance that

28. The above citations are from a letter by Russell quoted in T. D. Sullivan, et. al., *Speeches From the Dock: With Introductory Sketches and Biographical Notes* (Dublin: Gill and Macmillan, 1968), pp. 44-54 (47).

29. Ibid., pp. 31-44 (37f and 42f). For Roy Foster's comments see R.F. Foster, *Modern Ireland 1600-1972* (London: Penguin, 1988), p. 286.

the new liberated society of the future – where liberty and virtue shall be established – will recognise the vision by which he was actuated and thereby hold his character in esteem. Roy Foster's dismissal of Emmet's defence of his republican principles as 'attitudinizing', obscures the way in which Emmet's speech at the dock crystallises the clash of political ideologies which defined this revolutionary period in Irish politics. There are a number of textual variants of Emmet's speech. Some commentators think the reference to Ireland taking her place among the nations of the earth to be later embellishment designed to enhance Emmet's status as a martyr in the nationalist cause, but the idea that others might vindicate his motives and write his epitaph recurs.[30] Valuable light is shed upon an appropriate reading of Emmet by the testimony of one of his contemporaries. John Sheares on the night before his execution in 1798 wrote a letter to his sister, Julia, which expressed more or less precisely the same sentiments as Emmet:

> Justice will yet be done to my memory, and my fate be mentioned rather with pride than with shame by my friends and relations. Yes, my dear sister, if I did not expect the arrival of this justice to my memory, I should be indeed afflicted at the nominal ignominy of my death.[31]

The United Irish Society represented a wide coalition of political interests and it would be wrong to give the impression that it was dominated by activists with the religious interests of a Ledlie Birch or Thomas Russell. Nonetheless, it remains the case that as well as republican politics in Ireland sometimes being cast in religious terms, the very basis of the achievement of the 1790s was a political ecumenism: what the United Irish Society referred to as 'a cordial union of religious creeds'. At its inception, this new movement did not advocate independence from Britain. It was only the stubborn refusal of the Pitt administration to grant substantial reform, which convinced people separation would be necessary if democratic self-government was to be realised. It would come as a shock to some people to be reminded that at its birth Irish Republican-

---

30. For a discussion of the textual variants see R. Vance, 'Text and Tradition: Robert Emmet's Speech From the Dock', *Studies*, Vol. 71, no. 282 (1982), pp. 185-91.

31. R. Madden, *The United Irishmen, Their Lives and Times*, Vol. II, 1st series (London: 1842), p. 221.

ism accepted some form of political union with Britain. The point is worth labouring because there is a clear echo here with recent initiatives to create a democratic political culture that can unite people across the traditions in Northern Ireland and the precedence this is rightly taking over the question of national sovereignty.

It is perhaps significant that despite the defeat of the 1798 Rebellion, by the first half of the nineteenth century Ireland had produced Europe's first genuinely mass democratic movement in the Emancipation and Repeal agitations led by Daniel O'Connell. It was to be upon these foundations that the land and constitutional campaigns under Parnell were to secure parliamentary majorities for land reform and Home Rule. A generation later it was the extra-parliamentary resistance to a third Home Rule Bill introduced in 1912 which created the conditions for an insurrection in Dublin that in turn led to the formation of a democratic Irish state.

No matter how unsatisfactory certain aspects of the political life of the Irish Free State and Republic may have been, there can be no doubt that the end of British rule represented a major advance for democratic interests. Things worked out differently in the North, where Britain acquiesced with the continuation of Protestant domination through the partisan use of executive power by the unionist majority. The achievement of democracy in Ireland was thus only a partial success. It is this legacy, rather than partition as such, which still constitutes Ireland's most pressing political problem. The policy of direct rule from Westminster at best provided only a breathing space for redressing this democratic deficit. In the post-Franco era, Northern Ireland is the last remaining part of Western Europe yet to forge a democratic polity; and if the modern democratic revolution is to be brought to completion it will require the successful resolution of this state of affairs through seeing that the new political institutions become embedded, thereby securing a satisfactory democratisation of the Northern State.

The democratic failure in Northern Ireland has over the years been compounded by high unemployment and poor social conditions, which has meant that economic injustice has been associated with political division. Regrettably, in too many quarters adverse social conditions have in fact persisted throughout modern Ireland. The blighted urban areas of Dublin and Belfast are a reminder of how much progress still needs to made in establishing the citizenship of the disadvantaged and how apposite remains the desire of the United Irish Society 'to see a more equal distribution of the benefits and blessings of life through the lowest classes of the community, the stamina of society.'[32]

Ireland's difficulties and shortcomings must of course be seen in a wider context. It can scarcely be said that the democratic and social ideals of the modern period have triumphed in our present world when half its inhabitants still live under oppressive dictatorships and oligarchies of one sort or another. Even in Europe, which in the middle of the present century witnessed the triumph of democracy over barbarism, in the Balkans we have seen an ugly resurgence of tribalistic regression and atavism. European democracy has other worrying defects: the lack of accountability of such institutions as the European Commission and the central banks; the structural unemployment that has persisted; and the growing subordination of policy (and therefore people and communities) to the impersonal dictats of the market. These very limitations, however, point to the need for a renewal of redemptive hope rather than its abandonment.

THE SCOPE AND LIMITS OF CHRISTIAN SOCIAL UTOPIANISM

A reading of Christianity that remains in sympathy with its prophetic and socially utopian undercurrent will not be without its detractors. The main objection is that such a view presupposes an unjustified optimism with regard to human nature. Since this issue clearly has its bearing on the controversy surrounding postmodern scepticism, it merits close attention.

There is undoubtedly substance in the critique of eighteenth-century rationalism's excessive confidence in the power of human reason to transform society. In part this arose from the way in which the Enlightenment reflected the optimism of the bourgeoisie as the ascendant social class. The bourgeoisie was to prove to be a good deal less concerned to transform society once it attained power, though it passed on something of its, at times, overweening confidence in human malleability to the republican and socialist inheritors of its thinking.

32. Moody, 'The Political Ideas of the United Irishmen', p. 23.

Whether this warrants postmodernism's contrasting pessimism is another matter entirely. From a theological viewpoint, whilst it is right to strive for a greater manifestation of the Kingdom of God, under the conditions of history its presence will always remain provisional and incomplete. Such an acknowledgement need not, howevere, detract from the motivation for working for profound social change and can indeed fortify it by removing the burden of naïvety.

Although human beings are both made in the image of God and fallen, as David Jenkins has pointed out, 'realism about sin should not lead to cynicism about altruism and justice, or pessimism about the possibilities of collective organisation and communal caring.'[33] Often in political life the idea of original sin is misused, with plans to reform society and remove existing social evils dismissed out of hand as unfounded idealism. Yet to say that because human nature is fallen, there is therefore no hope for changing human society is surely defeatism.

In political theory a notable advocate of a pessimistic view of human nature was Thomas Hobbes. Describing the human condition in a state of nature, Hobbes saw fear and self-interest as leading to a state of 'war of all against all' ('*bellum omnium contra omnes*'). Hobbes sums up the unhappy consequences of such a prospect: 'No arts; no letters; no society; and which is worst of all, continual fear, and danger of violent death; and the life of man, solitary, poor, nasty, brutish and short.'[34] It was but a short step from Hobbesian pessimism to political absolutism, since if the human condition was naturally one of incessant conflict, a strong, centralised authority would be needed to control society. Regrettably, the Christian doctrine of original sin has frequently been pressed into support for auhtoritarian traditions in political thought.

To every movement there is a countermovement, and the struggle against the absolutism of the old order and for democracy, had a keen advocate in Jean Jacques Rousseau,[35] who significantly made his starting

33. 'The God of Freedom and the Freedom of God', *The Hibbert Lecture*, reprinted in *The Listener* (18 April 1985), pp. 14-17 (16).

34. See *Leviathan*, edited by C. B. Macpherson, (Harmondsworth: Penguin, 1968), pp. 185ff.

35. For an incisive discussion of Rousseau's political philosophy which captures the nuances and comments on the 'liberal' and 'illiberal' side of his thought see John Plamenatz, *Man and Society: A Critical Examination of Some Important Social and Political Theories from Machiavelli to Marx* (London: Longman, 1963) pp. 364ff.

point the conviction that human beings are sociable by nature. Although the natural goodness of human nature is corrupted by private property and modern civilization, Rousseau thought that a greater social harmony was desirable and could be fostered through new political institutions expressing 'the general will'.

What are we to make of these alternatives: innate self-interest and social disharmony, or human socialibility and the possibility of social harmony? It is questions such as these, and a sensitivity to their profoundly important implications, which show that it is vital that the disciplines of politics and theology cannot afford to keep a cosy separate existence. From a Christian point of view, the competing perspectives of Hobbes and Rousseau help alert us to a false dichotomy, since Christianity holds in tension the fact that human beings are fallen *and* that they are made in the image of God. Christian teaching concerning human nature has been preserved from an unremitting pessimism through its doctrine of *imago Dei*.

But, first, let us recognise the truth to which the doctrine of original sin points. Human beings possess human freedom, with all the possibilities for good and evil which that freedom entails. Sin is not a matter of necessity, since it implies freedom and responsibility. And yet in varying degrees in practice we all do sin because of our falleness which, since Augustine, has been explained in terms of a defect of will. Moreover, the wider pattern of bad choices and destructive actions in society as a whole, in their turn form the context in which other human choices are made. Human destiny is in fact shaped and circumscribed by a whole host of biological, economic, psychological and sociological factors. All this suggests the need for a recognition of the tragic element in human existence. This is at least part of the truth which lies behind the much misused doctrine of Original Sin, which Paul Tillich has argued points to the fact that 'every ethical decision is an act both of individual freedom and universal destiny.'[36]

The way in which individual and collective sinful actions so easily reinforce one another and impose their own destructive pattern of moral decline – unless arrested by some means – was all too evident in the dreadful events witnessed in the former Yugoslavia. Here we saw how an

36. *Systematic Theology*, Vol 2, (London: SCM, 1978) pp. 36ff. (38).

insistence on ethnic exclusiveness and superiority quickly leads to terri-
torial aggrandisement, which then necessitates 'ethnic cleansing', and
this in turn proceeds to violence and finally to unspeakable atrocity. Nor
were the rest of Europe's hands clean in all this. When Western strategic
economic interests were at stake, as in Iraq's invasion of Kuwait, intervention is swift; while in the case of Bosnia, action was half-hearted and
the prevailing attitude seemed to be that the situation is all too complicated, and in any case 'Am I my brother's keeper?'. Only after 200,000
people had lost their lives in the most appalling circumstances did the
West act decisively.

Thomas Hobbes could claim much support for his theories in events
in the former Yugoslavia. The collapse of communist political absolutism released the genie of a regressive nationalism and racism. What we
have seen in all this is how relatively thin is the veneer of modern civilization. On European soil the frightening dissolution of society into a Hobbesian '*Bellum omnium contra omnes*' was once again allowed to become a
tragic reality. In an Irish context, these events are a chilling warning of
the fearful prospect that could conceivably accompany an unwillingness
to face up to the challenges of creating a genuinely multi-cultural and
pluralist polity.

All this is evidence enough for what we may wish to say of the Fall and
Original Sin, and the actuality and potential for human destructiveness
that besets every human community.

At this point, however, it should be remembered that Christianity is
first and foremost a religion of redemption. Should not any movement
from politics to the Gospel also speak of divine grace, the image of God
in each one of us, and the possibility of a new beginning and moral regeneration? Original Righteousness is as important a truth as Original
Sin. The latter has not destroyed the former and those who think otherwise need look no further than Augustine's *The City of God*, where he
writes of the divine image: 'It is an image which by nature is nearer to
God than anything else in all creation, and one that by transforming
grace can be perfected into a still closer resemblance.'[37] A more recent
authority of relevance in this matter is Reinhold Niebuhr's rejection of

---

37.   *The City of God*, Abridged edition by V. J. Bourke from translation by G. G. Walsh, et al
      (New York: Doubleday, 1958), p. 235.

literalistic interpretations of the Fall which fail to set the understanding of the human creature as sinner in juxtaposition to the doctrine of *imago Dei*.[38] To achieve this balance in our understanding of human nature Paul Tillich has argued that theology

> must emphasize the positive evaluation of man in his essential nature. It must join classical humanism in protecting man's created goodness against naturalistic and existentialist denials of his greatness and dignity. At the same time, theology should interpret the doctrine of original sin by showing man's existential self-estrangement and by using the helpful existentialist analyses of the human predicament. In doing so, it must develop a realistic doctrine of man, in which the ethical and tragic element in his self-estrangement are balanced.[39]

Here it is of interest to examine in some detail the moral philosophy of Francis Hutcheson whose teaching, as has already been noted, had a seminal influence on the United Irish movement. Hutcheson's moral philosophy, which was forged in reaction to the emphasis on self-interest and rational calculation in Hobbes and Mandeville, was rooted in an estimation of human nature which stressed the human capacity for moral goodness.[40] Hutcheson adapted from the Earl of Shaftesbury the notion of 'moral sense', by which he meant the intuitive capacity through which we judge something to be virtuous or not. This moral sense informs us that the ultimate virtue is benevolence. Hutcheson sees the predisposition to virtue as being implanted in our natures, 'such that no education, false principles, depraved habits can entirely root this out'. This must be balanced, though, with Hutcheson's admission that

> the selfish principles are very strong, and by custom, by early and frequent indulgences, and other causes, are raised in the greater part of men above their due proportion, while the generous principles are little cultivated, and the moral sense often asleep.[41]

38. *The Nature and Destiny of Man*, Vol. 1, *Human Nature* (New York: Scribners, 1964), pp. 12ff. and 150ff.
39. P. Tillich, *Systematic Theology*, Vol 2, pp. 38f.
40. I have drawn upon Terry Eagleton's excellent treatment of Hutcheson's ethics in *Heathcliff and the Great Hunger: Studies in Irish Culture* (London: Verso, 1995), pp. 104-123.
41. Quoted by Eagleton, ibid., pp. 113 and 115.

There was thus a considerable degree of realism in Hutcheson's thinking. Indeed in his theory of government, it was primarily because human benevolence is not always sufficient to counter human self-interest,
that the institutions of civil society are made necessary.[42] The moral sense
and a high view of human nature may be foundational for him, but he is
not naive about self-interest. If he errs it is on the utopian side, though
he is not far away from getting an important balance right. An aphorism
coined by Reinhold Niebuhr perhaps negotiates successfully the rapids
that Hutcheson's moral theory and republicanism sought to traverse:
'Man's capacity for justice makes democracy possible; but man's inclina-
tion to injustice makes democracy necessary.'[43]

Hutcheson's understanding of human nature was indebted to the sev-
enteenth-century republicanism of James Harrington who held that
human beings had been invested by God with natures that fitted them
for self-rule and made them citizens rather than subjects. Often
Harrington called this 'reason' or 'virtue', but his whole discussion is
reliant upon the theological notion of people being made in the image
of God.[44]

Hutcheson and Harrington are a much needed corrective to the pessimism of much of the Protestant tradition. Fallen human nature may be
weakened and subject to the tragic universality of estrangement, but the
divine image in human beings still remains. Protestantism – in its anxiety to resist what it saw as the semi-Pelagianism of the Roman Catholic
Church – sometimes went too far in the other direction by stressing human depravity, and this has had destructive consequences in the political sphere.[45] In this regard it is of interest to note that the great Irish
Carolinian Divine, Jeremy Taylor,[46] offered an interpretation of Article
Nine of the Anglican Thirty-nine Articles which discussed Original Sin

---

42. See McBride, 'The School of Virtue ... ', p. 86.
43. *The Children of Light and the Children of Darkness: A Vindication of Democracy and a Critique of its Traditional Defenders* (London: Nisbet, 1945), p. vi. There were other occasions when the strong strand of Lutheran pessimism in Niebuhr got the better of
him.
44. See Pocock, *Virtue, Commerce, and History*, p. 41.
45. See Niebuhr's discussion in *The Nature and Destiny of Man*, Vol. 1, pp. 150ff.
46. For Taylor's discussion of Article Nine see *Whole Works* (London: Henry Bohn, 1867),
Vol II, pp. 571ff. The contribution of Taylor in this regard was brought to my attention by Henry McAdoo in his lecture *Jeremy Taylor: Anglican Theologian* (Tyrone: Church
of Ireland Historical Society, 1997).

in a way that was consistent with a much more positive conception of human nature. In his treatment of the doctrine, whilst acknowledging human weakness and 'infirmity', Taylor rejected the notion that human nature itself had become corrupt.

Good theology is often a matter of holding what at first might seem contradictory truths in a creative tension. It was with a fine theological sense that F. D. Maurice insisted that the Christian understanding of the Fall should always be considered after the doctrine of redemption. To make the doctrine of Original Sin a reason for rejecting any prospect of the social and moral regeneration of humankind would therefore be a travesty of the Christian message. Richard Tawney has pointed to this misuse to which the Christian doctrine of human nature is so often put:

> Granted that man's nature is such that evil is a permanent element in his life, that fact is not a reason for condoning the existence of such evils and incitements to evil as it is within his power to remove.[47]

Along with the misuse of the doctrine of Original Sin, the other popular objection to a Christianity at ease with its socially utopian undercurrent, upon which it is importnat to alight, however briefly, stems from the individualistic reduction of Christianity to the status of what Jürgen Moltmann has described as a '*cultus privatus*'.[48] Limiting religion to the realm of individual piety results in dualism and an impoverished 'spiritualisation' of the Christian message. To the charge that Christianity should concern itself with spiritual things, Tawney, a stalwart critic of the bourgeois social order, rightly responded by asserting that the form of social organisation society adopts, which in the case of capitalism is one 'dominated by a ruthless economic egotism', is a spiritual issue. A dualistic separation of the material and the spiritual runs counter to an incarnational faith. Resisting this tendency, Tawney contended:

> that the conduct of man in society forms a large part of human life, and that to resign it to the forces of self-interest and greed is to de-Christianise both it and the individual souls whose attitude and outlook are necessarily in large measure determined by the nature of

47. R. Tawney, *The Attack and Other Papers* (Nottingham: Spokesman, 1981), p. 175.
48. *Theology of Hope: On the Grounds and Implications of a Christian Eschatology* (London: SCM, 1967) pp. 304ff.

their social environment.[49]

The notion of there being two histories – the profane and the sacred – must be resisted. The redemptive work of Christ is universal in scope and therefore embraces the whole of reality. Thus Gustavo Gutiérrez writes:

> Salvation is not something other-worldly, in regard to which the present life is merely a test. Salvation – the communion of men with God and the communion of men among themselves – is something which embraces all human reality, transforms it, and leads it to its fullness in Christ.[50]

It is significant that the vision of the Heavenly City in both Old and New Testaments is the inclusive one of a new state or political society – a point which Terence McCaughey stresses, when he reminds us that Revelation Chapter 21 'speaks of a new community and State, but not of a new temple.'[51]

There is a certain arrogance about the individualistic pietism so prevalent in Western Christendom which views the Church as the repository of salvation. The Church may be a divine institution, but it is also a human one and as such stands equally in need of the transforming power of the coming Kingdom of God. More specifically, in the Irish context, if there is to be any candour, it should be acknowledged that there is indeed a sense in which far from being a part of the solution, the Church is very much a part of the problem. If we are to rid our society of sectarian strife then the policy for all our Churches must be one that recognises that the Church is in continual need of reform (*Ecclesia semper reformanda*). This will involve truly becoming a Church for the world, a Church that understands redemption as a reality occurring within the totality of human history. This redemption is but a prelude to the transcendent fulfilment of the Kingdom of heaven – also a fitting object of hope – though never a substitute for working for the realisation of the purposes of divine love in this world.

49. Tawney, *The Attack and Other Papers,* pp. 174-7.
50. *A Theology of Liberation* (London: SCM, 1974), p. 151.
51. *Memory and Redemption: Church, Politics and Prophetic Theology in Ireland* (Dublin: Gill and Macmillan, 1993), p. 8.

CHAPTER EIGHT

Remembrance and Redemption

The Great Hunger

To trace one's steps, slowly and respectfully, among the graves of those who have reached the goal of life in the ordinary course, fills one with holy warnings; to stand beside the monument raised on the battle-field to the brave men who fell there, calls up heroic echoes in the heart, but here is no room for sentiment; here, in humiliation and sorrow, not unmixed with indignation, one is driven to exclaim:

> Oh God! that bread should be so dear,
> And human flesh so cheap
>
> Canon John O'Rourke

Despite the suppression of the revolutionary energies of the remarkably advanced political culture of the 1790s, throughout the first half of the nineteenth century Ireland witnessed steady, if limited, progress in so-cial and democratic reform. Midway through the century an event of truly staggering proportions was cruelly to intervene. The Famine in all its starkness would seem to stand out as the definitive rebuttal of any attempt to view Irish history from a theological perspective as the outworking of a redemptive process. With this objection in mind this chapter tries both to come to some assessment of the Famine itself, and then to relate this to our contemporary world, so that what we under-stand today by the human redemptive process might be further illumi-nated. This is done through focussing on the question of responsibility for the Famine, then reflecting on the importance of the act of remem-brance itself, and finally considering the problems the Famine raises for an understanding of the outworking of divine providence.

THE FAMINE: NATURAL CATASTROPHE OR PUBLIC NEGLECT?

As Europe's last major subsistence crisis, the Irish Famine has a signifi-cant place within the wider European calendar. Indeed, given its dura-tion, and the horrendous scale of the fatalities and their proportion to the total population, it is little wonder that the Irish Famine ranks as one of the best known famines in recorded history. It is generally reckoned that between the years 1845 and 1851 over one million people died from starvation or disease. With a further two million escaping through emigration, Ireland's pre-Famine population of over eight million was nearly halved.

In the summer of 1845 the potato crop appeared to be doing well. It was when attempts were made to lift it that the panic struck. Nearly half the crop had failed and reports to this effect soon reached the Government. The fungus disease *phytophthora infestans* meant that the potatoes had either already rotted in the ground or perished within days. The blight was even more extensive in 1846, by which time fatalities were occurring. In 1847 the good yield could not compensate for the much reduced acreage of potatoes, and in 1848 the blight struck once again.

The export of corn during the Famine is sometimes cited as evidence that the crisis could have been averted. Although government requisition of all food stocks would have helped, it is doubtful whether this alone would have made a great difference. The magnitude of the disaster was such that what was needed was a degree of concerted government action that would have admittedly been of a high order. The practicalities of this and the political constraints of the time have been the subject of much debate. At one end of the spectrum of debate, Roy Foster describes the Famine as 'a subsistence crisis that was beyond the powers either of the existing state apparatus or the prevalent conceptions of social responsibility – in Ireland at least.'[1]

Robert Peel's government did in fact purchase Indian corn to exercise some control on prices by supplying the market and also set up public works schemes – an approach to policy, that, if it had been imaginatively pursued and given greater funds would have saved many lives.[2] Regrettably, the Russell administration which came into office in June 1846, took a less pragmatic approach and was strongly committed to not interfering with the market. The government's role was to be strictly

1. R.F. Foster, *Modern Ireland 1600-1972* (Harmondsworth: Penguin, 1988), p. 320.
2. For accounts of famine relief policy see T. O'Neill 'The Organisation and Administration of Relief, 1845-52' in R. D. Edwards and T. D. Williams, *The Great Famine: Studies in Irish History 1845-52* (Dublin: Lilliput Press, 1994), first published 1956), pp. 209-60.

limited and the costs of famine relief were increasingly foisted on the Irish landlords. Wage rates on public works were kept perilously low and many projects were mismanaged and eventually curtailed. Government spending was tightly restrained lest it prove a disincentive to private charity. When conditions worsened and deaths were occurring on a large scale, the government proved administratively incompetent and failed to purchase and distribute food to anything like the extent that was needed. Russell was informed of the reason why one state official in Ireland had resigned:

> He thinks the destitution here is so horrible, the indifference of the House of Commons to it so manifest, that he is an unfit agent of a policy that must be one of extermination.[3]

By 1847 people were dying in the ditches or after making their way to church graveyards. The workhouses were grossly overcrowded with the destitute and fever victims. In the West, whole families, in a desperate attempt to preserve a semblance of dignity, locked themselves in their cabins to die. In his moving account from the testimony of eye-witnesses Canon John O'Rourke quotes one such witness: 'the roads in many places became as charnel-houses and several car and coach drivers have assured me that they rarely drove anywhere without seeing bodies strewn along the roadside and that, in the dark, they had gone over them.' O'Rourke reports that the effects on children were especially harrowing: 'their faces were so wan and haggard that they looked like old men and women; their sprightliness was all gone; they sat in groups at the cabin doors, making no attempt to play.'[4]

These scenes were all the more shocking given their proximity to Britain's commercial and industrial wealth. Within Ireland itself, although some landlords were ready to make considerable sacrifices to relieve the distressful condition of their tenants, as a class the landowners did not respond effectively to the crisis. More than one third of them were absentees and some of those that were resident acted shamefully. The records show that evictions continued despite the suffering and hard-

---

3. Quoted in Peter Gray 'Ideology and the Famine' in Cathal Póirtéir, *The Great Irish Famine* (Dublin: Mercier, 1995), pp. 86-103 (102),
4. J. O'Rourke, *The Great Irish Famine* (Dublin: Veritas, 1989) (first published in 1874), pp. 190 and 197.

ship. The majority of Famine victims were in fact from the lowest rung in Irish society, the cottier class, of whom there were about three million. Thus in addition to the landlords, the remaining five million of Ireland's total population of eight million, must also bear some responsibility for the plight of those who starved.[5]

The tragedy was undoubtedly compounded by the archaic landown-ing arrangements that still prevailed in Ireland, which meant that a rela-tively small number of landed families owned the greater part of the country. The total rental income from Irish estates of ten million pounds imposed a heavy burden at the best of times. In 1846 John Stuart Mill broke off writing his *Principles of Political Economy* to campaign for land redistribution and peasant proprietorship to put an end to the rack-rent and eviction in famine-torn Ireland.[6] Had enlightened measures such as these been carried out many fewer would have died. Thus in a consider-able measure the underlying problem lay with the system of landowner-ship which the British sustained in Ireland.[7]

Many of the advocates of *laissez faire* policies saw the calamity that be-fell Ireland as a Malthusian corrective process. Some indeed positively welcomed the Famine, seeing in it the hand of providence. Buttressing political economy with a 'Christian' moralism, it was argued that divinely ordained natural economic laws should not be obstructed by govern-ments, since they are the means by which people are made subject to a moral discipline. This kind of thinking provided support for the popu-lar prejudice which saw the Famine as divine chastisement upon the in-dolent and feckless Irish. Charles Trevelyan took such a view:

> the cure has been applied by the direct stroke of an all wise Provi-dence in a manner as unexpected and unthought of as it is likely to be effectual. God grant that we may rightly perform our part and not turn into a curse what was intended as a blessing.[8]

5. Seán Mac Réamoinn rightly questions the 'received wisdom' that the Famine struck all our ancestors save 'those ruffian landlords' and, quoting Luke Dodd, refers to the 'class specific' nature of the Famine. See his essay 'With the Past, in the Present, for the Future' in D. Carroll, ed., *Religion in Ireland: Past, Present and Future* (Dublin: Columba, 1999), pp. 96-126 (111).

6. See Donald Winch's introduction to Mill's *Principles of Political Economy* (Harmond-sworth: Penguin, 1970), p. 32.

7. See T. Eagleton, *Heathcliff and the Great Hunger: Studies in Irish Culture* (London: Verso, 1995), pp. 22ff. and 60ff.

8. Gray, 'Ideology and the Famine', p. 93.

These remarks are all the more chilling given that they come from the treasury civil servant responsible for funds for famine relief! Trevelyan's constant anxiety throughout the crisis seems to have been that the destitute might receive too much help.

The prevalence with which the Famine was regarded as divine judgement is indicated by an address of thanks to an Arabian Sultan for his donation to the relief work, which baldly stated that 'it had pleased Providence in its wisdom, to deprive this country suddenly of its staple article of food'. Canon John O'Rourke describes this as a 'blasphemous attack upon Divine Providence'.[9]

In recent years revisionist historians have tended to play down British neglect and make allowances for the free-market dogmatism that characterised government policy. Although this is an understandable reaction to those populist nationalist interpretations that speak in lurid tones of a conspiracy to mass-murder, the argument that the ideology of *laissez faire* was so dominant that alternative policies could not have been countenanced should be contested. Even Adam Smith – the fountainhead of the classical tradition – accepted that the State must have a role in the maintenance of such public works and institutions as are beneficial to society and which otherwise would not exist. John Stuart Mill, perhaps the most influential intellectual at the time, had argued the case for government intervention in areas where the market was manifestly failing.[10] The inheritance of the Romantic and early Socialist critiques of market individualism, the Chartist Movement, and in a more modest way the general impetus surrounding the formation of the Christian Socialist Movement, would be examples of popular developments which show that the political culture of the 1840s was by no means as monolithic as some might suggest.

At the height of its industrial power Britain undoubtedly had the means to prevent famine. Indeed, the contrast between the imperial capital boasting British preeminence through the Great Exhibition at Crystal Palace in 1851 and the shameful neglect of Ireland's cottier class, could scarcely have been more poignant. Those closest to the suffering cer-

9. O'Rourke, *The Great Irish Famine*, pp. 182f.
10. See his *Principles of Political Economy*, edited by D. Winch (Harmondsworth: Penguin, 1970) (First published in 1848). In his introduction Winch discusses the limits of *laissez faire* in Mill's thought.

tainly did not regard it as inevitable and unpreventable. When deaths
were commonplace throughout West Cork, Randolf Routh, who was involved with relief operations, claimed: 'food is not lacking but rather the
money to buy it'. Another observer of events in West Cork, the Revd R.
Townsend, was in no doubt where to place the blame. 'The principles of
political economy', he contended, 'have been carried out in practice to
a murderous extent'.[11] The ageing Daniel O'Connell was sharply critical
of relief policy and pointed to the £20 million compensation granted to
former slave-owners in the colonies. Recent research by Joel Mokyr in
his book *Why Ireland Starved?* tellingly contrasts government expenditure on the Famine of £9 million with the £70 million spent in the Crimean
campaign of the next decade.[12] It would seem that imperial interests
were deemed of more importance than the well-being of the citizens of a
supposedly equal 'Union'. Even the relief that was given took the form
of a loan that had to be repaid with interest as the crisis was still unfolding.

Historical assessments of this kind have an important bearing on the
present. When the Famine is viewed primarily as a natural calamity, it
makes it a good deal less contentious and political an issue. As well as
reacting to more tendentious nationalist accounts, revisionist historians
have been concerned that an anti-British slant might give valuable propaganda to 'terrorists'. But genuine reconciliation will not be achieved by
suppressing the conflict and pain of the past. The dereliction of moral
duty by Britain during the Famine years bore eloquent testimony to its
unfitness to govern Ireland. The imperial Parliament, it would seem,
wanted the benefits of the Act of Union but not its obligations. One
hundred and fifty years later, the wrong done to Ireland still needs to be
more fully acknowledged. The statement made by Tony Blair shortly after he took office as British Prime Minister is therefore to be welcomed.
'Those who governed in London at the time', Blair conceded, 'failed
their people through standing by while a crop failure turned into a massive human tragedy.' In correspondence with the Foreign Office I was
advised this did not constitute an apology, which is surely warranted; it is

11. Quoted in P. Hickey 'The Famine in the Skibereen Union (1845-51)' in Póirtéir, *The
    Great Irish Famine*, pp. 185-203 (188, 203).
12. See Cormac Ó Gráda, *Ireland: A New Economic History 1780-1939* (Oxford: Clarendon,
    1994), pp. 191 and 176.

nonetheless a significant contribution to the improvement of Anglo-Irish relations and also to helping heal the wounds arising from other past antagonisms.[13]

THE ACT OF REMEMBRANCE

As we have already seen in respect of the Famine, the way we view our past is always filled with consequences for the present. The commemoration of that dark chapter in Irish history not only raises issues of historical interpretation, but is also a moral, political and theological act.

It is natural enough to want to retreat mentally when faced with the weight of suffering and human tragedy that the Irish Famine must have involved. When charitable societies sent people to investigate some of the horrific reports that were emerging from Ireland, word quickly went back that the accounts had certainly not been exaggerated. 'In their opinion', recorded one observer, 'it was impossible to exaggerate the dreadful condition in which they found the people.'[14] Given the enormity of the catastrophe, it is understandable that commentators should sometimes describe the Famine as Ireland's Holocaust. It may not have involved the calculated use of technology to deliberately inflict genocide, and the comparison is therefore not apt, but people knew about the deaths and what was happening on their very doorstep and often did nothing.

In trying to relay the horror and misery of such events we certainly do come up against the sheer inadequacy of language. Does this mean we should not attempt the task? In relation to the Holocaust George Steiner has argued:

> The world of Auschwitz lies outside speech as it lies outside reason. To speak of the *unspeakable* is to risk the survivance of language as creator and bearer of humane, rational truth.[15]

Steiner is right that pained silence has its place when reminded of

---

13. Downing Street Press Release, 31st May 1997, and a reply from the Foreign Office dated 11th August 1997 to a letter I had sent to the Prime Minister seeking clarification.
14. John O'Rourke, *The Great Irish Famine*, p. xvi.
15. Quoted in M. Kelleher 'Irish Famine in Literature' in Póirtéir, *The Great Irish Famine*, pp. 232-47 (232).

such things, but this alone would risk colluding with the silence of a world content to ignore the victims.[16] Despite its inadequacies, speech is an integral part of the act of remembrance without which we would de-humanise ourselves through our insensitivity to the plight of our fore-bears. We need accounts of even the most terrible of things if we are really to let them touch us. The function of literary representations of the horrors of famine is therefore, as John Banville's novel *Birchwood* would suggest, 'so that tears might be shed and the inexpressible ex-pressed'.[17] The alternative to speaking of such things is repression and, given Ireland's colonial past, most would agree that there has been too much of that in the Irish psyche.

There is in fact a significant literary record of the Famine which re-cent scholarship has done much to bring to our attention. Chris Morash has produced an anthology of nineteenth-century Famine poetry which provides an impressive record of the varied responses to the traumatic events that had convulsed Ireland.[18]

In 'An Irish Mother's Lament', Elizabeth Willoughby Varian contem-plates a mother's grief in losing her child and is forthright in attributing blame for Ireland's sorrows upon the landlords:

Oh! terrible the inward strife that rends the mother's heart;
They only know who've felt the pang, how hard it is to part.
Was there not plenty in the land? the earth gave forth her store –
The glad and fruitful mother earth, with riches brimming o'er.
Not for the slave who till'd the soil the garner'd wealth was won;
Our tyrant masters gorged their fill, and murder'd thee, my son!

It is the landlord class who are again singled out for condemnation in a poem of Lady Wilde's, which speaks of 'whitening bones' rising 'from the cabins and the ditches' on judgement day:

16. See R. Williams, 'Remembering for the Future' in his *Open to Judgement: Sermons and Addresses* (London: Darton, Longman and Todd, 1994), pp. 237-42. I have drawn on this address in my discussion below.
17. See Kelleher 'Irish Famine in Literature', p. 246f.
18. See Kelleher, 'Irish Famine in Literature' and her *The Feminization of Famine: Expres-sions of the Inexpressible (Cork: Cork University Press, 1997)*; C. Morash, *The Hungry Voice: Poetry of the Irish Famine* (Dublin: Irish Academic Press, 1989). The poems quoted below are to be found on pp. 74f., 222 and 138 of Morash's anthology.

For the Angel of the Trumpet will know them as he passes.
A ghastly, spectral army, before the great God will stand,
And arraign ye as our murderers, the spoilers of our land.

Not surprisingly, the sentiments in the poetry of the period run in a number of directions and we find some echoes of the tendency to attribute the Famine to divine providence. With the melancholy James Clarence Mangan, the Famine is seen as divine chastisement:

The land expires beneath Thy frown,
Abroad the red sword striketh down.

Here though, the theme of judgement has the added twist that it is linked with the purifying of the remnant few, as part of an unfolding millenarian prospect.

Richard D'alton Williams in his 'Vesper Hymn to the Guardian Angels of Ireland' also views the Famine in terms of apocalyptic woes and trials that refine and prepare the way for a new era when 'Love, Peace and Plenty, replenish the land'. D'alton Williams was a member of Young Ireland and his poetry – albeit somewhat exotically – relates the Famine to nationalist hopes and aspirations. With Mangan and D'alton Williams, divine providence is not cited to endorse the teachings of political economists, and instead the crucible of the Famine is seen as heralding a new Ireland set free from the tyranny of the past.

An interesting feature of much of the poetry is that in contrast with the fatalism and resignation that characterised many people's reaction to the Famine, again and again the writers reach for religious imagery to express an impassioned sense of outrage that carries a political message. It is this strong element of protest and expectation that gives so many of the poems their vitality.

Revulsion at the denial of the value of human life in the past can become the well-spring for discontent within our contemporary world, and these poems are illustrative of the way in which the act of remembrance can become politically subversive should it begin to change our perspective upon the present. As well as honouring the dead, this indeed is part of the purpose of remembrance, since a wholesome remembrance is not passively sentimental but has a menace about it. Thus Herbert Marcuse has rightly observed:

Remembrance is no real weapon unless it is translated into historical action. Then, the struggle against time becomes a decisive moment in the struggle against domination.[19]

Marcuse was influenced by the work of the Jewish literary critic and messianic thinker, Walter Benjamin, for whom the idea of a redemptive relation to the historical past was a central concern. For Benjamin, history is not concerned with 'homogeneous, empty time, but time filled by the presence of the now.' The task of the historian is therefore to seize hold of the messianic element in the past and press it into the service of the present. The historian, he writes:

> grasps the constellation which his own era has formed with a definite earlier one. Thus he establishes a conception of the present as the 'time of the now' which is shot through with chips of Messianic time.[20]

Counterposing his conception of history to the dominant 'official' history of the ruling classes, which is written from the perspective of the victors, Benjamin spoke of the need to 'blast open the continuum of history'. To do this revolutionary vision must be informed by a passionate recollection of the messianic-laden past:

> To articulate the past historically does not mean to recognise it 'the way it really was' (Ranke). It means to seize hold of a memory as it flashes up at a moment of danger … In every era the attempt must be made anew to wrest tradition away from a conformism that is about to overpower it. The Messiah comes not only as the redeemer, he comes as the subduer of Antichrist. Only that historian will have the gift of fanning the spark of hope in the past who is firmly convinced that *even the dead* will not be safe from the enemy if he wins.[21]

Put more simply and less abstractly (and therefore at the risk of over-simplifying), the point Benjamin would seem to be making is that it is possible to look back at history and see moments of real inspiration and liberative potential; these occur both at times of human freedom's ad-

---

19. Quoted in M. Löwy, *On Changing the World: Essays in Political Philosophy, from Karl Marx to Walter Benjamin* (New Jersey/London: Humanities Press, 1993), p. 137.

20. 'Theses on the Philosophy of History' in W. Benjamin, *Illuminations*, edited by Hannah Arendt (London: Fontana, 1973), pp. 255-66 (263 and 265).

21. Ibid., p. 257.

vance and even at its times where human fulfilment is denied but there still lies a protest and a menace. Untiring in his search for the messianic moment, Benjamin cautioned that the apparent normality of the present should not be allowed to bewitch us. Even the despair-engendering obscenities of fascism heightened the sense of the need for a revolutionary break and thereby pointed towards the messianic realm of freedom.[22]

In somewhat similar vein it might be said that in the sheer negation of human life in the Famine there lies a revolutionary moment. Thus the act of remembrance can be harnessed in the direction of a break with the history of oppression. Something of this sort occurs in one of Richard D'alton-Williams' poems, where the terror of the Famine is contrasted with the longed-for moment of redemption:

Come! come to us, Angels of Hope and of Healing,
With chaplet of snowdrop and plume of the dove –
And, like rainbow-clad show'rs to the fainting earth stealing,
Come green-winged Mercy and fire-arrowed Love![23]

This emotionally charged reaching for millenarian language has its place in inspiring and sustaining vision. It also serves as a reminder that, at the very least, a serious commemoration of the Famine should instill in us the determination that in the world today such things should never be allowed to happen again.

Such a determination, if it is to be effective, must in turn involve a readiness to formulate practical measures in response to the subsistence crises in our contemporary world. Some of the political commitments that this might entail include: the repudiation of callous economic indifference and the dogmatic certitudes of those in favour of unrestrained market forces; a willingness to control banking institutions' policies towards poorer countries in the interests of preventing material deprivation; a recognition of the need to curtail arms sales that fuel regional conflicts and produce widespread disability and population displacement; a taking of responsibility for environmental policies that expose many parts of the hemisphere to greater risk; an acceptance of the necessity of higher levels of aid and at least some degree of regulation of basic com-

22. Benjamin's *Theses* should be seen in the context of fascism: see J. Roberts, *Walter Benjamin* (London: Macmillan, 1982), pp. 198, 208.
23. Morash, *The Hungry Voice*, p. 241

modity prices for primary producers in more impoverished jurisdictions; and finally, a readiness to defend basic human rights, including the most basic right of all, the right to life, which must imply the right of the poor to sustenance. These are the kind of measures that need to be taken if a compassionate moral response to the Famine is to be translated into meaningful and effective political action in the present.

The overall goal of the elimination of primary poverty within one generation is a realistic one that should be seen as a moral imperative. It is chilling to think that the grinding poverty we still see in many parts of the southern hemisphere is justified on more or less the same grounds as was the Famine. Thus when the most rudimentary basic health programmes of poorer countries are routinely abandoned at the insistence of international banking institutions, it is the need to ensure 'the efficient operation of market forces' that is so often cited. The language may be sanitised but the reality is not. Such actions and the disease and death that follow are not brought about by God. They are, as Cardinal Daly has reminded us, 'the will of people'. Condemning the gross disparities in wealth in our contemporary world, Cardinal Daly writes:

> People may call it the necessary and progressive and proper play of market forces. In Famine times they proclaimed that 'free trade' and the inescapable 'iron law of economics' were the engine of progress. The economic theories of then and today are not fundamentally dissimilar. Their consequences are very similar.[24]

The task of creating a more equitable international order and ensuring that basic human rights are honoured and held as sacrosanct will require the concerted action of the community of nations. Although Ireland is but a small part of a much larger jigsaw, it has a potentially significant contribution to make in mapping out a new vision of global responsibility and world community. The Irish public has a particularly good track record on supporting overseas aid and leaders like Mary Robinson have done much to articulate the positive role Ireland might have to play in international relations. This wider vision needs to be an essential part of our conception of politics if the commitment to social justice and democracy, which lies at the heart of all that is best in the

24. *Irish Times*, September 25, 1995.

nationalist ideal, is to have substance.

Ireland would be forgetful of her past struggles for social justice and political freedom if she turned a blind eye to oppression in other parts of the world today. We need remembrance because in the act of commemoration, through imaginatively bringing past suffering into focus in our minds and insisting that the victims of the past are not consigned to oblivion, we are moved to inquire about the victims of our own generation. By challenging the tyranny of yesterday, and foreclosing its domination through speaking for the downtrodden and naming the dead, we also serve notice on current oppression that seeks to marginalise or destroy.

Remembrance (*anamnesis*) lies at the heart of the Christian faith, which has its origin in the memory of Jesus who died in solidarity with the victims of the rich and powerful of this world. In the subversive act of the Eucharist we remember and celebrate Christ's self-giving and the unyielding love and hope for humanity expressed in his proclamation of the Kingdom of God: the equality of table fellowship pointing towards the coming reign of righteousness. This celebration takes place in the context of belief in the divine love as a transforming power within history that will ultimately prove triumphant over history, since through the resurrection of Christ the verdict of the oppressor is overturned and God shows himself to be the God of the vanquished and humiliated.

THE FAMINE AND A GOD OF LOVE

Even if remembrance of the Famine can become redemptive for the present, and even if we believe the dead are raised, we are still left with the question: how can such horrendous suffering be compatible with a God of love? At a human level, blame can be ascribed, but does this absolve God from ultimate responsibility? The idea of the Famine as divine judgement is rightly dismissed as a slander upon God. As one writer puts it: 'If bad men slaughter, charge it not on GOD'.[25] But this still leaves the difficulty of how can the world be governed by a gracious providence when such things are allowed to occur? The lines of a poem by Denis Florence McCarthy, entitled, 'A Mystery', poignantly express the perplexed disbelief many would feel at the thought of an all-powerful deity

25. Morash, *The Hungry Voice*, p. 203.

who permits people to die of starvation:

> God of Justice! God of Power!
>   Do we dream? Can it be?…
> Is it right, is it fair
> That we perish of despair
> In this land, on this soil
>   Where our destiny is set,
> Which we cultured with our toil
>   And watered with our sweat?[26]

If God is all-loving and omnipotent why is it that there is so much evil and suffering in the world? 'Theodicy' is the word used to described theological efforts to address this question. The standard modern formulation of the conundrum is that provided by David Hume:

> Is he willing to prevent evil, but not able? then he is impotent. Is he able, but not willing? then he is malevolent. Is he both able and willing? whence then evil?[27]

The classic 'free-will defence', which stems from Augustine of Hippo, maintains that if God grants human beings genuine free will, this cannot logically exclude the possibility of that freedom resulting in evil actions. The other main attempt at an explanation is that of 'soul-making' theodicies, stemming from Irenaeus, which see evil and suffering as part of the fabric of a universe in which human beings undergo a moral and spiritual improvement.[28]

Both these responses have foundered as adequate explanations of the sheer scale and enormity of evil and suffering in our world. Many would hold that even if the universe had entailed terrible suffering for only one child, and God had foreseen this, then irrespective of any future blessedness, he surely should not have created it.[29]

It would no doubt be possible to spend a good deal of time speculating about the merits of a range of possible universes and what restric-

---

26. Ibid., p. 190.
27. See K. Surin, *Theology and the Problem of Evil* (Oxford: Blackwell, 1986), p. 2.
28. A recent exponent of the Irenaen view is John Hick, *Evil and the God of Love* (London: Collins, 1968).
29. Here I have in mind two classic texts: F. Doestoevsky's, *The Brothers Karamazov* (London: Quartet, 1990) and A. Camus' *The Plague* (London: Penguin, 1998).

tions a genuinely free creation would involve. It seems reasonable to suppose that the generation of higher forms of life requires an evolutionary process that will have negative as well as positive consequences. This will entail both suffering in the natural world and suffering arising from the misuse of human freedom. Although God may not directly will this suffering, and is active in trying to redeem its consequences, it is nonetheless permitted and God is therefore ultimately responsible for it.[30]

Whatever we might think about permissible alternative universes, in the end we have to deal with the universe in which we live. Within this world pain and evil are to be found side by side with love, joy and beauty. It is also undoubtedly true that it is often through evil and suffering that love and moral virtue do emerge, though this still leaves the difficulty of whether the latter can be said to be of such inestimable value as to thereby justify human suffering, much of which is destructive and seemingly with no purpose or redemptive value. Indeed, it would be offensive to innocent victims to suggest that what they are enduring has anything to do with their spiritual development.

In Judaeo-Christian thinking human wickedness – especially in its more extreme forms – has been closely linked with a belief in evil spirits and the Devil. Many theologians, while acknowledging the usefulness of the category of the demonic in describing the insidious and the often structural nature of evil, would want to de-mythologise the idea of a metaphysical world of spirits. Even if a more traditional view is taken, provided a primitive dualism is ruled out (as it has been in classical Christianity from Irenaeus and Augustine onwards), the existence of fallen angels does not remove divine sovereignty and therefore responsibility. Nor can it be said to remove human responsibility, since in the Genesis myth the serpent only provides the source of temptation.[31]

---

30. Keith Ward mentions death, competition for survival, failure to achieve new modes of life, along with the suffering perpetrated by free moral agents. On the issue of divine responsibility he writes: 'Though God does not intend every instance of suffering, God does intend a universe in which some such suffering will inevitably occur. God is the source of that suffering, and bears responsibility for it. But it makes a profound difference to the situation if God does not desire it for its own sake, but rather intends that it should be diminished and abolished whenever that is possible, whether by divine or creaturely action.' See Keith Ward, *Religion and Creation* (Oxford: Clarendon Press, 1996), pp. 220ff.

31. See P. Tillich, *Systematic Theology*, Vol 2, (London: SCM, 1978), pp. 38f.

Some theologians have argued that God would be justified in creating a world which included evil and suffering if the Creator was ready to
share in the world's pain.[32]

The idea that God cannot suffer stems from the classical Greek philosophical conception of God, and is rooted in the belief that the divinity
is pure activity, the sum of all perfections, timeless, immutable, above
this transient world of alteration and decay, beyond the passions, and
therefore cannot be subject to change from anything external. Such was
the strength of this conviction that both Augustine and Aquinas followed
the classical tradition in this matter. Christ's death on the cross was thus
in certain respects to prove problematical not only to sophisticated Greeks
and the Jewish world, but also mainstream Christianity![33]

A prominent example of a theologian eager to provide an alternative
to a doctrine of God founded on classical Greek thinking is Jürgen Moltmann, who sees the cross as evidence of divine participation in human
suffering and is ready to affirm that the eternal God suffered in Christ.
Moltmann maintains that the traditional belief in divine impassibility
must be abandoned: the Triune God is not beyond the passions and is
capable of suffering.

Expounding this theme of divine participation in suffering, making
use of Hegel, Moltmann speaks of the 'universalizing of the historic Good
Friday of the god-forsakeness of Jesus, so that it becomes a speculative
Good Friday of the god-forsakeness of all that is.'[34]

Here Moltmann makes the rather large assertion that through the
suffering of Christ the Triune God has come into contact with all human
suffering. A case can certainly be made that along with the physical cru-
elties to which he was subject, Christ would have suffered great mental
anguish, given that he was a person of great love and sensitivity who was
rejected, betrayed and saw all his finest hopes for the people he loved so

32. Surin, *Theology and the Problem of Evil*, pp. 67, 112ff.
33. A point which is no better illustrated than by the traditional formulation of the doctrine of the incarnation at the Council of Chalcedon in 451. This formulation, which
taught that the divine and human nature of Christ were united in a single person,
also upheld the teaching that since the divine nature could not suffer, Christ suffered
in his human nature alone. For a recent stimulating discussion of the classical doctrine of divine immutability see Ward, *Religion and Creation*, especially pp. 192ff.
34. *Theology of Hope: On the Ground and the Implications of a Christian Eschatology* (London:
SCM, 1967), p. 169.

cruelly dashed.[35] It might therefore be true that, in some qualitative sense at least, Christ can be said to have plumbed the depths of human suffering as one who was 'a man of sorrows and acquainted with grief'.

Moltmann has other grounds in addition to his Christology for pressing the claim that there is a direct divine participation in human suffering. He follows the Jewish theologian, Abraham Heschel, who has argued that through the fellowship of God's covenant with his people, God becomes capable of suffering. The bond is too close for it to be otherwise: our pain is felt by God and becomes part of the divine agony. This involves much more than divine sympathy since God, in this view, is affected by our pain. Drawing upon the Spanish mystical philosopher Miguel de Unamuno, Moltmann states directly that 'God participates in the world's pain and suffers in all who suffer.'[36] This is possible because the world is within the divine being and God therefore suffers with the creation.

To speak in this way of God's presence in both the suffering of Christ and in suffering humanity, gives grounds for hope not found in traditional theism's teaching that God is beyond the passions. Yet whatever comfort this may provide, it still cannot be said to justify the creation of a world in which is found the harrowed pain of famine victims.

Probably the most powerful theological response to the problem of evil has been that advanced by forms of 'process' theology, which combine an emphasis on divine involvement with suffering with the idea that God's being itself is inextricably entwined with the creation.[37] Here the traditional description of divine omnipotence is attenuated and the clas-

35. On the theme of betrayal see J. Hillman, Betrayal, (London: Guild of Pastoral Psychology, 1971), pp. 5-26. Hillman writes: 'In the story of Jesus we are immediately struck by the motif of betrayal. Its occurrence in threes (by Judas, by the sleeping disciples, by Peter) – repeated by Peter's betrayal thrice – tells us of something fateful, that betrayal is essential to the dynamics of the climax of the Jesus story and thus at the heart of the Christian mystery. The sorrow at the supper, the agony in the garden, and the cry on the cross seems repetitious of a same pattern, restatements of a same theme, each on a higher key, that a destiny is being realised, that a transformation is being brought home to Jesus. In each of these betrayals he is forced to the terrible awareness of having been let down, failed, and left alone. His love has been refused, his message mistaken, his call unattended, and his fate announced.' (p.11)

36. *Trinity and the Kingdom of God* (London: SCM, 1981), pp. 25ff. (39). On Heschel see also Ward, *Religion and Creation*, pp. 19ff.

37. For an introduction to process theology see J. Cobb and D. Griffin, *Process Theology: an Introductory Exposition* (Belfast: Christian Journals Ltd, 1977).

sical view that creation proceeds from the overflowing of the divine love and adds nothing essential to the being of God is qualified. This allows for a more meaningful integration of the redemptive process within he divine life and thereby underlines the significance that other theological perspectives give to redemptive history.[38] Moreover, it might be asked, can a deity that is unaffected by creation be invoked as a focus of hope in the light of tragedies on the scale of the Irish Famine. The divine life must surely be affected in a most profound way by such happenings. Within the Godhead the memory of such events must always remain and in some way be incorporated into the divine identity. If this is the case, then human suffering must in some sense be constitutive of the very being of God.

There is also merit in the questioning of more traditional notions of divine omnipotence. At the very least we are dealing with a teaching that can only be understood eschatologically and when cleansed of worldly pre-conceptions. In many people's experience invocations of the power of God often seem like whistling in the dark. Personal misfortune or observing the plight of others makes careless talk about God's power insensitive and inappropriate. We need perhaps to ask what we mean by the word 'power' when we apply it to God. Christ certainly exercised power in a very different way to what people expected: he did not take up the sword to lead Israel in revolt; he refrained from using his strong personality to dominate others; he could not compel people to love one another; he was unable to prevent his enemies plotting against him; he could not stop it if someone to whom he had offered the hand of friendship betrayed him; he was crucified in weakness between two thieves. Why then is it that Christianity speaks of God's power being manifest in the crucified Jesus? What kind of power is revealed in that place of suffering and dereliction?

The incarnation involved a voluntary self-emptying (*kenosis*), whereby Christ 'though he was in the form of God, did not count equality with God as a thing to be grasped, but emptied himself and took the form of a servant' (Philippians 2:6-7). Here Kingship and Lordship are redefined

---

38. A useful critique of the classical view and defence of a more Hegelian and process theology viewpoint is found in Keith Ward, *God: a Guide for the Perplexed* (Oxford: Oneworld, 2002), pp. 140ff.

in terms of trasformatory dynamic of sacrificial care and servanthood. The divine self-limitation did not mean that Christ was without power. Yet, crucially, his power was not power as the world knows it, but something much deeper, namely, the creative power of suffering love. This love was the secret of Christ's spiritual strength. It was the driving force behind his proclamation of the Kingdom of God, his recklessness in risking all in his hopes and dreams for others, his readiness to face tribulation and not count the cost, and his final obedience unto death.

In contrast with the superficiality of some forms of pietism, this would suggest that very often it is precisely when things are going wrong that this kind of power is most evident. It is manifest when people go on believing despite times of doubt and uncertainty; when they go on hoping despite the fact that so many hopes have been dashed; and when they go on loving despite the hostility and resentment that may be directed against them. To follow the way of the Messiah is to be moved by the kind of love which made him so open to the needs of others, especially the poor and heavy laden, on whose behalf he strove valiantly for God's Kingdom of justice and righteousness.

The incarnation and the cross subvert what we normally might think of power relations and tell us that the place where we will find God in the world is not with the dominant, but in a committed and loving solidarity with the victims and those who suffer. It is in the context of this identification that we know God's power to be the power of suffering love.

The principle of divine self-limitation should be extended beyond the incarnation to how we understand divine action in the world generally. If the cross of Christ is the supreme revelation of God, then it would surely suggest that in a very real sense God too is weak and vulnerable.[39] When applied to our thinking about creation, the idea of divine *kenosis* goes some way to accounting for this divine weakness. In order for there to be space for a creation that is genuinely free, the act of creation must have involved a voluntary divine self-emptying. In the interests of allowing the creation its freedom there must, in part at least, be a divine letting go. The granting of this freedom has both glorious and tragic consequences; and, given the divine self-limitation, it is in weakness and pow-

---

39. See Donald MacKinnon, 'Epilogue – *Kenosis* and Self-Limitation' in his *Themes in Theology: The Three-fold Cord* (Edinburgh: T. & T. Clarke, 1987), pp. 229-36.

erlessness that God suffers with the world. The divine presence within the world is, therefore, primarily that of suffering love brooding over the creation and longing for its fulfilment. Through the Spirit the divine creativity is operative, but always in harmony with human freedom and the dynamics of the natural world. Divine grace – as Aquinas insisted – does not stand opposed to nature but works through it. Talk of miracles still has its place if by this we do not mean the suspension of the dynamics of nature, but those truly marvellous events that we see in people's lives that attest to divine grace. Such events would include a renewal of faith, a rekindling of hope, a deepening of charity, a healing of broken relationships, and even sometimes, given that human beings are an organic and psychosomatic unity, physical healing itself.

A proper recognition of the divine self-limitation entailed in the act of creation will have important implications for the way in which we understand providence. Faith in providence is not an optimism that excludes the possibility of failure and the tragic dimension of human life. What it does affirm is that, in spite of the negativity in human existence, the divine life continually directs all things to their fulfilment and will ultimately triumph.

In order to co-operate with the loving purposes of God for the world there must be a willingness to resist the causes of human suffering; the strength to accept weakness and vulnerability; the courage to demonstrate the creative power of suffering love; the wisdom to show that divine power is manifest in acts of mercy and forgiveness; and the readiness to involve ourselves in risk and the possibility of failure. In the divine economy, after all, failures remain precious, for they stand under the shadow of that other failure at Calvary's Hill. Against this background there is no place for triumphalism. The only assurance that is given is the eschatological hope that in the end the divine love will prevail.

This admittedly more nuanced conception of divine action in the world is a good deal more in keeping with both human experience and divine revelation than those forms of pietism that speak as though God constantly intervened supernaturally within the created order. The Enlightenment's destruction of the theology stemming from this kind of pietism should be welcomed. This rather shallow and dishonest thinking is both contradicted daily by human experience and fails to appreciate the full profundity of God's revelation in the crucified Jesus. It in fact presents us with an irrational and immoral monster of a God who selectively helps some while leaving others bereft.

In his *Letters and Papers from Prison*, Dietrich Bonhoeffer goes perhaps to unjustified lengths in stressing the starkness of divine self-limitation and all that this entails when he says that we have to live in the world '*etsi deus non daretur*' (as though God had not been given). His meditation on this theme is nonetheless suggestive in regard to the connections that should be made between the cross and our understanding of divine action generally.

> God would have us know that we must live as men who manage our lives without him. The God who is with us is the God who forsakes us (Mark 15.34). The God who lets us live in the world without the working hypothesis of God is the God before whom we stand continually. Before God and with God we live without God. God lets himself be pushed out of the world on to the cross. He is weak and powerless in the world, and that is precisely the way, the only way, in which he is with us and helps us. Matt 8.17 makes it quite clear that Christ helps us, not only by virtue of his omnipotence, but by virtue of his weakness and suffering.
>
> Here is the decisive difference between Christianity and all religions. Man's religiosity makes him look in his distress to the power of God in the world: God is the *deus ex machina*. The Bible directs man to God's powerlessness and suffering; only the suffering God can help.[40]

If because of the divine *kenosis* we should understand the divine love in the world as weak, vulnerable and open to suffering, then this undoubtedly presents us with a view of God that is perhaps less offensive in face of the reality of evil than a detached remote deity. Added to this, the Christian faith holds out the eschatological prospect of the ultimate rescuing of victims and the triumph of the divine love over evil. And yet, even if all this is true, it still leaves us with the reality of anguished memory and the sheer terror of human history.

The conclusion which has begun to emerge in this theological wres-

40. *Letters and Papers from Prison* (enlarged edition), ed. E. Bethge, (London: SCM, 1971), pp. 360f.

tling with the problem of suffering in our own time is that any attempt by
human beings to justify God in the face of human suffering is unacceptable. An agnostic silence is deemed more appropriate than echoing Augustine's dismissal of the problem with the retort that God 'judged it
better to bring good out of evil than to preclude evil from existing.'[41]
Instead of trying to elaborate a satisfactory theodicy, the theological en-
terprise should be moving in a more practical direction, and should be
asking: what is God doing in the world to overcome evil and suffering
and, even more pertinently: what are we ourselves doing?

Such a perspective brings with it the reminder that rather than being
agents for compassion and action to prevent the tragedy of the Famine,
Christians, with forms of piety that mirrored the prevailing economic
individualism, were to a large degree responsible for what happened.
The Church of Ireland Archbishop of Dublin, Richard Whately, accused
the poor of being responsible for their plight and vigorously opposed
action by the State to relieve want.[42] As has already been noted, there
was no shortage of Christian opinion providing a religious gloss for harsh
economic doctrines that consigned so many to ignominious deaths. Although there were, thankfully, some notable exceptions to this hard-
heartedness, and the Quakers especially did much to relieve the suffering, the historical record remains a chastening one for Christians.

Moreover, there are some disturbing echoes with our contemporary
world where the continued popularity of forms of Christianity that reduce the Gospel message to one of private individual salvation can scarcely
be denied. When faced with the wounded and suffering of the world this
kind of self-indulgent introverted piety has no programme of social and
political action to relieve distress and need. There is something deeply
contradictory and profoundly disturbing about this.

In focussing attention on a more practical response to the problem of
human suffering, Christians are put on the spot as to whether they really
have got in touch with God's longings and hopes for the world. The
commitment to justice and building a better world is laid upon Christ's
disciples because his proclamation of the Kingdom bore witness to the

41.	E. Evans, *Saint Augustine's Enchiridion or Manual to Laurentius Concerning Faith, Hope, and Charity* (London: SPCK, 1953), p. 25.
42.	Ó Gráda, *Ireland: A New Economic History*, p. 193.

fact that such a world is willed by God. Moreover, the importance of this redemptive process is better appreciated when it is seen as part of the unfolding of the divine life itself. Irish history's darkest moment, the Famine, does not contradict this. It may point to the tragic dimension within human life, but also, understood aright, nothing could more starkly underline the importance of the Christian striving for redemption as something that takes place within the social domain.

It is wiser to take a more engaged approach to the problem of evil and suffering. Rational explanations run the risk of falling into complicity with innocent suffering. Moreover, if we are to acknowledge the mystery, terror and beauty that surrounds us in our apprehension of nature and the divine, then there are surely occasions when rational explanation must give way both to action and to a more emotional, searching, and troubled exploration and questioning.

If we believe God to be all-loving, then extreme suffering must be deeply felt within the divine life, which must be committed to doing all that can be done to prevent it. Everything that is possible within the boundaries of the relationship between God and the creation is brought into action: it would be inconceivable to think otherwise. When the suffering continues, within the divine brooding anger and sorrow must surely abound. But what about doubt, recrimination and self-questioning? The God who created is the God who weeps over creation – like Christ did over Jerusalem. Emotionally at least, there is scope here for a split personality. And rightly so, for it would be outrageous to think that God does not recoil at human suffering to such a degree that the very decision to create is brought into question. Given the outcome of that decision, some mystical writers have not unreasonably speculated that there might even be a dark side to divinity.[43]

Traditional theism has in fact accepted that God is bound by necessity, though this is seen as an internal rather than an external constraint.[44] Creation necessarily involves finitude and with it estrangement. We also need to remember that an understanding of God as Trinity points to a plurality as well as a unity within the plenitude of the divine being. The

---

43. Most notably, perhaps, Jakob Böhme.
44. See Keith Ward's discussion of necessity in *God: a Guide for the Perplexed*, pp. 124ff. and 223f.

insistence on the oneness of the Godhead should not therefore be an impediment to using different names for God such as Providence, Holy Charity, Love, Mystery, Wisdom, the All-merciful, each of which, like Father, Son and Spirit, is expressive of different aspects of the divine character. Rather than postulate a dark side to the divine nature, it is perhaps sufficient to acknowledge that within the many-sidedness of God there must exist some divine relation not only to the presence within the creation of structures and dynamics that are part of the outworking of divine care but also to nature's darker and more tragic side.

We only see through a glass darkly and, with that in mind, should not be neglectful of those things we can and ought to hold on to. We should remember God's passion for the world in Jesus Christ which brought the divine love into fellowship with other victims in other places, and pointed to the Triune God's suffering with the whole creation. In the cross the sorrow and pain of the world have been taken into the very heart and being of God. In a creation marred by evil, the divine love chose not to stand aloof but instead sought to oppose evil through setting about redeeming its effects by absorbing its consequences and entering into solidarity with us.

We should take solace from the empty tomb and resurrection, wherein we rejoice in the love that has 'come again like leaves that springeth green', showing the mystery at the heart of world, the beauty that lies beyond tragedy and darkness. The risen Christ remained the crucified Christ: the gaping side was still there. Yet as the ascended Christ, his wounds were in the process of being transfigured in a sacred joy that lies beyond pain.

There is wonder in the creation of love out of darkness and nothingness: a love that comes not from the Saviour alone but which through grace is born within each one of us. And who can really say whether or not it is better to have love after darkness and pain than no love at all?

Yet the darkness was allowed; and, if that is so, should not the love that resides in the human family speak words of forgiveness not only to fellow sinners but to God as well? Perhaps Christ, who readily submitted to the Baptism of John to fulfil all righteousness, will gladly step aside to let there be a celestial silence before such words are spoken somewhere in heaven's place.

CHAPTER NINE

Ethical Rebellion or Rebellious Ethics?

Paramilitary Violence in Northern Ireland

> All that I have said and done
> Now that I am old and ill
> Turns into a question till
> I lie awake night after night,
> And never get the answers right.
> Did that play of mine send out
> Certain men the English shot?
>
> – W. B. Yeats

Although the scale of human suffering in the Great Famine stands on its own, Irish history has had other deeply tragic aspects. Not least of these has been the recurrent warfare and hostility associated with Ireland's colonial relationship with Britain, and the internal strife this has so often promoted. The Troubles of the 1970s to the 1990s are regrettably but the latest manifestation of a long-standing history of enmity and conflict. Since each generation must carry responsibility for its actions, it is important that the ethical issues surrounding the resort to paramilitary violence are addressed.

This chapter will consider this violence in the light of the just war/ rebellion tradition. The hopes aroused by the cessation of hostilities and the significant (even if sometimes faltering) movement in the direction of building a peaceful and democratic society, provides the immediate context for such a moral audit. As part of the forgiveness and healing that needs to accompany the search for a sustainable peace, this kind of examination can play an important role in re-evaluating the past and is a very necessary part of the political process.

It was to his credit that at the end of his life Yeats was concerned about the influence his patriotic play *Cathleen ní Houlihan* may have had upon the generation of the 1916 Rising. We would all do well to adopt the same moral seriousness in relation to the conflict in Northern Ireland. Yeats' self-questioning makes the point that moral responsibility for situations of armed civil conflict extends far beyond the direct participants. Those who exercise political power or influence have special obligations, but, in varying degrees, every member of the community must acknowledge their part in the making of a society where communal violence has erupted. By each of our actions or inactions, choices and possibilities for others are generated or denied. Thus when people do violent things that they would not do in other situations, any resulting guilt is not theirs alone.

This does not mean that the notion of individual responsibility should be abandoned, but it does suggest that we should recognise, as Paul Tillich put it, that human existence is 'rooted both in ethical freedom and in tragic destiny.'[1] In the case of Northern Ireland we must accept that we have all contributed to the tragic destiny in the grip of which the violent and the victims have been more directly caught. One particularly virulent component of this tragic destiny is undoubtedly the sectarianism that is so endemic in Irish society and about which we have done far too little.[2]

THE CHURCHES' RESPONSE TO THE TROUBLES

During the civil conflict in Northern Ireland the Churches have, rightly and roundly, condemned paramilitary violence. It has not, however, always been clear whether this condemnation stems from anything other than a general abhorrence of violence.[3]

Such a stance would in fact raise as many questions as it answers. What about the State's use of arms as the civil power or at times of war? Are there no situations where recourse to armed rebellion against the State might be justified? The distinction that is sometimes made between 'force' and 'violence', whereby force is used to describe the coercive action of the civil power, begs the question of moral legitimacy. If force is understood to be the justifiable use of violence, there is no reason why in some

---

1. *Systematic Theology*, Vol. 2 (London: SCM, 1978), p. 38.
2. This matter is taken up at the conclusion of Chapter 10.
3. See *Violence in Ireland: A Report of the Churches*, Revised ed. (Belfast and Dublin: Christian Journals Limited and Veritas, 1977), which includes in an appendix some of the more important official statements made by the different denominations.

situations this may not apply to those engaged in rebellion. Christian moral reflection upon paramilitary violence cannot be confined to abstract moralising as though it could somehow conduct its investigations and reach its conclusions in isolation from the complexities of a political analysis of given situations. An assessment must be made of both the particular circumstances and the wider context in which violence occurs, in order to determine whether it might or might not be morally justified.

A common response – often found in the media – is to dismiss the perpetrators of paramilitary violence as wicked and deranged persons. It is also assumed that the immorality of their actions is self-evident to everyone. But is it not the case that paramilitary organisations would be unable to function effectively if there did not exist a significant body of tacit support for their activities within at least certain sections of the community? No doubt, some paramilitaries do not enjoy the best of mental health, and it might be true that many of their supporters are thoroughly irresponsible and immoral people, but this alone does not explain the widespread incidence of armed conflict we have witnessed in Northern Ireland. What does – unpalatable as it may be – is the fact that there have been a significant number of quite rational and sane people who have firmly believed that in Northern Ireland resort to force was quite justified.[4]

Part of the violence that has occurred falls into the category of defending 'our' people: the IRA saw itself as responding to the unjustified encroachments of the military or loyalists, while Protestant paramilitaries sought to contain the IRA threat. The Provisional IRA, however, had ambitions that went far beyond defending beleaguered Catholic residents: it was also its declared aim to impose a United Ireland by armed force. In the light of this threat, loyalist paramilitaries have had the larger

4. On the question of whether terrorists are psychotic, Anthony Clare writes: 'Seriously psychotic people do not hunt in groups, bombing, mutilating and machine-gunning their victims. Indeed, contrary to public perception, mentally ill individuals are rarely violent at all. On those rare occasions that they are, their violence is almost invariably random, pointless, arbitrary. IRA violence, and UVF violence too, is not random, pointless, arbitrary. It is chillingly conceived, methodologically planned and ruthlessly executed. To call IRA terrorists psychotic is to give the mad a bad name.' *The Sunday Independent* (Dublin: 15 August 1993). Dr Clare is Clinical Professor of Psychiatry at Trinity College, Dublin.

agenda of preparing for the possibility of full-scale civil war. The Provisional IRA defended the use of violence on the basis that they do not recognise the authority of the State. The attitude of their loyalist counterparts towards the State has been more ambivalent: they recognise the State, but do not think it is doing its job effectively.

In this situation a blanket condemnation of all violence is insufficient since it does not adequately address the issues at stake. The same is true of condemnations that dismiss all paramilitary violence as terrorism. Terrorism only accurately describes some instances of violence, and, more often, it would be appropriate to speak of guerrilla activity. A serious examination of the Christian case against paramilitary violence will quickly find that what is being wrestled with is in fact a fairly complex issue: the application of the just war tradition in the Irish context. It might be better to speak of 'just rebellion theory', since what we are dealing with in the Northern Ireland conflict is not war between states, but war within a state. The justification of rebellion, however, involves moral considerations of a broadly similar kind to those of the just war tradition.

APPLYING THE JUST WAR TRADITION TO THE TROUBLES

The just war tradition can be traced back to Ambrose and Augustine, but underwent substantial refinement and development by canonists during the medieval period. The classic expression of just war theory is found in Thomas Aquinas and still forms the basis of current thinking.[5] Under the heading of the right to make war (*jus ad bellum*), the theory begins with a consideration of the circumstances where recourse to war is justified, and offers several criteria: there must be a just cause; war must be sanctioned by legitimate authority; there must exist a right intention; the good to be achieved must outweigh the harm done (the proportionality principle); war must only be undertaken as a last resort.

The theory also makes provision, under the heading *jus in bello*, for

---

5. Aquinas provided, with commentary, a summary of previous thinking, and it was to his work that later theologians turned. For discussion of the historical background and development of the Just War tradition see J. T. Johnson, *Just War Tradition and the Restraint of War: A Moral and Historical Account* (Princeton: Princeton U. P., 1981), pp. xxiff., and E. McDonagh, *The Demands of Simple Justice: A Study of the Church, Politics and Violence with Special Reference to Zimbabwe* (Dublin: Gill and Macmillan, 1980), pp. 60ff. In the brief account of Just War theory below I have largely followed Johnson's summary of the theory.

restraint in the conduct of war. Here it offers the criteria of discrimination and proportionality, which are usually understood as involving noncombatant immunity and restrictions on the type of weapons used.

Because Christian moral reflection upon the resort to arms cannot avoid a detailed political analysis of the circumstances in which it occurs, the rebellion of 1798, the 1916 Rising, the Anglo-Irish War of 1920-1, and the Irish Civil War, would all require lengthy separate evaluation.[6] Moreover, in conflicts where there are several different protagonists, separate moral considerations will apply. The following application of just war theory to paramilitary violence in Northern Ireland is restricted to a consideration of the Provisional IRA's paramilitary campaign and the action of the British armed forces. The issues raised by Protestant paramilitarism are not expressly addressed, though there too questions need to be faced about whether there existed a just cause, whether the activity was sanctioned by a legitimate authority and how the principle of proportionality applied.

Just cause and right intention

It would be widely accepted that the right to self-defence is a fundamental right of nations, communities or individuals, and therefore constitutes a just cause. Following the disturbances in the late 1960s associated with the civil rights campaign, the first wave of paramilitary activity did in fact initially adopt a defensive posture. It is often forgotten that at this stage the IRA was reluctant to take up arms and had been committed to a policy of political campaigning. Besieged Catholics, threatened by loyalist vigilantes and even sometimes by undisciplined elements within the Royal Ulster Constabulary, in fact taunted the IRA with the slogan that IRA meant 'I Ran Away'. The new, more militant Provisionals did not wait for very long on the sidelines, and the defensive role quickly escalated into a campaign of ruthless ferocity to overthrow the State and impose a united Ireland by force of arms.

Leaving to one side for the moment the actual methods deployed, it is necessary to consider the arguments that can be marshalled on behalf of such wider aims. At this point the question of just cause merges with

---

6. Elsewhere in this volume there has been some discussion of whether recourse to arms was justified in the case of the Easter Rising. See Chapters Three and Four on Connolly and Pearse.

the third criterion, that of right intention.

The case that the State in Northern Ireland lacks legitimacy is not without foundation. From its inception, the Northern State did not adequately endeavour to represent the interests of the whole community. The situation was, no doubt, compounded by the failure of many nationalists to recognise the legitimacy of the State or participate in its political institutions. Unashamedly, however, unionist politicians proclaimed that they wished to sustain 'a Protestant Parliament for a Protestant People'. The franchise was restricted, proportional representation was revoked and gerrymandering took place; Special Powers legislation suspended *habeas corpus* and involved a level of coercion incompatible with a democratic polity; the Catholic/Nationalist minority were discriminated against in employment and housing and were underrepresented in public life.

Moreover, throughout the civil conflict of the 1970s and 1980s, British policy failed either to reform the old unionist state or create new viable democratic structures. Progress in redressing social disadvantage and ending discrimination was also desperately slow.[7] In the circumstances of the continuance of a policy of direct rule, which was in fact only intended as a temporary expedient, it could reasonably be argued that the objective of creating a democratic state in Northern Ireland represented a just cause.

But this is not what the Provisional IRA sought. Indeed they opposed efforts to achieve such an objective – most notably the power-sharing executive of the early 1970s – on the grounds that it would be merely shoring up the Northern State. The creation of a united Ireland was its primary aim. It was argued that partition was imposed on the basis of a sectarian headcount, and that the majority in the whole of Ireland favoured its end. Unionists, for their part, insisted on their right to maintain the British way of life which was seen as more consistent with their Protestant roots and argued that the majority within Northern Ireland favoured the *status quo*.

7. See M. Farrell, *Northern Ireland: The Orange State*, 2nd ed., (London: Pluto Press, 1980); E. McCann, *War and an Irish Town*, 2nd ed. (London: Pluto, 1980); G. Adams, *The Politics of Irish Freedom* (Kerry: Brandon, 1986). John Whyte points out in his *Interpreting Northern Ireland* (Oxford: Clarendon, 1990), p. 180, that many of the conclusions of these authors are supported by scholars who do not share the same ideological stance.

Historically, Republicans have in fact been divided on the question of the imposition of a united Ireland by force. De Valera was not always unequivocal on the matter, but it is significant that the transcripts of the Treaty debates of 1922, released in 1972, show that he advised the Dáil in private session that he did not think a policy of force with Ulster would be successful and said it 'would be making the same mistake with that section as England had made with Ireland.'[8] Although Michael Collins had been willing to supply the IRA in the North with weapons to protect the Catholic population, he also averred the use of force to coerce Ulster:

> By force we could beat them perhaps, but perhaps not. I do not think we could beat them morally. If you kill all of us, every man and every male child, the difficulty will still be there. So in Ulster. That is why we do not want to coerce them.[9]

A united Ireland might be a legitimate aspiration, but democratic principle would suggest that the only acceptable path to such a goal is through consent and not coercion. The use of armed force to create a united Ireland cannot therefore be considered to have been a just cause. It is therefore something of a breakthrough that the principle of consent is now accepted by all the main parties to the conflict.

Legitimate authority

The second criterion, that of legitimate authority, raises the question of whether only the State is entitled to wage war. Many Christians would hold this view on the basis of Paul's exhortation in Romans 13 to be subject to the authorities because they have been 'instituted' by God. But Scripture itself is by no means always consistent in its teaching regarding the State. Thus, in Revelation 13, we find that the State is seen as being under demonic control.[10] There has, in fact, since the Reformation period been a strong Christian tradition which holds that in circumstances where the State has become oppressive and has abused its au-

---

8. See C. Cruise O'Brien, *States of Ireland* (London: Hutchinson, 1972), p. 295.
9. See J. Lee, *Ireland 1912-1985: Politics and Society* (Cambridge: Cambridge University Press, 1989), pp. 60f.
10. For a recent discussion of biblical teaching on the relation between church and state see W. E. Pilgrim, *Uneasy Neighbours: Church and State in the New Testament* (Minneapolis: Fortress Press, 1999).

thority, revolt might be morally justified. Indeed, modern democratic theory is based on the idea of a social contract whereby the State derives its authority from the popular will. In the absence of that consent the State can no longer command the loyalty of its citizens and action to overthrow it might be admissible.

The British government's claim to a legitimate mandate in Northern Ireland may be a legally valid one, but this mandate was diminished by the absence of democratic structures within Northern Ireland which commanded the consent of the whole community, and the persistence of the social disadvantage experienced by Catholics. There has also, at times, been some confusion as to what exactly that mandate is for. In a post-imperialist era the idea of British rule in Ireland is not without its difficulties. British rule in Ireland has been oppressive and unjust.

The injustice goes back a good deal further than the Act of Union of 1800, though it is interesting at this point to note that it seems to have been forgotten that the Orange Order opposed this measure. John Beresford, the Grand Master of the Orange Order, may not have been the most advanced democrat, but he had grasped the inequity involved in Ireland's incorporation into the Imperial Parliament: 'Proud of the name Irishman, I hope never to exchange it for that of Colonist, or to see my country governed by laws exacted by a Parliament over which she has no control'.[11]

Given the injustices entailed in the imperial relationship that formerly existed between Britain and Ireland, the only terms in which British involvement might have credibility is to prevent bloodshed and secure a political resolution of the conflict acceptable to both traditions. The guarantee to the unionists that a united Ireland will not be imposed, should not be used to justify acquiescing in any unionist blocking of the political process.

The absence of the normal processes of political life in Northern Ireland throughout the Troubles undoubtedly created instability and a dangerous political vacuum. The Provisional IRA, however, cannot be said to have possessed a rival legitimate authority to the British government in the way that Sinn Féin could claim through its majority in Dáil Éireann

11. See F. Campbell, *The Dissenting Voice: Protestant Democracy in Ulster from Plantation to Partition* (Belfast: The Blackstaff Press, 1991), p. 112.

during the War of Independence. Although the Army Council of the Provisional IRA considered itself as a government in waiting, which owed allegiance solely to the Republic first proclaimed in 1916 and to the first of Dáil 1919, this scarcely constituted a democratic mandate. It should not be forgotten that during the Civil War, the IRA opposed Dáil Éireann and has repeatedly done so.

It may be true that Provisional IRA paramilitaries have enjoyed a degree of tacit support in the North, but a popular mandate cannot be said to have existed. The comparison sometimes made with the African National Congress, which did have massive popular support, is demonstrably false, given Sinn Féin's overall electoral performance. Even on its best showing Sinn Féin had only a part of the nationalist vote, and an even smaller proportion of the total vote.

Proportionality

The criterion of proportionality applies to the total cost of war. It also applies to the question of restraint in the conduct of war (*jus in bello*). Both the actual and potential costs of the Provisional IRA campaign to unite Ireland have been, by any civilized moral calculus, unacceptable. Moreover, in the conduct of its campaign, discrimination and proportionality have not figured prominently. Even if a guerrilla campaign may make certain difficulties inherent, non-combatant immunity has too often been largely ignored.

Nothing better illustrates the falsity of the claim of the Provisional IRA to be the true heirs of the 1916 Rising than its record on the use of violence. The leaders of the Easter Rising, sensitive to the corrupting nature of violence, from the outset were insistent that the rebels abide by the highest of standards. The final paragraph of the 1916 Proclamation included the words: 'We pray that no one who serves that cause will dishonour it by cowardice, inhumanity, or rapine.' It was the death of three civilians, caught in crossfire, which induced Pearse to offer unconditional surrender when some of his comrades wanted to beat a line of retreat. At his trial Connolly did not offer a defence, but when critical references were made to the treatment of prisoners he responded vigorously and defended the conduct of the rebels.[12]

12. Pearse's conduct stood in marked contrast to some of his writing on the purifying nature of violence, but was consistent with his decision back in 1914 not to distribute

Last resort

The question of last resort is particularly important in a situation where there are possibilities of democratic alternatives. The absence of democratic forums in the North throughout most of the Troubles may have been a grave handicap, about which far too little was done by the British authorities, but there did exist democratic structures that could be appealed to in Britain and the Republic of Ireland. Thus although the democratisation of the Northern State constitutes a just cause, even in the context of direct rule, non-violent methods would have been likely to be much more effective and held out sufficient prospect for change. The Social Democratic and Labour Party's strategy of working to achieve change by non-violent means was therefore in Northern Ireland the correct one. The irony and tragedy of failing to recognise this has meant that the prospect of some form of federal, or even united Ireland, has been pushed further into the future by the bitterness and divisions that the Troubles have fostered.

THE MORAL RECORD OF THE BRITISH STATE

If paramilitary violence is to be criticized, so too should the unjustified use of violence by the State. Moral criteria must be applied every bit as severely to governments. When the British government criticises the paramilitaries it can hardly be said to occupy the moral high ground. Throughout the period of the Troubles there have been many instances where there must be concern about what is sometimes described as the 'institutionalised violence' of the State: the brutality with which security measures have often been implemented, the record on internment and the use of torture, the allegations over instances of a shoot-to-kill policy, the findings of the Stevens Report concerning collusion between the security forces and loyalist paramilitaries. Democracy cannot be defended when the organs of the State act outside the law and by methods that deny basic human rights. Back in November 1971 Cardinal Conway and his episcopal colleagues rightly balanced their condemnation of para-

---

the explosive bullets landed at Howth. See J. Lee, 'In Search of Patrick Pearse', in M. Ní Dhonnachadha and T. Dorgan, eds., *Revising the Rising* (Derry: Field Day, 1991), pp. 122-38 (134) and J. Lee, *The Modernisation of Irish Society 1848-1918* (Dublin: Gill and Macmillan, 1973), p. 156. On Connolly's trial see C. Desmond Greaves, *The Life and Times of James Connolly* (London: Lawrence and Wishart, 1972), p. 421.

military violence with the following statement:

> It is also our duty, however, to condemn another form of violence
> which is also shameful and contrary to the law of Christ. We refer to
> the process known as 'interrogation in depth' as it is often been prac-
> tised in Northern Ireland in recent months. Men have been kept
> hooded and standing, with arms and legs outstretched, practically
> continuously for days and nights on end until, from exhaustion (lead-
> ing to repeated collapses), darkness, noise and thirst, they felt they
> were going out of their minds and prayed for death.[13]

Civilized and democratic governments have no legitimate reason to
behave in such a fashion, which, in any event, is counter-productive in
political terms, since it alienates precisely those sections of the community to which advocates of armed struggle make their appeal.

Responsible government should focus its attention on backing up the
brokering of political solutions with tackling the underlying causes of
the conflict. The current welcome progress towards a sustained peace
does not alter the fact that the record of successive British administrations in this respect has been abysmal. It is difficult to believe that it has
not over the years occurred to some of the more agile minds in the British political establishment that Provisional IRA and loyalist paramilitarism
are indications of a deep-seated social dislocation and malady, and it is
this fractured social order which must first be reconstituted, if it is not to
remain a breeding ground for such excesses. Yet for most of the Troubles all we seemed to get from successive British governments was a series of half-hearted economic and political measures. It would be com-
placent not to recognise that the danger is always there that political
progress will be halted if substantial measures are not taken to tackle the
problem at the social and economic level with sustained vigour. Deprivation and sectarianism feed off each other: worsened conditions promote
sectarianism which in turn damages business confidence further. This is
the vicious circle that needs to be broken.

In any moral audit of the conflict in Northern Ireland a shade more
candour about the role of government is a healthy thing. One can be

13. Quoted in *Violence in Ireland: A Report of the Churches*, pp. 123ff. (126). For a discussion
of the use of torture in Northern Ireland and the judgement of the European Court
of Human Rights see Lee, *Ireland 1912-1985: Politics and Society*, pp. 438ff.

forgiven for suspecting that at least some political leaders have been able to use public revulsion at particular outrages to distract attention from government incompetence. And the laudable instinct of the public to rally round when democracy is threatened has helped the poll ratings at some wobbly moments. There is perhaps enough of a grain of truth here to raise questions about the seeming lack of political will during much of the Troubles to address the social ills that would have had a serious prospect of effecting change.

DEEP HURT AND DEEP HEALING

Candour also requires an acknowledgement that it is not only successive governments which have failed seriously to address the economic and political causes of the conflict in Northern Ireland. The Churches have too often issued calls for peace and reconciliation that have not addressed the underlying social realities. In the words of the prophet Jeremiah they have 'healed the wound of my people lightly', and spoken of `peace, peace, when there is no peace' (Jeremiah 6:14). The Christian vision of the Kingdom of God is not a superficial peace, and includes the hope of justice with all its manifold implications. That should have been said more clearly and the implications spelt out more fully.

A reconciliation that does not meet the demands of justice is bogus. For there to be genuine reconciliation, repentance and forgiveness entail the settlement of former wrongs and injustices. When people have been denied rights and have suffered economic disadvantage, reconciliation implies restorative justice. It offers a way out of the cycle of violence and revenge, by creatively bringing together the willingness to forgive the wrongs of the past with the desire to make space for a new future where injustices are removed. Too often repentance and forgiveness are understood in an individualistic manner, they also have a public and political dimension that urgently needs to be retrieved.

After so many years of violence the hurt is very real and very deep. The search for a sustainable peace will only really flourish when this is acknowledged and forgiveness is sought not only by former paramilitaries, but also by all in Church, state and society who have not done all they ought to have done. There is still much lying awake at night for us all to do.

CHAPTER TEN

Liberation Theology and the Search for Peace in Ireland

Without peace all other dreams vanish and are reduced to ashes.
– Jawaharlal Nehru

Through stressing the centrality of the struggle for democratic rights and social advancement, an attempt has already been made to view Irish history from the 'underside', where the experience of the marginalised and those denied basic human freedoms is allowed to speak. It has been evident that it has very often been energies from 'below' that have been the decisive factor in producing political change. In the preceding chapters a number of theological themes have already been considered that merit a place within the larger project of articulating what a broadly liberation theology perspective might involve in an Irish context. The present chapter addresses some of the methodological issues that arise from using a liberation theology model, and goes on to examine how such a model might be adapted and applied to the political conflict in Northern Ireland arising from competing conceptions of national identity.

APPLYING A LIBERATION THEOLOGY METHODOLOGY

In the highly polarised societies of the Southern hemisphere a social analysis of class conflict and oppression which draws upon the Marxist tradition is still widely seen as providing an essential tool for understanding the reality of life under such conditions. In these countries, identifying those social and political forces that are the expression of the struggle for justice of the exploited and dispossessed, does not pose great difficulties. Severe deprivation is the lot of the vast majority of the population, and the daily fight for democratic rights and improved social conditions is set in the context of the perception that very often it is a rapacious, unrestrained capitalist system with powerful multi-national corporations which is frustrating these aspirations and hopes. It is therefore not surprising that the two hallmarks of the theology that has been forged in this context have been the acceptance of a class-conflict social analysis and the adoption of what is referred to as 'the option for the poor'.

The term 'Liberation Theology' was first used to describe the more socially committed theology that emerged after the Second Vatican Council at the meeting of Latin American Bishops at Medellín, Columbia, in 1968. In the general ferment following Vatican II it was increasingly felt that to be faithful to the Gospel, the Church must articulate a response to the reality of political domination and economic exploitation which characterises the plight of the majority in Latin America. The classic text of this period was *A Theology of Liberation* by Gustavo Gutiérrez.[1] In addition to an emphasis upon class division, Gutiérrez espoused a 'dependence theory', whereby countries at the periphery suffered from structural imbalances that favoured more powerful nations. This aspect of the analysis contrasted with Marx's recognition of the progressive role of capitalism – despite its injustices – in terms of developing the forces of production and thereby the preconditions for socialism, and shows that from its inception liberation theology has made a fairly eclectic use of Marxism.

The new orientation in theology quickly spread to poorer countries in other parts of the hemisphere, and soon began to present a challenge to the more traditional theologies of Europe and the United States that did not adequately address class polarisation and the plight of the marginalised.

The basic method used in liberation theology has been variously outlined by thinkers such as Juan Luis Segundo and Leonardo Boff. The starting-point for this theology is an active involvement with the oppressed, which leads on to a social analysis of the situation, and is in turn followed by theological reflection and pastoral action. Here theology is seen as a second order activity, which is rooted in a practical engagement on behalf of the poor in their struggle for justice. In his account of the method of liberation theology Leonardo Boff writes:

> It begins with indignation at the poverty experienced by God's children, a poverty that God surely does not will … The second step is

---

1. G. Gutiérrez, *A Theology of Liberation* (London: SCM, 1974).

the investigation of the ways that produce such wanton misery on one side and scandalous wealth on the other. Here, the historical, social, political and economic analyses are brought into play. Third, this reality of misery, already deciphered with socioanalytic tools, is read with the eyes of faith and theology, discerning the paths of sin and the avenues of grace. Finally, pastoral activity is developed that enables the Church and all Christians to help in the process of complete liberation.[2]

Boff has undoubtedly identified crucial elements in the process of theological engagement and reflection, even if the acknowledgement that poverty is not God's will in stage one suggests that theology cannot neatly be confined to stage three!

How does such an approach translate into an Irish context? Although poverty is evident enough in many parts of Irish society, it does not exist to the same degree or on anything like the same scale as among the poorer nations. Despite the problem of low pay in many sectors, the unacceptable level of unemployment blighting some communities, the disadvantage experienced by women and the generally high incidence of social exclusion in Irish society, many of those who have work are reasonably well-off. In these circumstances, the option for the poor may still remain valid as an act of human solidarity with the sizeable body of people marginalised from the mainstream of economic life. It will need, however, to be complemented with a commitment to engagement with a wider social constituency, if the political forces to create a more just and caring society are to be mobilised.

Alongside the social and economic sphere, though not unconnected with it, a particularly pressing issue in an Irish context is how might a liberation theology perspective be applied appropriately in relation to the political conflict in Northern Ireland arising from competing aspirations in relation to political identity. In many of the emerging countries at the periphery of the capitalist system, the endeavour to create a more just society is directly linked to the struggle for national liberation. This

2. L. Boff, *Church: Charism and Power: Liberation Theology and the Institutional Church* (London: SCM, 1985), p. 20. For Segundo's account of the method of liberation theology, see his discussion of the 'hermeneutical circle' in *The Liberation of Theology* (New York: Orbis, 1976), pp. 7ff.

kind of tie should not, however, be seen as an automatic one. The crucial criterion here is whether or not particular national movements promote human rights, social justice and democratic freedoms. If this is the
case, a theology that is genuinely liberative may enter into a critical solidarity with a given national movement. What theology should never do
is become captive to nationalist ideologies that are destructive of human
freedoms. The question of whether a liberation theology outlook implies support for the nationalist cause must therefore be carefully exam-
ined before rash assumptions one way or the other are made.

It was indicated in the Introduction that, although human alienation
and marginalisation take manifold forms, this study has deliberately focused its attention upon a concern with social justice and democracy in
the specific context of conflicting political identities. It was noted too
that there has not been a great deal written upon the specific manner in
which liberation theology might be applied in the Irish context. It is also
true that in some instances what has been written is far from satisfactory.

Writing at the close of the 1980s, Joseph McVeigh, who has made what
is probably the most sustained contribution in this general area, has been
unabashed in his use of a liberation theology model to justify support for
Sinn Féin and, by extension, the armed struggle. His analysis stresses the
politically reactionary role of Christianity since Constantine and shows
at some length the way in which, throughout Irish history, the Roman
Catholic hierarchy has either tacitly or actively supported the status quo
of injustice and oppression. For McVeigh, this is all of a piece with the
stance taken by the Roman Catholic authorities in Ireland on partition,
social inequality and the British presence in Northern Ireland. He sees
British involvement in Ireland as the continuation of colonial rule and
closely links the persistence of poverty and injustice in the North with
partition. Calling for a 'theology of liberation' instead of 'a pro-estab-
lishment theology of obedience', McVeigh argues that the Church should
side 'with the oppressed Irish nationalists of the North in their struggle
for social justice'.[3]

3. *A Wounded Church: Religion, Politics and Justice in Ireland* (Cork and Dublin: Mercier
    Press, 1989), pp. 10f. A more recent attempt from a Sinn Féin perspective to look at
    liberation theology also fails to take the issue very far or show much discrimination.
    See (coincidently the same surname!) Jim McVeigh, 'The Irish Church and Republi-
    canism – *the Need for a Liberation Theology*', *The Furrow*, Vol. 50, No 1 (January 1999),
    pp. 3-7.

McVeigh is quite right on a number of matters. Throughout much of Irish history the Roman Catholic hierarchy has adopted a reactionary posture on political issues. James Connolly pointed this out back in 1910 in *Labour, Nationality and Religion*. The situation since Connolly was writing would provide further support for such a view, and although more recently the picture may be more nuanced, it can scarcely be denied that Irish Roman Catholicism has continued to be characterised by a deep social conservatism. Such an admission does not, however, mean that McVeigh's assessment must be right because it differs from the Church's stance!

There are several other sleights of hand. On the question of the tradition of 'just revolution', McVeigh is correct in drawing attention to the way in which this has been used by liberation theology to support armed struggle in certain countries. But this in itself scarcely resolves – as McVeigh seems to think it does – the question of whether paramilitary violence has been justified in the particular circumstances that prevailed in Northern Ireland.[4]

McVeigh's description of Britain's historic relationship with Ireland as an imperial and colonial one is beyond dispute. Where his argument falls down is in the assumption that this is still the case. 'An Irish liberation theology', he writes, 'will reflect the experience of the Irish people as an oppressed and colonised nation which has not yet achieved full political and economic freedom and control over its own affairs.'[5] An examination of the capital transfer figures from Britain to Northern Ireland is alone sufficient demonstration that the British interest in Ireland is not motivated by imperial economic advantage.

Although in his discussion of partition, McVeigh is right to point to its negative economic consequences, he overstates his case. The problem is as much one of market inefficiencies involved in the way partition has reduced the overall level of economic activity throughout Ireland, North and South, as it is a matter of partition being part of an imperial design

4. McVeigh, *A Wounded Church: Religion, Politics and Justice in Ireland*, pp. 65ff. McVeigh writes: 'The Church's theology of the Just Revolution was clearly on the side of the oppressed and allowed for the taking up of arms to get rid of an unjust and intolerable tyranny. The problem is that there has never been any discussion about this within the Irish Church.' (66).
5. J. McVeigh, *Renewing the Irish Church: Towards an Irish Liberation Theology* (Cork and Dublin: Mercier Press, 1993), p. 11. See also pp. 90f., 99, 106f., and 130.

to secure colonial exploitation.

What McVeigh is really offering us is an uncritically assimilated version of the Sinn Féin viewpoint in theological dress. His general approach, it must be conceded, does conform to the methodological process outlined by Boff and Segundo in the famous 'hermeneutical circle', which moves from the engagement arising from the preferential option for the poor, towards social analysis, and only then to theological reflection, and, finally, pastoral action. Where McVeigh gets into difficulty is at the second hurdle in his social and political analysis, which is marred by the fact that he is unable to escape from his own captivity to a Sinn Féin outlook. Moreover, it must be added that given the changing perspectives now being articulated by Gerry Adams and others, McVeigh's whole approach is in consequence now looking distinctly out of date.

What then might be an appropriate social analysis for the contemporary Irish context?

As has been said, the traditional approach of liberation theology is to use a social analysis informed by Marxist theory. But is this viable in view of the collapse of the totalitarian collectivist societies of the former Eastern bloc? The failure of the Soviet experiment in socialism has certainly discredited Leninism and Stalinism, though this does not mean that a democratic socialism informed by insights derived from Marx and the Marxist tradition is thereby ruled out. Likewise, social democrats whose analysis favour strong public services and policies to redistribute wealth still have a case to make. Contrary to what seems to be an unstated assumption of many commentators at the right of the political spectrum, the disintegration of Soviet totalitarianism does not thereby vindicate unbridled free-market capitalism. The kind of analysis with which a genuinely liberative theology should be concerned is one that is critical of tyranny, injustice and oppression in all its manifold forms. Writing in 1937, and sensitive to the suppression of political freedoms in the Soviet Union, Richard Tawney put the point succinctly: 'Tyranny and economic injustice are both abominations. Christians are not compelled to choose between them. They can and should repudiate both.'[6]

Liberation theology in fact has stressed that it wishes to make only a

---

6. 'A Note on Christianity and the Social Order' (1937) in his *The Attack and Other Papers*, (Nottingham: Spokesman, 1981), pp167-92 (172).

limited use of Marxism as a tool of social analysis. In practice, this has meant the acceptance of some of the insights derived from Marx's critique of capitalism and his theory of historical development. There is nothing wrong with this. The Christian religion does not possess its own political theory and there is no reason why it should not make an instrumental use of political ideas of a secular provenance, whether it be Marxism or other areas of political theory. The Christian faith does not operate in vacuum but in a given cultural context with which it should be engaged: the important point is that the engagement should be a critical and productive one.

In the Irish context, an effective social and political analysis must be able to offer a coherent assessment of both the social problems that mar Irish society and the running sore of the national question. In Chapter Six an attempt has already been made to address the former concern through adopting policies that will ensure wealth and opportunity are spread more equitably. The present chapter underlines the need for such policies and suggests that dealing effectively with social exclusion and political conflict (which are intertwined) will necessitate the enlisting of a wide social constituency. Although the remainder of this chapter will focus primarily on issues of political identity the wider social context must always be kept in mind.

To begin our task of examining political identity, there will need to be some preliminary treatment of the nationalist and unionist ideologies which dominate the political landscape in Northern Ireland. The discussion below outlines some of the salient features of these ideologies and offers a critique of them. This is followed by an attempt to articulate a more satisfactory social and political analysis.

COMPETING IDEOLOGIES: UNIONISM

As a political movement, Unionism has its origins in the Home Rule crises of the late-nineteenth and early-twentieth centuries.[7] Prior to that,

---

7. For the discussion below, see P. Buckland, *Irish Unionism 1 The Anglo-Irish and the New Ireland 1885-1922* (Dublin: Gill and Macmillan, 1972) and *Irish Unionism 2 Ulster Unionism and the Origins of Northern Ireland 1886-1922* (Dublin: Gill and Macmillan, 1973); also Jennifer Todd, 'Unionist Political Thought, 1920-72' in D. George Boyce, et al, eds, *Political Thought in Ireland Since the Seventeenth Century* (London: Routledge, 1993), pp. 190-211

in Ulster, political divisions found expression largely through the main-stream British political parties. It was only when the prospects of a Dublin parliament raised fears of a Roman Catholic ascendancy and that Home Rule might mean Rome Rule, that unionism emerged as an organised political body. Unionism successfully mobilised a cross-class opposition to Home Rule, which incorporated an emphasis upon the settler past, the cultivation of Protestant values and identity, contractual allegiance to the British Crown and participation in the imperial project of Empire. The Orange Order grew rapidly in strength during this period, its populist loyalism linking the folk memories of 1689/90 with the defence of Protestantism in Ireland. The unionist case was pressed in economic terms, and in the campaigning literature of the period a sharp contrast was portrayed between the prosperous industrial North-East of Ireland and the backward peasant economy of the South. It was during this period that the Home Rule movement under the direction of the Nationalist League became more overtly nationalist with strong clerical support and there emerged in a pronounced form the polarisation of Irish politics upon Catholic Nationalist and Protestant Unionist lines that was thereafter to do so much to shape the course of Irish politics.[8]

During the latter part of the nineteenth century, it must be conceded that the economic and structural ties of Empire were undoubtedly significant, and widely perceived as such. Thus unionists could rely on strong support within the British political establishment. By the time of the Anglo-Irish War British interests had, however, shifted sufficiently for Lloyd George's administration to be willing to grant devolved government in the 1920 Government of Ireland Act and an Irish Free State in 1922.

After partition the new unionist state formed in the 1920s did not succeed in integrating the Roman Catholic population, and this reflected the failure of unionist political theory to articulate an adequate concern for the democratic rights of the nationalist minority. Although, with some justification, unionists could point to the economic advantages of the Union, this alone was unlikely to satisfy the aspirations of Roman Catho-

8 . The elections of 1885 and 1886 were particularly crucial in this respect. See Brian Walker, 'The 1885 and 1886 General Elections – A Milestone in Irish History' in his *Dancing to History's Tune: History, Myth and Politics in Ireland* (Belfast: Institute of Irish Studies, 1996), pp. 15-33.

lics who felt excluded. In the late 1960s under Terence O'Neill a more liberal and modernising unionism did emerge, though it had only limited success in its programme of democratic reform.[9]

Within contemporary unionism, two main strands can be discerned, which might perhaps usefully be described as liberal unionism and militant unionism.[10] The liberal unionism favoured by some elements within the professional and middle classes is clearly embarrassed by the tribalism evident in the Democratic Unionist Party and sometimes within the Ulster Unionist Party, and takes a much more pragmatic view of the British connection. Here the combination of a greater cultural affinity with Britain and a concern to maintain the perceived economic advantages that flow from British involvement, provide the motive to support the maintenance of the Union. This more confident form of unionism is more ready to acknowledge some of the mistakes of the past, and accepts the need for change and the introduction of improved democratic processes. The case for a more liberal unionism has undoubtedly been strengthened since the loyalist ceasefires by the way in which some of the former paramilitaries seem to be ready to think in bolder new ways instead of clinging to the slogans of the past.

The general outlook of militant unionism is more strident and sectarian in tone. Although it may be claimed its support for the Union, pleas for more draconian security measures, and wistfulness for the return of the old Stormont Parliament is not anti-Catholic, much of the rhetoric of militant unionist leaders with its constant references to 'our people', along with the sectarian mentality promoted by the Orange Order, would seem to belie this, as indeed would the various parades which are perceived as an assertion of Protestant supremacy. With militant unionism and much of Orangeism the emphasis is upon a self-identity that has traditionally seen Protestants as God's chosen people. The siege of Derry and other events in the unionist calendar, which are directly associated with a highly selective reading of the Old Testament, act as symbols to fortify this sense of Protestant election and identity. From the mid-nineteenth century onwards, the traditional religious motifs of unionism have

9.   Todd, 'Unionist Political Thought, 1920-72', especially pp. 197, 202ff.
10. There are also many different strands within these categories. For a recent discussion of different types of unionism, see J. McGarry and B. O'Leary, *Explaining Northern Ireland: Broken Images* (Oxford: Blackwell, 1995), pp. 92ff.

been closely allied to extreme evangelicalism and a biblical fundamentalism.

During the Troubles, a species of this highly conservative form of unionism to a disturbing degree set the agenda and did much to create the climate sustaining the paramilitary violence of the Ulster Volunteer Force and Ulster Defence Association. A potent mixture of religious fanaticism and political demagogy has been used to heighten the sense of insecurity of the more threatened sections of the loyalist population. Protestant condemnations of popery and theological ideas drawn from later Calvinism, such as the doctrine of double predestination, have been used to justify the denigration of the Roman Catholic tradition. The extremism of this exotic brew is proportionate to the uneasy, partly repressed, awareness that in Northern Europe at the close of the twentieth century, a political culture based upon Protestant hegemony might no longer be viable.[11]

When it comes to a consideration of Britain's relation to Ireland, militant unionism, with its enthusiasm for God and Empire, looks distinctly anachronistic in the context of the degree of secularisation of British society, the end of Empire during the period since partition, the loss of those traditional industries like shipbuilding which provided much of the economic rationale for continued ties with Britain, devolved government and the growing pressure for independence in other parts of the United Kingdom, and the degree of European integration in the post-Maastricht and post-Nice era. These changes are reflected in the fact that the traditional affinities between the Conservative Party and unionism, which proved such a potent factor in the past, are no longer widely felt.

Militant unionists, and sometimes more moderate unionists, have too often viewed the Northern Ireland situation as essentially a security problem soluble by strong law and order measures. This fails adequately to address the democratic deficit, and other injustices of the past, and the continuing high level of unemployment and social deprivation that blight many areas of Northern Ireland and have done so much to fuel the conflict.

11. I have drawn on Terence McCaughey's account of unionism and orangeism in his *Memory and Redemption: Church, Politics and Prophetic Theology in Ireland* (Dublin: Gill and Macmillan, 1993), pp. 20ff. and 42ff.

Too often in the past the dominant stance within unionism has been the more militant and strident in tone. The initial reaction of both the Ulster Unionist Party and the Democratic Unionist Party to the Downing Street Declaration and the Framework Documents often made it look as though the only response to proposals for change would be a repeated and resounding 'No'.

Within the Ulster Unionist Party over the years the more liberal voices have undoubtedly had difficulty in sustaining their position. James Molyneaux's decidedly precarious support as leader is a case in point. On more than one occasion unionists would have been better advised to enter into talks from a position of strength, rather than risk being marginalised through their own unwillingness to respond more positively to proposals. Once the principle that no constitutional change shall take place without consent was accepted as a binding commitment by the two sovereign governments and affirmed by referenda North and South, it surely provided the basis for a more confident unionism that is ready to argue its case and press for the kind of changes that might make Northern Ireland more attractive to all its people. By too often complaining of betrayal and a reluctance to enter all-party talks, the unionist cause was weakened because unionists themselves were frequently seen as looking backwards and not forwards. David Trimble's leadership of the Ulster Unionist Party has no doubt been marked by a concern not to move too far ahead of his constituency, but people have rightly looked to him to articulate a more pluralist politics and on occasions he has shown great courage in doing this.

Thankfully, the acceptance by Sinn Féin of the principle of consent made it a good deal easier for Trimble to sign up to the Good Friday Agreement, which paved the way for the Northern Ireland Executive that has, despite the twists and turns, showed what a new more inclusive politics might look like.

COMPETING IDEOLOGIES: NATIONALISM

Although this section will deal mainly with the Provisional IRA and Sinn Féin, it should be noted at the outset that throughout the Troubles the majority of nationalists in the Republic and in Northern Ireland have been constitutional nationalists for whom the aspiration to achieve a united Ireland has been set in the context of a commitment to the use of exclusively democratic means. Thus the Social Democratic and Labour Party favour a negotiated political settlement and an 'agreed' Ireland, with democratic institutions that afford parity of esteem and recognise the identities of both traditions. The SDLP have consistently maintained that major constitutional change would require the consent of the majority within Northern Ireland.[12]

Although the Provisional IRA and Sinn Féin are separate organisations and therefore, from time to time, there may be differences of emphasis and sometimes strains in their alliance, the closeness of their relation justifies considering them together. Modern IRA/Sinn Féin has included two main strands, both of which formerly embraced a physical force strategy in relation to the Northern conflict. First, it has represented people motivated by a nationalist ideology solely concerned with the reunification of the national territory. The second strand, that of socialist republicanism, has had wider objectives and has seen the British presence in Ireland in terms of class conflict and anti-imperialist struggle.

The Sinn Féin outlook is not deliberately sectarian. Indeed socialist republicanism would make much of the need to raise the consciousness of class interests with members of both religious traditions. In practice, though, Sinn Féin draws its support exclusively from Roman Catholics and its activities have clearly promoted sectarian strife. The other major criticism must be that in making the question of national freedom paramount, both strands within IRA/Sinn Féin have failed to address constructively the socio-economic agenda. This is reflected in the fact that the community work on social issues that has been undertaken by Sinn Féin has not been used primarily to advance an effective response to those problems, but to heighten people's indignation in order to enlist political support for objectives it has been simultaneously prepared to pursue by the ballot and the bullet.[13]

Sinn Féin sees the British presence as the primary cause of the violence in Northern Ireland and insists on the right of the Irish people to

12. See McGarry and O'Leary, *Explaining Northern Ireland*, pp. 59ff
13. Gerard Quinn describes Sinn Féin's complaints about discrimination as 'a cynical exercise for propaganda purposes' in his 'Northern Ireland: Social Policy and Economic Privilege', *Studies*, Vol. 81, No. 322 (Summer 1992), pp. 191-202 (198).

self-determination. It is argued that this right should be exercised by the population of the whole island. Hitherto, it has been maintained that, although in a united Ireland unionists will be welcomed as equal citizens, the principle of self-determination does not extend to the right of unionists to maintain a separate state. The more recent historic acceptance of consent within Northern Ireland for constitutional change represents an enormous advance in this respect, and one that I have argued elsewhere is consistent with the expressed views of both Michael Collins and Eamon deValera.[14] The principle of self-determination cuts both ways, since if the right of the unionist majority within Northern Ireland to impose its will on the minority is rejected, so too should the right of the majority in the whole island to impose its will on the unionist minority.[15]

The socialist republicanism of Sinn Féin, which is espoused by the organisation's leading political spokesperson, Gerry Adams, has in recent years been characterised by a greater willingness to pursue constitutional politics to the point now of accepting places in a Northern Ireland Government. Whether this is partly opportunist or not, it does indicate a changing stance, illustrated by the fact that old abstentionist policies have been long since abandoned. The cessation of hostilities and the readiness to enter into the democratic process means the new thinking has won widespread support within Sinn Féin.

Despite these welcome developments, Sinn Féin has not jettisoned many of its old shibboleths. For example, although Adam's presentation of the argument might of late be a shade more nuanced, the notion that the Irish conflict is an anti-imperialist struggle[16] is looking distinctly dated even if only employed for rhetorical purposes within his own constitu-

14. See Chapter 9, p. 171.
15. For the earlier Sinn Féin standpoint see G. Adams, *Free Ireland: Towards a Lasting Peace*, revised edition (Kerry: Brandon, 1995), pp. 232ff. The self-determination issue is discussed at length in McGarry and O'Leary, *Explaining Northern Ireland*, pp. 35ff. and 121ff.
16. Adams, *Free Ireland: Towards a Lasting Peace*, pp. 88ff. My use of the word 'nuanced' might be a shade generous since the two final (and more recently written) chapters do not contest statements by British ministers that Britain no longer has any 'selfish, economic or strategic interest' (pp.201ff., especially pp. 203 and 227). For socialist republican interpretations of Britain's role in Ireland see E. McCann, *War and an Irish Town*, 2nd ed. (London: Pluto, 1980) and J. Whyte, *Interpreting Northern Ireland* (Oxford: Clarendon, 1990), pp. 175ff.

ency. In the last century British Rule could legitimately be seen in terms of imperialist domination, but this view is now outmoded since there is no obvious economic benefit to Britain in maintaining armed forces and large treasury subsidies. It may be true that there is a residual defence/security interest,[17] but with the ending of the Cold War and the increased enthusiasm of the Republic of Ireland for European integration, this is no longer especially significant. We may, no doubt, assume that at this stage people like Adams may be ready to admit more in private than they would concede in public, though the logic of his position would suggest that at some point the new thinking will involve an acknowledgement of the need for a revised attitude on a whole series of issues and the development of a more sophisticated political discourse.

The Hume-Adam's agreement, which paved the way for the 1994 ceasefire, and the more recent historic Good Friday Agreement, would certainly seem to indicate that a return to the constitutional nationalism which the IRA and Sinn Féin once derided is now overwhelmingly favoured. This progress must be consolidated since the punishment beatings and the shadowy murders of drug dealers sit uncomfortably with a willingness to move towards a democratic and genuinely 'republican' polity. Such progress holds out the prospect that with new political institutions, power-sharing and the acceptance of reformed policing structures, a climate might be sustained that could lead to successful democratisation and a society more at ease with itself.

SOCIAL AND POLITICAL ANALYSIS

In order to develop a critical stance in relation to the competing political ideologies in Northern Ireland it is necessary to articulate a more satisfactory social and political analysis. A reading of the situation which constructively illuminates the political culture of that society might then become the basis for a theology that is genuinely liberative. The analysis that is offered below makes use of insights derived from a non-deterministic reading of Marxist social theory and a consideration of some theoretical reflections on the nature of nationalism.

Although much has been written about the conflict in Northern Ire-

17. See Anthony Coughlan's discussion in his 'Northern Ireland: Conflicts of Sovereignty', *Studies*, Vol. 81, No. 322 (Summer 1992), pp. 180-190 (185f. and 190).

land, surprisingly little political assessment has been offered which gets beyond descriptive accounts of the entrenched positions of the main protagonists. In venturing into this void there is a danger in being only able to skim the surface of what are, by any estimation, major issues which have a bearing far beyond Ireland. Taking a position in relation to the appropriate utilization of a Marxist social analysis and attempting an examination of the nature of nationalism will involve wrestling with two of the defining problems of our time. The tragedy of Northern Ireland – like many other tragedies of our generation – has been that the conflict has been played out on the basis of political outlooks that are, to say the least, seriously deficient.

The first point that needs to be stressed is that if a Marxist social analysis is to be adequately pursued, the religious dimension of the conflict should be addressed in conjunction with social and economic factors. Socialist republicans in Sinn Féin have been incorrect in thinking that a Marxist analysis of the situation in Northern Ireland justifies a narrow class politics. Thus, although Sinn Féin acknowledge that religion has been a cause of division in Irish society, it does not take religion sufficiently seriously in its analysis and thereby it does not effectively contest the religious sectarianism sustaining extreme nationalism and unionism.

Manifestly religious loyalties and their associated conceptions of national identity have proved stronger than class loyalties.[18] That this should be the case is only problematic for a determinist reading of Marxism. Marx's view that the thinking of social classes is related to material circumstances, i.e., the particular mode of production and associated relations of production in any given society, should not be taken to imply that human culture is merely a reflection of material conditions. Although in his materialist conception of history Marx saw ideologies as being rooted in social and economic circumstances, he recognised that ideological conflict in turn played a crucial role in historical development and that there was considerable scope for contingency.

This is evident in his own historical writings, where he does not confine his discussion to economic and technological factors. Thus in *The Class Struggles in France* and *The Eighteenth Brumaire of Louis Bonaparte*, Marx attended closely to the ideological and political aspects of these

18. Eamonn McCann concedes this point in his *War and an Irish Town*, pp. 88 and 120.

struggles. He did not see his theory of history as implying that all intellectual and cultural phenomena are a direct expression of the economic
relations of production. He was ready to allow for a considerable degree
of autonomy for legal, moral and spiritual ideas.[19] Within the Marxist
tradition, the significance of ideological and cultural factors for the process of historical change has been given a renewed emphasis by the Italian Marxist, Antonio Gramsci, whose work has provided a major corrective to economistic readings of Marx.

All this would suggest that a Marxist analysis of Northern Ireland that
does not give a prominent role to religion is in fact flawed. Indeed, it
would be quite consistent with a Marxist analysis to argue that in particular historical conjunctures it is possible that religion might prove to be
the dominant factor. In the Irish context, where religion has been closely
entwined with the two main political traditions, it would be foolish not
to accept that religion has in fact played a central role. Unpalatable
though it may be, the Christian Churches have reinforced the competing conceptions of national identity, and the history of the twentieth
century would certainly suggest that it would be a grave mistake to un-
derestimate the degree to which national identity can command people's loyalties and passions.

The other respect in which the IRA/Sinn Féin approach has lacked
discrimination is that too little account is taken of the economic interests maintaining the *status quo*. Although class stratification and polarisation clearly exist among Protestants, empirical studies show that, taken
as a whole, economic advantages in terms of access to work and higher
paid employment are enjoyed by Protestants. There can only be said to
exist a unified class interest between poorer Roman Catholics and poorer
Protestants (who certainly exist in many beleaguered communities but
are a smaller proportion of the total Protestant population). In Northern Ireland levels of unemployment and access to higher paid jobs show
that Protestant religious allegiance has often been accompanied by a
tangible material benefit derived from that allegiance and this extends
quite far down the social ladder (See Chapter 6, p. 112 above).

The narrow appeal to disadvantaged Protestants is much too restricted

19. See J. Marsden, *Marxian and Christian Utopianism: Toward a Socialist Political Theology*
    (New York: Monthly Review Press, 1991), Chapter 2.

a basis for the much needed co-operation across the religious divide. Middle-class members of both communities also share an interest in securing political change.

The tragedy of Northern Ireland is that social discontent has not united people of all social classes and religious affiliations in the conviction that something must be done to address the pervasive injustices which are ultimately in the interests of no one. There is no reason why socialists should not welcome cross-class alliances in the interests of promoting both social reform and the democratisation of the Northern State.[20] If socialists had been ready to embrace co-operation between different social classes, the history of Europe in the twentieth century may well have taken a different course, with the defeat of fascism being secured without the agonies of war. Socialists in Northern Ireland should be more ready to work with other parties who do not necessarily share the same goals, since progressive social and economic measures and the making of significant progress in the achievement of democratic structures are valuable in their own right. Members of Sinn Féin ready to embrace fully constitutional politics, the SDLP and liberal unionists represent a powerful coalition of political forces able to take Irish politics forward. John Hume was right to have identified this objective and to have struggled for it with such vigour and determination. It has been upon this basis that substantial political progress has undoubtedly been made.

Having identified how Marxist theory might more constructively illuminate Irish politics, it would be unwise not to acknowledge the shortcomings of Marxism which have a bearing on the Irish context. After two world wars and the disintegration of Eastern Europe there can be little doubt that the Marxist tradition has seriously underestimated the power of nationalism in the modern world. To his credit, James Connolly sensed this lack, and against the bland internationalism of many socialists of his generation, argued that the national and social struggle need to be linked in the interests of both democracy and socialism. Clearly, as a political phenomenon, nationalism needs to be taken much more seriously than has hitherto been the case. An examination of nationalism

20.   John Whyte includes a chapter on Marxist interpretations of the Northern Ireland conflict in his *Interpreting Northern Ireland*, pp. 175ff. For a recent critical treatment of the various types of Marxist analysis that have been applied in Ireland, see McGarry and O'Leary, *Explaining Northern Ireland*, Chapters 2 and 4.

that might provide some criteria to distinguish between the healthy and destructive aspects of the various components of contemporary Irish political culture is therefore urgently needed.[21]

Modern nationalism is an extremely diverse and complex phenomenon. Sometimes nationalist movements have involved the unification of formerly separate states. Nineteenth-century Germany and Italy would be instances of this. More often, though, nationalism is separatist. A classic example here would be the nation-states emerging from the break up of the Austro-Hungarian Empire. Frequently a particular language and culture become powerful tools in the process of nation-building, though many national projects are intentionally multi-cultural. Nationalist movements have sometimes proved to be aggressive and militarist, elevating the interests of a given nation above that of others; but nationalism can take a polycentric form, whereby the rights of each nation are valued, and thereby be consistent with the comity of nations.

The beginnings of modern nationalism as a political doctrine can be traced to two sources. The first is associated with the French Revolution and the concept of popular sovereignty. Here the nation is understood to consist of people inhabiting a particular territory who through democratic political institutions give expression to a common citizenship despite diverse cultural differences. It is only when the people themselves exercise sovereignty that they can identify with the nation. Rousseau stressed that in a democratic republic the citizen should be attached to the nation by bonds of loyalty and affection. Here the nation is not conceived in ethnic or linguistic terms, but as a body of citizens exercising democratic rights and being responsible for maintaining the liberty of the nation.

The Romantic movement in Germany gave rise to another conception of nationalism, which defined itself in predominantly cultural and organic terms. Outlining his idea of the nation-state, J. G. Herder stated that 'the natural state, therefore, is *one* people with *one* national character.' For Herder, although each nation has its own national distinctiveness, no nation occupies a privileged position and all nations make a contribution to the general development of humankind. It was only with

---

21. The discussion that follows has drawn closely upon John Schwarzmantel's *Socialism and the Idea of the Nation* (Hertfordshire: Harvester Wheatsheaf, 1991), pp. 25ff.

Fichte and later developments that the tendency was established to view the German nation as pre-eminent and for an irrationalist devotion to the fatherland to replace the concern with democratic ideals.[22]

When romantic nationalism assumes a form which allows for a cultural inclusiveness, democratic structures and a respect for other nations, it is compatible with the definition of the nation associated with the French tradition of popular sovereignty. In such a form romantic nationalism has the distinct advantage of strengthening national cohesiveness with ties and bonds that supplement the common commitment to political liberty. At its best, the Young Ireland movement of the mid-nineteenth century achieved this objective, the general enthusiasm for Wolfe Tone being indicative of Young Ireland's adhesion to democratic principles. The fostering of national identity in the context of a commitment to democratic ideals is extremely important. When this is not done and people's need for a sense of cultural identity is ignored, it leaves a dangerous vacuum, which has so often provided an opportunity for tyranny. Prime examples of such tyranny would be fascism's xenophobic nationalism or Marxism's undifferentiated internationalism which in the Soviet Union led to totalitarian rule. At its best, romantic nationalism has thus been a valuable corrective to the rather too austere and abstract concept of nationalism associated with much of the Enlightenment and the French Revolution.

It is only when romantic nationalism takes an exclusive form involving national self-elevation and a disregard for democratic rights that it should be opposed. Fascism would be the extreme example of this form of nationalism. The glorification of the nation which we find in modern fascism was rooted in a reactionary preoccupation with the soil and racial group. As a means of retrieving a threatened identity, fascism tapped a deep vein when it responded to the insecurities of the uprooted recently industrialised European masses amid the trauma of economic depression. It appealed to the more vital and elemental realm within human existence, but did not channel the expression of these vital needs and powers in directions consistent with true human fulfilment. Rather

---

22. Ibid., pp. 33ff. (35). Also J. Talmon, *Romanticism and Revolt: Europe 1815-1848* (London: Thames and Hudson, 1967), pp. 85-134. Herder's cultural nationalism should be seen in the context of his commitment to democratic principles.

than being an indication of national resurgence, fascism was evidence of a deep-seated social dislocation and malady.

In a not altogether dissimilar fashion extreme nationalism and unionism (which is also a form of nationalism) have appealed to insecurities that are widely felt, and offered a sense of identity through a destructive assertion of the rights and interests of one section of the community. It should not be forgotten that it is precisely this deliberate nurturing of sectarian attitudes which has created the climate where violence has occurred. People should be proud of their culture, traditions and loyalties, but ways must be found of fostering a sense of identity that involves the recognition of others. This will mean disavowing both an Irish nationalism that sought to create a confessional state and the unionist failure in the past to defend the rights and interests of all members of the community.

In the work of cultural reconstruction that is needed in Irish society, finding ways to give a constructive expression to the basic human need for a sense of identity must become the central task. This is something that can be done without people retreating into sectarian ghettos. Societies are enriched and not diminished by the fact that they are not ethnically, religiously or culturally monochrome.

Human identity is found in much more complicated and flexible forms than some would seem to allow. What at first might seem unconventionalities – if not contradictions – often turn out to be quite liberating. In an interview in the *Irish Times*,[23] the singer and musician Eleanor McEvoy said that not all her male fans were entirely happy with the lyrics of the *Woman's Heart* album – 'only' a woman's heart. In Joyce's *Ulysees*, Leopold Bloom, the androgynous 'womanly man', defies the tyranny of convention.[24] John Stuart Mill once remarked:

23. *Irish Times*, Friday 6th August 1993.
24. On the question of cultural identity, see Declan Kiberd's *Anglo-Irish Attitudes*, A Field Day Pamphlet, No.6 (Derry: Field Day, 1984), and 'The Elephant of Revolutionary Forgetfulness' in M. Ní Dhonnachadha and T. Dorgan, eds., *Revising the Rising* (Derry: Field Day, 1991), pp. 1-20 (Kiberd refers to Joyce's portrait of Leopold Bloom on p. 16, and in the same paragraph he astutely observes: 'It was the British imperialists who had created the notion of a necessary antithesis between things English and Irish, but a sharp critique of such thinking was implicit in the writings of the generation of 1916.'). A more recent treatment of culture and identity in an Irish context is found in Declan Kiberd and Edna Longley, *Multi-Culturalism: The View from the Two Irelands* (Cork: Cork University Press, 2001).

But the women, of all I have known, who possessed the highest measure of what are considered feminine qualities, have combined with
them more of the highest *masculine* qualities than I have ever seen in
any but one or two men, and those one or two men were also in many
respects almost women. I suspect it is the second-rate people of the
two sexes that are unlike.[25]

These insights can be extended beyond sexual identity. The nationalist and unionist divide is not nearly so great when both are informed by
a generous vision of political community. In its religious and cultural life
Irish society would surely be enriched by a creative interaction of different traditions which avoided a false polarisation or the mind-set that sees
political life as a zero-sum game, whereby gains for one tradition must be
a loss for another. People who value their Protestant heritage and British
roots and affinities need not abandon them should they also wish to
consider themselves Irish.[26] Many Scottish and Welsh people readily think
of themselves as British. A large number of Americans still consider themselves Irish. Both nationalists and unionists have been slow to adopt a
more flexible approach on this issue. There needs to be a recovery of
the more expansive conception of national love, rooted in a zeal for the
democratic ideal, which we find in the republicanism of Francis
Hutcheson, who, in 1729, commented:

Here we may transiently remark the Foundation of what we call *national Love*, or *LOVE* of one's *native Country*. Whatever Place we have
liv'd in for any considerable time, there we have most distinctly
remark'd the *various Affections* of *human Nature*, we have known many
lovely characters; we remember the *Associations, Friendships, Familys, natural Affections*, and other *human Sentiments*; our *moral Sense* determines
us to approve these *lovely Dispositions*, where we have most distinctly
observ'd them; and our *Benevolence* concerns us in the Interests of
those persons possess'd of them. When we come to observe the like as
distinctly in *another* Country, we begin to acquire a *national Love* towards it also; nor has our *own* Country any other preference in our

25. See K. Britton, *John Stuart Mill* (Harmondsworth: Penguin, 1953), p. 37.
26. For a recent discussion of issues and findings concerning Irish identity see Walker,
  Dancing to History's Tune, pp. 110-27.

Idea, unless it be by an Association of the pleasant Ideas of our Youth, with the *Buildings, Fields* and *Woods* where we receiv'd them. This may let us see how *Tyranny, Faction,* a *Neglect* of Justice, a *Corruption* of Manners, and *any thing* which occasions the Misery of the Subjects, destroys this *national Love,* and the dear Idea of a COUNTRY.[27]

As far as the nationalist tradition is concerned, the only Irish nationalism worthy of the name is an inclusive one that confers citizenship upon all members of the national territory, irrespective of their religion, ethnicity, or cultural attachments and emotional affections for another country. This is the tradition of the European Enlightenment mediated through the United Irish Society. There is nothing specifically Irish about this tradition of political liberty: the tree of liberty also grew upon Albion's soil. Perhaps the day might come when it will be possible to celebrate 1688, 1798 and 1916, not as sectarian victories or defeats, but as part of a process, at once valiant, troubled and ambiguous, through which both the Irish and English asserted their democratic rights against the unjust usurpation of power.

Unionism, likewise, needs to distance itself firmly from an ethnic or religious political identity. It should abandon its links with the Orange Order and encourage Roman Catholics to join unionist political organisations. It should also take a hard look at what is entailed in unionist British identity. Many aspects of this identity, such as a common language and support for parliamentary traditions of government, would in fact apply to the Republic. This still leaves unionists' specific attachment to the British Crown and constitution. This is only a problem when it is rooted in a supremacist attitude that sees British political institutions as more advanced than those of the Republic. Such a claim smacks of an unhealthy cultural imperialism and can be countered by the observation that the Republic can boast an elected President, proportional representation and a developing constitution, while Britain lacks a written constitution, has a hereditary monarchy, a second chamber still in need of reform, an English established Church, and an electoral system that often leads to unrepresentative government.

---

27. Quoted by Seamus Deane in 'Swift and the Anglo-Irish Intellect', *Eighteenth-Century Ireland,* Vol 1 (1986), pp. 9-22 (16).

To minimise the differences between Irish and British culture in this way is not to dismiss them, and if people in Northern Ireland feel themselves to be more British than Irish, they are fully entitled to seek to give this sense of identity an institutional expression in the form of a commitment to the Union with Britain. But this must be done on the basis of an inclusive civic unionism that is ready to acknowledge the failures of the past, prepared to show a greater sensitivity to the aspirations of many citizens of Northern Ireland to a united Ireland and eager to sustain new democratic structures acceptable to all members of the community. A willingness to be less dogmatic and countenance greater flexibility on the constitutional status of Northern Ireland is also required. The right to Union with Britain is not an inviolable divine right but one that – like the wish for a united Ireland – must be advocated by peaceful and democratic means of persuasion.

THEOLOGICAL REFLECTION AND PASTORAL ACTION

The above analysis has identified a whole series of issues with which the Churches need to engage. These issues find their place within an overall theme that can be summed up as the need to create a more egalitarian society characterised by justice, peace and a fundamental respect for human dignity and democratic freedoms.

This theme is in fact central to the Christian vision of the Kingdom of God and is therefore deeply theological. The Kingdom of God, meaning simply the reign of God, is present whenever God's liberating and transforming rule becomes manifest. Within the Gospels, this Kingdom is seen as encompassing social and political life. This is evident in Jesus' reference, at the outset of his ministry to his mission to 'preach good news to the poor, proclaim release to the captives, recovery of sight to the blind, and set at liberty those who are downtrodden' (Luke 4:18). The reign of God is the subject of many of the parables and the constant focus of Jesus' ministry. In Matthew 12:20 we read: 'He will not break a bruised reed or quench a smouldering wick, till he brings justice to victory'. Thus along with personal repentance and faith, the Kingdom involves the transformation of oppressive social structures which marginalise and exclude. This must be stressed, given the virulence of more individualistic expressions of the Christian faith in contemporary Ireland.

As the reign of God, the Kingdom that was inaugurated in Christ's ministry, still awaits its final consummation – it is an eschatological Kingdom. This universal and eschatological dimension of God's purposes in salvation is deeply rooted in both the Old and the New Testaments. The trauma of Israel's experience of exile, the removal from the sacred land, and the loss of temple and king, eventually brought with it the profound lesson that the sovereignty of Yahweh extends over all the earth. In the epistles of the New Testament we find that the lordship of Christ begins to be interpreted as having cosmic significance. The risen Christ reigns in glory at the right hand of God, and the outworking of his purposes is to take place on the stage of world history. The breadth and scope of this vision again point to a corresponding understanding of salvation that includes the eschatological hope of justice, peace and social harmony.

This Christian hope does not therefore offer a superficial peace and reordering of things, but is one of a new human flourishing and social wholeness. As Enda McDonagh reminds us, 'peace' (*shalom*) is concerned with the historical order:

> the peace to be given by the God of Israel and of Jesus Christ has this worldly, historical and social implications … Empty or oppressive orderliness does not reflect the biblical sense of peace. In the Hebrew tradition *shalom* signifies a rich reality of wholeness; well-being and flourishing which extends from the cosmos through society to God. It is a covenant reality, at once gift and task…. The richness of [this] reality is not easily translatable into words available in the Greek or Latin tradition. The Septuagint Greek tradition of the Hebrew scriptures uses more than twenty terms to convey the range and richness of *shalom* … The recovery of the density and dynamism of the Hebrew 'wholeness and flourishing', both economic and social, is essential.[28]

In Ireland today it is therefore a primary responsibility of the Christian Churches to issue a prophetic challenge to a society ready to tolerate marked disparities in wealth and opportunity. Throughout Ireland, both North and South, there still persists what is by Western European standards a high degree of social deprivation. Such injustice is unaccept-

28. E. McDonagh, *Between Chaos and New Creation* (Dublin: Gill and Macmillan, 1986), pp. 45f.

able both in its own right and because of its consequences for our political culture, especially in the North, where its corrosive effects have done so much to sustain political division.

It is important to have set this wider context, which relates the whole question of political justice to the Christian vision of the Kingdom of God, before venturing a theological engagement and critique in regard to the more specific issue of sustaining democratic politics amid competing conceptions of political identity.

As has already been indicated, in their extremist and sectarian forms both nationalism and unionism betray some of the racist characteristics of fascism. The ease with which people speak of 'Catholic Nationalism' and 'Protestant Unionism' should be a cause for shame. To define national identity in such tribal terms is unacceptable. Jewish prophetism, as Paul Tillich pointed out, freed itself from primitivist ties to soil, land and race, when it insisted that such ties are always provisional and subject to the ethical obligation expressed in the 'demand of justice'. A society's true interests are denied when the poor are oppressed or minorities excluded. All existing social relationships are in fact brought into question through the prophetic expectation of the coming reign of divine justice and the arrival of a 'new heaven and a new earth'.[29]

These biblical motifs suggest that it is on the basis of a partial reading of scripture that tribalist nationalists and unionists – whether the mystically inclined wing of Sinn Féin or fundamentalist Orangemen – look to the Christian tradition to fortify their claim to the status of being a chosen people. Israel's experience of the Exodus should not be used to justify such an exclusivity, since this liberative event serves as a paradigm for Yahweh's universal saving purposes – a message which is put succinctly by the prophet Amos:

> 'Are you not like the Ethiopians to me, O people of Israel?' says the Lord. 'Did I not bring up Israel from the Land of Egypt, and the Philistines from Caphtor and the Syrians from Kir?' (Amos 9:7).

This message concerning a universal salvific purpose lies at the very heart of the divine liberative mission, against which all false gods and

29. *The Socialist Decision*, trans. by F. Sherman with introduction by J. R. Stumme (New York: Harper and Row, 1977), pp. 18ff.

ideologies will fall. The radical inclusiveness of this message was unequivocally endorsed by Christ himself: 'I tell you, many will come from east
and west and sit at table with Abraham, Isaac and Jacob in the kingdom
of heaven' (Matthew 8:11). Theological teachings which lead to the denigration or exclusion of others must therefore be vigorously contested.

On the Protestant side, the doctrine of double predestination and the
associated idea of the Protestant population as God's chosen people must
therefore be rejected. Apart from the monstrous view of God which this
doctrine entails, the notion that some are destined to be damned has
been used, along with anti-papal sentiments, to justify the political exclusion of Roman Catholics. This teaching has in Irish history been closely
linked with the contestation of the land. The iconography of Orange
Order banners, which selectively use Old Testament stories to suggest
parallels that ally Protestants with the people of Israel, offer a false and
misleading understanding of Protestantism. The misuse of Scripture in
this way has often resulted in an idolatrous attempt to claim divine sanction for a narrowly conceived and backward-looking perception of Protestant political interests in Ireland.[30] When Protestants make too close
an identification of the Gospel with their own religion, they forget that
the Reformation principle *Ecclesia semper reformanda* also entails a critique
of their own tradition. The problem with Orangeism is not therefore its
Protestantism, but that it is not Protestant enough! It seems to have forgotten that the new covenant which Christ instituted is a universal one
between Christ and humanity which has broken down the barriers that
divide. There is no chosen people, since all are one in Christ.

The besetting sin of theological exclusivity is not of course all on the
Protestant side. The current unwillingness of the Roman Catholic hierarchy to enter into a more serious dialogue and closer communion with
other Churches on an equal basis has also had damaging consequences.
Substantial progress was undoubtedly made in the Second Vatican Council, but much more is needed on questions such as the sacraments and
the validity of holy orders.

The Churches need to make their calls for peace and forgiveness more

30. See McCaughey, *Memory and Redemption*, pp. 22ff. Also A. Buckley, 'The Chosen Few:
      Biblical Texts in the Regalia of an Ulster Secret Society', *Folk Life*, Vol. 24 (1985/6),
      pp. 5-24.

effective by a readiness to acknowledge the ways in which religion has been a divisive force in the past. If repentance should lead to amendment of life, this has consequences for the Churches too, which must give active consideration to the way in which they have actually reinforced the religious and cultural divisions which in turn have helped sustain destructive political divisions.[31]

Along with the Churches formally dissociating themselves from sectarian attitudes, this process must extend to those areas of their institutional life that contribute to the division within society. Serious questions need to be asked about the less than enthusiastic response to integrated education, policies on inter-Church marriages, the Churches' role in relation to state policy on divorce and the general lack of progress in ecumenical relations towards a fuller communion.[32] The discussion below confines itself to a treatment of the failure in ecumenical witness, not least in responding to sectarianism, which has undermined an effective prophetic engagement with society.

The ecumenical movement in Ireland clearly has a crucial role to play both as a witness to the fact that the religious divide can be bridged and as a catalyst for the rebuilding of relationships within the wider community. It is therefore regrettable that ecumenical relations, while personable among Church leaders, sometimes have little impact at the local level. As well as Church leaders shaking hands and working together, there need to be local initiatives in the places where it matters. Enda McDonagh rightly reminds us that

> The closer the Irish Churches come together as believing and worshipping communities in shared Christian faith, hope and love, the more liberated they become from their traditionally divisive, ethnic, cultural and political affiliations.[33]

One area where scope already exists for much greater co-operation is our common Baptism, which is accepted by all the main Churches. If members of the Roman Catholic Church were invited to attend Protestant Baptisms, and *vice versa*, it would be a significant step in undermin-

---

31. For a sociological study of this issue, see Duncan Morrow, et al, *The Churches and Inter-Community Relationships* (Coleraine: University of Ulster, 1994).
32. Terence McCaughey discusses these matters in *Memory and Redemption*, pp. 79-102.
33. McDonagh, *Between Chaos and New Creation*, p. 160.

ing the corrosiveness of sectarian division.[34]

It would, of course, be wrong to suggest that the reconciliation of diverse cultural traditions is not a difficult and costly process. There is, as Alan Falconer has reminded us, too much easy talk of reconciliation. Discussing the reconciliation of different ecclesiastical polities, Falconer stresses that human reconciliation is in fact always a process:

> reconciliation of memories, then, involves the process of seeking for-giveness, accepting responsibility for the past actions of 'our' commu-nity which belong to the memory of both parties, and by appropriat-ing the history of the other who has been shaped by 'our' past actions to learn from their experiences which are not shared with 'us'. Through this process of forgiveness both are empowered to be and to enter a new relationship which is able to embrace the memories of the hurt and alienation.[35]

This is a task that can only be faithfully implemented with the aid of our Church historians. As Joseph Liechty has pointed out, the roots of sectarianism are not found on the fringes of Church life, but as part of the mainstream of the major traditions. He identifies three doctrines of the Reformation period which proved particularly pernicious in this re-spect: 'providence; one true Church, outside of which is no salvation; and error has no right.' Here providence was understood not in a gen-eral sense, but in support of the claim that God is on the side of the 'elect' or 'true Church'. It was the combination of either of the first two doctrines with 'error has no right', which meant that religious coercion was so widely deemed as justified.[36]

---

34. Ronald Preston makes the point in *Confusions in Christian Social Ethics: Problems For Geneva and Rome* (London: SCM, 1994), pp. 166f.

35. 'The Reconciling Power of Forgiveness', in A. Falconer, ed., *Reconciling Memories* (Dub-lin: Columba Press, 1988), pp. 84-98 (95).

36. See 'Christianity and Identity in Ireland: A Historical Perspective' in *Christianity, Cul-ture and Identity*. Conference: Evangelical Contribution On Northern Ireland (ECONI), 4 November 1995, pp. 1-7. Also more recently Joseph Liechty and Cecelia Clegg, *Moving Beyond Sectarianism: Religion, Conflict, and Reconciliation in Northern Ireland* (Dub-lin: Columba, 2001), pp. 67ff. This text which arose from a research project spon-sored by the Irish School of Ecumenics is rooted in community involvement and adult education initiatives and usefully documents people's contemporary experi-ence of the dynamics and function of sectarianism. Regrettably, its historical discus-sion of sectarianism in the Churches is not supplemented by an examination of the history of political thought and therefore no attempt is made to marshal the insights

Although it should not be forgotten that in the post-Reformation pe-riod the policy of all the main traditions was to persecute when practica-ble, in the Irish context the issue which stands out is the support of the Protestant established Church Ascendancy for the suppression of the rights of Roman Catholics and Dissenters. This tragic history still has to be more squarely faced. Disestablishment went some way to liberating the Church of Ireland from this role, but the ease with which it sup-ported the continuation of Protestant domination in Northern Ireland means that some very tangible expressions of regret for the past still need to be made. In this regard it is a welcome development that Arch-bishop Robin Eames, referring to Northern Ireland, has said in an arti-cle in August 2001: 'there was discrimination and there was injustice.'[37] If statements like this were expanded and the injustices identified, the episcopate of the Church of Ireland could do much good by placing on record a formal apology for its past associations. Issuing such apologies has a healing role, not least because it shows that wrongs that still cause pain are acknowledged and owned. It also frees those who issue them to move forward to a better self-understanding.

It is significant that as recently as 1999 a collection of essays, *A Time to Build: Essays for Tomorrow's Church*, intended as an appraisal of the Church of Ireland on the threshold of the new millennium, despite some excel-lent material, does not devote attention to the issue of Ascendancy or its continuation in modified form in Northern Ireland.[38] The opening es-say discusses the 'discomfort' experienced by Protestants in the Free State and the insensitivities of the *Ne Temere* stipulations for inter-Church mar-riages. This is true, but it does not constitute anything like an approach-ing equivalence with the historic injustices inflicted upon Catholics. The other notable omission in this text is that there is no attempt to forge links with the very rich tradition of Anglican social thought stemming from F.D. Maurice, through Charles Gore, Henry Scott-Holland, Rich-ard Tawney and William Temple. This tradition was never reflected in

---

of the inclusive politics of Irish Republicanism at its inception. The text's prescriptive recommendations in consequence remain too generalised and are weak in several vitally important respects.

37. 'Christian Ministry in a Divided Community', The Joseph Winter Lecture, *Church of Ireland Gazette*, 3rd, 10th, 17th August 2001.

38. Edited by S.R. White (Dublin: APCK, 1999).

any indigenous sense within the Church of Ireland and this is directly related to its Ascendancy past which made it unreceptive to developing a more prophetic voice. There is no reason why this should remain so and the welcome concern in some of the essays for issues of social justice will only be strengthened by drawing upon the fertile inheritance of Anglican social thought.

In addition to the question of Ascendancy, the other matter which any candid examination of the history of the Church of Ireland raises, is the way in which as an institution it has actively fostered sectarian prejudice. The anti-Roman Catholic invective in the one hundred and four Irish Articles compiled by Archbishop Ussher and the Thirty-nine Articles are part of this heritage. It is therefore to be welcomed that the General Synod has recently distanced itself from certain references in its historic formularies, including the Thirty-nine Articles adopted by the Church of Ireland in 1634.[39] Given that the essence of sectarianism is to frame a religious self-identity in specific opposition to that of others, the paragraph in the 1870 'Preamble and Declaration' of the Church of Ireland rejecting 'innovations in doctrine and worship', which is clearly intended as a condemnation of Roman Catholic doctrine was particularly regrettable.[40]

Within Presbyterianism, the anti-Catholic teachings in the Westminster Confession likewise need to be disavowed. There has already been valuable progress in this direction. In 1988 the General Assembly passed a resolution which, while affirming Christ's headship of the Church, went on to state

> that the historical interpretation of the Pope of Rome as the personal and literal fulfilment of the biblical figure of 'the Anti-Christ' and 'the Man of Sin' is not manifestly evident from scripture.[41]

Regrettably, more conservative and often fundamentalist perspectives

---

39. See *Journal of the General Synod*, 1999, p. 199.
40. The paragraph reads: 'The Church of Ireland, as a Reformed and Protestant Church, doth hereby re-affirm its constant witness against all those innovations in doctrine and worship, whereby the Primitive Faith hath been from time to time defaced or overlaid, and which at the Reformation this Church did disown and reject.' *The Book of Common Prayer* (Dublin: APCK, 1960), p. 346.
41. See J. Dunlop, *A Precarious Belonging: Presbyterians and the Conflict in Ireland* (Belfast: Blackstaff, 1995), p. 112.

which view salvation in terms of strict adherence to 'sound' Protestant doctrine and a highly individualistic faith have often been more evident. When allied with political extremism this religious fundamentalism can prove a potent mixture, as can be seen in the Free Presbyterian Church with the political demagogy of Ian Paisley and the frequent denigration of the Roman Catholic tradition.

This sectarian history stemming from the Reformation, which is common to the rest of Europe, in Ireland has undoubtedly been compounded by the close relationship that has existed between the Protestant Churches and the Orange Order. From its founding in the 1790s, through bringing together religious and political identity in an exclusive manner, the Orange Order has played a significant role in exacerbating sectarian tensions.

It is to be regretted that throughout the period of the recent Troubles the Church of Ireland and the Presbyterian Church have been unwilling to dissociate themselves from ties with the Order. In those areas where a witness of this kind would be as costly as it would be effective, individual clergy need to have their hands strengthened. This could be achieved by support from Church leaders and debate at the General Synod of the Church of Ireland and the General Assembly of the Presbyterian Church. In the Church of Ireland, in order to avoid the spectacle and scandal associated with protests in places like Drumcree, legislation should be passed to prohibit the use of churches by the Orange Order. Episcopal appeals over these matters have been largely ignored and a crisis in authority has been allowed to develop, with considerable confusion about where the Church stands, which makes the compelling case for a legislative response long overdue. Opposing sectarianism by such measures should be seen as a basic point of Gospel obedience and credibility.

There is clearly something profoundly wrong when in a society that has been so marred by violence, marches that strain relations within the community and provoke civil disorder often set out from or end with Church services. Even if clergy do not attend these services, by permitting their churches to be used in this way, clergy and congregations are, if only tacitly, lending support to, and implying divine approval for, demonstrations of a sectarian nature.

Given the fragility of the political situation, action is urgently needed over this matter. It is regrettable that an otherwise excellent report [42] on sectarianism by the Irish Inter-Church Meeting in 1993 did not give greater attention to the role of the Orange Order. The report on sectarianism presented to the General Synod of the Church of Ireland in 1999 did discuss the role of the Orange Order but the Synod failed to act.[43] The 'Scoping Study' on sectarianism presented to the 2003 Synod was little more than a survey of attitudes within the Church of Ireland, and precipitated a debate that avoided the more substantive issues. The idea that sectarianism can be meaningfully addressed by avoiding Drumcree is to embrace a discipleship without cost or integrity.[44]

An argument can be made for action along the lines of the South African example in relation to apartheid and making the disavowal of any ties with Orangeism a *status confessionis*. This term was first used in the Reformation to define matters vital to the being of the Church and was raised by Dietrich Bonhoeffer with regard to the perils posed by Nazism.[45] At the ver least, attention should be focussed on effective measures to ensure that church premises are no longer made available to the Orange Order. Many individual Church of Ireland members would no doubt wish to retain their membership of the Order, but crucially the Church of Ireland itself would no longer be associated with the Order.[46] Moreover, those clergy faced with contentious marches would not be put in an isolated and vulnerable position, since it would be the collective authority of the Church of Ireland that was being asserted. It would be

42. *Sectarianism: A Discussion Document. The Report of the Working Party on Sectarianism* (Belfast: Irish Inter-Church Meeting, 1993). A description of the Orange Order is given in an appendix on pp. 147ff.
43. Joseph Liechty is right to point out that the fact that this report was commissioned is to be welcomed as an indication of a greater awareness of the problem of sectarianism. See his recent article 'Sectarianism and the Churches: The Legacy and the Challenge' in D. Carroll, *Religion in Ireland: Past, Present and Future* (Dublin: Columba, 1999), pp. 86-95.
44. Gareth Higgins, *The Hard Gospel: Dealing Positively with Difference in the Church of Ireland (A Scoping Study Report to the Sectarianism Education Project,* (General Synod of the Church of Ireland, 2003). A descriptive rather than a prescriptive approach is also found in Robin Eames' discussion of the Orange Order in his essay 'The Religious Factor' in D. Murray, *Protestant Perceptions of the Peace Process* (Limerick: University of Limerick Centre for Peace and Development Studies, 2000), pp. 101-35 (especially 116ff).
45. See Preston, *Confusions in Christian Social Ethics,* p. 69.
46. Earl Storey has produced a useful discussion of the relationship between the Church of Ireland and the Orange Order in *Traditonal Roots: Towards an appropriate relationship between Church of Ireland and the Orange Order* (Dublin: Columba, 2002).

for the security forces to ensure church property was respected and the Church of Ireland would not be responsible for any lapses in this regard. Parades themselves would continue to go ahead, though hopefully wiser counsels within the Orange fraternity will be heeded when the case is made for reaching accommodations with residents that avoid enflaming a discord which is ultimately in no one's interests, either politically or economically. Thankfully most parades are non-vexatious and Orange members who value the peace dividend will want to keep it that way.

Finally, it is worth stressing that there is nothing wrong with the aspiration of the Orange Order to maintain the Union. The policy of ending ecclesial links with the Order should not therefore be seen as an attack upon unionism. Indeed the unionist case is only strengthened when it is aligned to a non-sectarian politics. This point is appreciated by many forward-thinking unionists who are able to see the wisdom of seeking to distance their party from the Order. In such circumstances it is surely not asking too much that the Protestant Churches should do likewise and thereby place their voices unequivocally behind calls for a more inclusive conception of political community.

In this respect more might have been hoped for from the Moving Beyond Sectarianism programme of the Irish School of Ecumenics. The final report of this project by Joseph Liechty and Cecelia Clegg published in 2001 is in many regards impressive.[47] They rightly emphasize the 'systemic' nature of sectarianism, which makes it incumbent upon people to see that, even if only in inadvertent ways, everyone contributes to the problem. This makes them hesitant about apportioning blame in any given quarter and suspicious of the anti-sectarian approach, preferring a less judgemental 'moving-beyond-sectarianism' that seeks to redeem, transform and heal distorted expressions of human identity.

The difficulty is that they take the merits of this strategy too far in the rather soft line adopted in relation to the Orange Order. Although aware of the Order's alignment of religion and politics, they suggest that if purged of destructive elements, it might still have a valid role. But surely the essence of Orangeism is to uphold what are seen – albeit falsely – as Protestantism's political as well as religious interests. The iconography

47. Liechty and Clegg, *Moving Beyond Sectarianism*, especially pp. 9ff, 24ff, 104ff, 112,126ff and 153ff.

of banners and selective use of Scripture surely make this patently clear. To dismiss opponents of the Orange Order as 'liberal' sectarians runs the risk of collapsing into a post-modern relativism that abandons any public commitment to democratic values.

This criticism throws into sharp relief a major weakness in the analysis of sectarianism that is offered by Liechty and Clegg, namely, its failure to concentrate sufficient attention upon those forms of sectarianism that are essentially anti-democratic because they seek to deny the political rights of others. It is when this barrier is crossed that prejudice is politi-cised to unacceptable proportions. When this occurs, Christians of all persuasions should unite in rejecting such a denial of human freedom and the equality of all in Christ. This is why the Protestant Churches' failure to distance themselves from the Orange Order is so detrimental. If we really are to move beyond sectarianism in Ireland, it will require the Churches themselves to leave behind their own captivity to the per-nicious cancer of sectarianism within the body politic.

From a theological perspective the fact that sectarianism should be so endemic should come as no surprise. It is certainly illuminated by what we understand by Original Sin. When creatively applied, the traditional doctrine comes to powerful expression in the way in which in sectarian-ism we find human sinfulness entwinned within the very fabric of soci-ety. As such, it forms part of the sociological and psychological factors that go make up the 'tragic destiny' in which we are all caught yet for which we remain responsible.[48] The doctrine also sheds light upon the dynamics of sectarianism as a virulent example of the temptation to deal with insecurity by taking refuge in the egoism of collective pride and destructive self-assertion.[49]

All this would support the conviction that the funding of programmes to combat sectarianism should be seen as a vitally important pastoral priority for the Churches. Regrettably, this recognition only serves to underline how deeply damaging it is for Protestantism in Ireland that its inappropriate relationship with the Orange Order means it is fundamen-

---

48. See Paul Tillich, *Systematic Theology*, Vol. 2 (London: SCM, 1978), p. 38.
49. Here I have drawn upon Reinhold Niebuhr's discussion of collective pride in *The Nature and Destiny of Man*, Vol. 1, *Human Nature* (New York: Scribners, 1964), pp. 208ff.

tally compromised on this issue and therefore lacks moral and intellectual credibility.

Irish Roman Catholicism also has major strides to make. Arguably no part of the Roman Catholic Communion has a greater historic responsibility and opportunity to promote increased reconciliation with worldwide Protestantism than the Irish Roman Catholic Church. The revised attitude to sister Churches in the Second Vatican Council needs to be built upon. It would have a major impact and set a marvellous precedent if television screens the world over saw Irish Roman Catholics and Protestants at a special service of reconciliation in Belfast sharing bread together and calling with one voice for forgiveness, healing and renewal in this troubled island. In this regard, Brian Lennon, S.J., has cited the Decree on Ecumenism (par 8) of the Second Vatican Council and the Directory on Ecumenism (1993), both of which permit eucharistic hospitality in pressing pastoral circumstances, in his call for more flexibility on this issue by the Irish Roman Catholic Church.[50] Does not the historical turning-point facing Irish society with the setting up of new political institutions constitute a pastoral emergency that would justify eucharistic sharing at important ecumenical gatherings?

The questions of Eucharistic sharing and the case for Protestants distancing themselves from the Orange Order were in fact put to leaders of all the Churches at a meeting in 1996. As a member of the theological sub-committee of the Irish Inter-Church Meeting, along with two colleagues, I was delegated to present the sub-committee's recommendations. They met with a cool reception. The recommendations had been part of the concluding section of a report entitled *Freedom, Justice and Responsibility in Ireland Today*, which was published in 1997, omitting this aspect of the report's challenge to the Churches.[51] The report drew attention to the close identification between political identity and religious affiliation, and the way in which religion so often reinforces political divisions. The final recommendations were seen as a bold attempt to address this in a way that would deal a formidable blow to the triumphalism and sectarianism that bedevils both Churches, and give real sub-

---

50. Brian Lennon, *After the Ceasefires: Catholics and the Future of Northern Ireland* (Dublin: Columba Press, 1995), pp. 99ff.

51. *Freedom, Justice and Responsibility in Ireland Today*, Report of the inter-church Meeting (Dublin: Veritas, 1997).

stance to the rather too easy verbal condemnations of sectarianism.[52]

Regrettably, in 1998 the Catholic Bishops' Conferences of England & Wales, Ireland, and Scotland, produced a booklet, *One Bread One Body*, which was rather negative on the scope for Eucharistic sharing. Ironically, the document's theology of the Eucharist which drew heavily upon Vatican II was very inclusive in its scope and stood in marked contrast with the final restrictive pastoral stipulations. Responding to the document, Enda McDonagh, making the plea for greater openness to Eucharistic sharing, adroitly points out that agreed statements between the Reformed Churches and Roman Catholic Church have already laid the basis for this, and maintains that a more generous approach 'has many gospel analogies in Jesus' feeding of the multitudes and his fellowship meals with the excluded.' [53] The papal encyclical *Ecclesia de Eucharistia* of 2003 would suggest that the Vatican is all too aware of the pressure for change. In the Irish context of continuing sectarian division and the need to sustain political progress, the failure to make any headway in this matter is particularly disappointing.

On the issue of sectarianism, which, as we have seen, is not consigned to the margins of ecclesial life, it must be said that there is much that is theologically suspect in ecclesiastical provincialism of whatever variety. As F. D. Maurice never tired of insisting, the unity of the Church is something that is already established and is founded on our relationship with the Father who has drawn us into fellowship with the Son through the Spirit. Whether it be Protestant national Churches or the Roman Catholic Church, Maurice considered it a mistake when any given body of believers, on doctrinal, historical or other grounds, started to perceive themselves in exclusive terms. It is not 'systems of doctrine' but a living relationship with Christ as Lord and Saviour that is the sole ground for unity.

---

52. The report's recommendations and the reaction to them by Church leaders is discussed in an article by Gerry O'Hanlon 'The Churches in Ireland Today – *Kairos* or Lost Opportunity?', *The Furrow*, Vol 48, No 7/8 (July/August 1997), pp. 399-405.
53. *One Bread One Body: A teaching document on the Eucharist in the life of the Church, and the establishment of general norms on sacramental sharing* (Dublin: Veritas, 1998). For Macdonagh's response see 'Invite and Encourage – a millennial proposal for sharing the Eucharist', *The Furrow*, Vol 50, No 1 (January 1999), pp. 18-25 (23). Gerry O'Hanlon has continued to press the case for eucharistic sharing in 'The Good Friday Agreement: A Christian Perspective' in Dermot Lane, ed., *New Century, New Society: Christian Perspectives* (Dublin: Columba, 1999), pp. 102-111.

With this deeply incarnational faith and emphasis firmly upon the organic unity that arises from what God has done for us in uniting us with Christ, Maurice dismisses the sectarian mindset. 'If we were forced to form conceptions about a Son of God,' he writes, 'there could be no consent'. 'If he is revealed to us', he continues, 'as the centre of our fellowship, the only-begotten Son of God, in whom we are made sons of God; the weary effort is over'. Maurice's conviction concerning unity, universality and catholicity, was rooted in his cogent presentation of the truth to which the Church must bear witness concerning humanity's relationship with Christ. It is not enough, he writes, 'to bring the sinner, weary, heavy-laden, and hopeless, to Christ'; we must also proclaim 'that Christ is in every man – the source of all light that ever visits him, the root of all righteous thoughts and acts that he is ever able to conceive or do'.[54] Maurice fully recognised that people may neglect or even oppose this inheritance, and that we know not where the justice and mercy of God begin or end; nonetheless the inheritance remains as gift to all humanity.

Seen in this light, the Church should not be a source of sectarian division but must testify to the unity of all humanity. Its role is to help heal the division and enmity within society, and it can only preach a message of reconciliation effectively by itself being a sign of unity. This theme has been lucidly expounded by the Latin American liberation theologian, Gustavo Gutiérrez, who responds positively to the emphasis in the Second Vatican Council upon the Church as a sacrament of the universal work of salvation. He refers to *Lumen Gentium*'s description of the Church as a sacrament of 'the unity of all mankind' and goes on to conclude:

> In a radically divided world, the function of the ecclesial community is to struggle against the profound causes of the division among men. It is only this commitment that can make it an authentic sign of unity.[55]

Amid the historic divisions and the deep injustices by which Irish society is still so marred, these words constitute a profound call to repentance. Beyond repentance there is hope. Perhaps hope may yet surprise

54. F. D. Maurice, *Theological Essays* (Cambridge: Macmillan, 1853), pp. 416f. and p. 65.
55. Gutiérrez, *A Theology of Liberation*, pp. 260 and 278.

and delight us by its triumph. A sentiment brilliantly captured by Seamus Heaney in words which bring to politics religious vision.

> History says: *Don't hope*
> *On this side of the grave.*
> But then, once in a lifetime,
> The longed-for tidal wave
> Of justice can rise up,
> And hope and history rhyme.
>
> So hope for a great sea-change
> On the far side of revenge.
> Believe that a further shore
> Is reachable from here.
> Believe in miracles
> And cures and healing wells.[56]

---

56. Seamus Heaney, *The Cure at Troy: a version of Sophocles' Philoctetes* (New York: Farrar, Strauss and Giroux, 1991), p.77.

Index of Names